P9-DIG-783

SUNNY DAYS

THE CHILDREN'S
TELEVISION REVOLUTION
THAT CHANGED AMERICA

David Kamp

Foreword by Questlove

SIMON & SCHUSTER

New York   London   Toronto   Sydney   New Delhi

Simon & Schuster
1230 Avenue of the Americas
New York, NY 10020

First Simon & Schuster hardcover edition May 2020

SIMON & SCHUSTER and colophon are registered
trademarks of Simon & Schuster, Inc.

For information about special discounts for bulk purchases,
please contact Simon & Schuster Special Sales at 1-866-506-1949
or business@simonandschuster.com.

The Simon & Schuster Speakers Bureau can bring authors to
your live event. For more information or to book an event, contact
the Simon & Schuster Speakers Bureau at 1-866-248-3049
or visit our website at www.simonspeakers.com.

Interior design by Lewelin Polanco

Manufactured in the United States of America

1   3   5   7   9   10   8   6   4   2

Library of Congress Cataloging-in-Publication Data
has been applied for.

ISBN 978-1-5011-3780-8
ISBN 978-1-5011-3782-2 (ebook)

PHOTO & ART CREDITS

Page x: David Attie/ Michael Ochs Archives/ Getty Images; page 2: Classic Picture
Library/ Alamy Stock Photo; page 22: Courtesy of the Jim Henson Company;
page 32: CBS/ Photofest; page 38: Courtesy of WQED Multimedia; page 48: David
Attie/ Archive Photos/ Getty Images; page 64: Courtesy of Everett Collection;
page 74: Gjon Mili/ The LIFE Picture Collection via Getty Images; page 88:
Bettmann/ Getty Images; page 100: Baltimore Sun Media. All rights reserved;
page 114: Courtesy of Everett Collection; page 128: Grey Villet/ The LIFE Picture
Collection via Getty Images; page 140: Album/ Entertainment Pictures via ZUMA
Press; page 158: Barbara Alper/ Archive Photos/ Getty Images; page 172: ABC/
Photofest; page 186: *Top photo*, courtesy of Everett Collection. *Bottom photo*,
WPIX-TV, courtesy of Carole Demas Collection; page 203: PBS/ Photofest; page
220: WGBH Media Library & Archives; page 238: ABC Photo Archives/© BC/
Walt Disney Television via Getty Images Photo Archives; page 262: Dan Herrick/
ZUMA Wire; illustrations on pages 31, 47, 171 by Joe McKendry.

For my mother

CONTENTS

— — — — — —

FOREWORD

Growing Up in a
Brand-New TV Community
BY QUESTLOVE

O ne of the ways I recognize that time has passed is to watch television and think about the difference between TV when I was a kid and TV now. I grew up in the seventies, which means that there was not only no streaming but no cable. I grew up in the glory days of the Big Three networks—NBC, ABC, and CBS. But kids had a fourth network: PBS. To me, as a kid, it was the most important network of them all.

When I was very young, I watched *Sesame Street*, and I learned all the things that it set out to teach me: letters and the words they made, numbers and the ideas they suggested. I also learned about cities, and how TV shows could depict them honestly if they wanted to. There were plenty of cities on other shows, grown-up shows with cops or with young people living in apartments (small apartments—this was long before *Friends*). But none of those cities were familiar to me the way that *Sesame Street* was. It was urban, maybe the most urban show on the air. On *Sesame Street*, "urban" meant what it is supposed to mean: a cityscape filled with different kinds of people, as well as busy stoops and storefronts where these people went to talk and joke and eat and sing. This was a community in the literal sense, which, to us kids watching at home all over America, became a community in the figurative sense.

When I stop to think about the urban world of *Sesame Street*, I find my thoughts turning to race. *Sesame Street*, in a move that was radical for its time, included all kinds of races: African American, Latin American, and more. Plus, it had Americans who were not even exactly people. They were puppets—or, more specifically, Muppets. From very early on, I thought about who these urban Muppets were, race-wise. How could you map them onto the human world? Were they their own race, or many different races? They were not white, certainly. They were of color: red, purple, blue. But Ernie didn't seem like the same kind of thing as Grover, and Grover didn't seem like the same kind of thing as Oscar the Grouch, and none of them were the same kind of thing as Big Bird. (Nothing was the same kind of thing as Big Bird.) After a little while, I stopped trying to divide the Muppets into races, or stopped trying to fit them into the human race.

But even this rule had an exception: Roosevelt Franklin, a *Sesame Street* Muppet who was clearly supposed to be African American. I could tell partly because of his speaking voice. Though I didn't know it at the time, that voice was provided by Matt Robinson, who also played the original Gordon on *Sesame Street* (and whose daughter would grow up to be the actress and singer Holly Robinson Peete), but I could tell that the show was trying to create a black Muppet. Roosevelt Franklin was a breakout star, not so much for his energy (though he had plenty) but for his philosophy. He understood the world and tried to understand more. He understood himself and tried to understand more. I remember watching him in the early years of the show, and then feeling upset when he seemed to appear less and less. Even when I was young, Roosevelt's disappearance seemed like a mystery and an injustice.

Later, I came to understand a little of how and why this happened. This book, *Sunny Days*, fills in the story, and tells a hundred other stories of children's television in those days, and how *Sesame Street* and its educational-TV brethren—shows like *The Electric Company, Zoom,* and *Free to Be ... You and Me*—shaped kids like me, and kids not like me, and how our generation was the recipient of some of the best, most interesting, most idealistic, most flawed, and sometimes most problematic uses of this amazing medium. When I read *Sunny Days*, I can once again see all the faces, human and Muppet and otherwise. I can hear all the songs. Most important, I can feel all the things I felt back then, and I'm grateful for it.

*Danny Seagren, Jim Henson, and Frank Oz bring Ernie
and Bert to life in the early days of Sesame Street.*

INTRODUCTION

The Age of Enlightenment Jr.

On the last Friday of July in 1970, David Brinkley, the eminent NBC newsman, paid curious tribute to his departing coanchor, Chet Huntley, whose final evening on the air it was. Noting that Huntley was retiring to his native Montana, where he kept a ranch, Brinkley addressed his broadcast partner on the long-running *Huntley-Brinkley Report* with more wistfulness and anxiety than his wry demeanor usually allowed. "When you are out there under clear skies and clean air," Brinkley said, "maybe, once in a while, you'll think of those of us still here—fighting the traffic, the transportation breakdowns, the strikes, pollution. And wondering what is left that we can eat, drink, smoke, or breathe that will not kill us, and wondering what horror will be visited upon us next."

Brinkley was hardly alone in suggesting that American society, and perhaps life on earth, was about to come to an ignominious end. The news offered ample evidence. A year earlier, the river running through Cleveland, the Cuyahoga, had caught fire, its murky waters slicked with oil runoff from the factories along its banks. The protests against the Vietnam War were growing ever more rancorous, and sometimes deadly: in April 1970, four students were killed, and nine more wounded, when National Guardsmen opened fire on demonstrators at Kent State University in Ohio. Much of academia, meanwhile, was consumed by the Malthusian fear that population growth was outpacing humanity's ability to feed itself; Paul Ehrlich, a Stanford biologist, had gained a measure of celebrity for his 1968 book *The Population Bomb*, which forecast that, "in the 1970s, hundreds of millions of people will starve to death in spite of any crash programs embarked upon now."

It was a noisy, transgressive moment culturally, during which Crosby, Stills, Nash & Young's lament for the Kent State dead, "Ohio," was banned from many AM radio stations, and *Midnight Cowboy*, an artful character study of the friendship between a male prostitute and a con man, set against the backdrop of New York City at its entropically scuzzy nadir, became the first X-rated film ever to win the Academy Award for Best Picture.

Another journalist of Chet Huntley and David Brinkley's vintage, the veteran newspaperman Edward Robb Ellis, kept detailed diaries of this period. Surveying the events unfolding before him as 1970 dawned, he presented an outlook even more apocalyptic than Brinkley's. "I doubt whether I shall live through this decade of the seventies, or wish to do so," Ellis wrote. "Although I consider myself fairly youthful in my attitudes, quick to confess my mistakes when they are pointed out to me, eager to change and adapt to a changing environment, I sense that I cannot alter my nature and beliefs sufficiently to accept all the values of those younger than myself. . . . It is possible that not since the decline and fall of the Roman empire (a long process, not an abrupt event) has the world known such a climactic turning point in human affairs."

— — —

It's startling to read and view these accounts knowing that they belong not to some unfathomably distant era but to a time when I was very much alive. I was a kid in 1970, living, like many others, blissfully oblivious to the end-times rhetoric, contentedly navigating the world at hip height.

It would be easy to attribute this disconnect to the simple fact that we were preschoolers, not yet equipped with the cognitive ability to keep tabs on current events. But something else was going on. A separate, more optimistic contingent of Americans witnessed the same societal stresses that the pessimists did, but, rather than wringing their hands in lamentation, they felt a call to action.

In the early months of 1970, just a few miles up the road from Ellis's Chelsea apartment and Huntley's Rockefeller Center perch, in an old RKO movie theater on Manhattan's Upper West Side that had been converted into a soundstage, a group of men and women of various ages and races were convening daily to finish up the first season of a children's TV program that was still considered an experiment, not yet assured a second season. Its theme song began with a bass-heavy musical figure approximating a toddler's expectant gambol toward a playground—*womp-womp, womp-womp, womp-womp, wompa-domp*—and a chorus of children singing, "Sunny day, sweepin' the clouds away . . ." It was called *Sesame Street.*

Sesame Street was revolutionary in many ways, not least in its *embrace* of urban shabbiness, its comfort in the very conditions that the no-hopers bemoaned. As a *Time* correspondent who visited the show's set that year noted, "The place is in the unavoidable present; the clothing of the cast is well worn, the umber colors and grit of inner-city life are vital components of the show."

Yet *Sesame Street*'s creative team infused this set with joy, effecting an innovative visual blend of scruffiness and gentle psychedelia that was enchanting to children, if sometimes confounding to adults. Today, *Sesame Street* is a beloved institution, its songs, look, format, and such Muppet characters as Big Bird and Oscar the Grouch familiar to several generations. But at the time of its development, the show was so radical as to be literally unimaginable to those not involved in it. Loretta Long, who played Susan, *Sesame Street*'s sunshiny maternal figure, recalled putting a scare into her parents back home in rural Michigan when, in 1969, she described her new job, which, to them, sounded like a drug-induced hallucination.

"I said to my mom, 'It's an educational show, and I'm going to be sitting on a stoop talking to an eight-foot yellow bird!' As it was coming out of my mouth, I knew it was a mistake," she said. "My mother got real quiet. She handed the phone to my father. He was very direct: 'You going to do this when you come home from your real job, right, baby?' 'Well, Daddy, this is going to *be* my real job!' I was so glad that I didn't talk about Oscar. They already were thinking that I was having a breakdown. If I'd said, 'And this thing is going to jump out of a trash can and yell at you,' my mother would have been on the first train, *smoking*, coming to get her child."

As unhinged as the show sounded to the uninitiated, what it stood for was hope. The streetscape was concrete, but the emphasis, metaphorically, was on the little shoots of greenery that sprouted through the cracks in the pavement. Three and a half years before *Sesame Street*'s November 1969 premiere, on PBS, the idea for the program had been hatched by two friends at a dinner party: Joan Ganz Cooney, a producer of documentaries for public television, and Lloyd Morrisett, a vice president at the philanthropic Carnegie Corporation. Deep in conversation at Cooney's New York apartment, they identified a social problem, that poor children were entering kindergarten without the learning skills of their middle-class counterparts, and a potential solution, to use television to better prepare these disadvantaged kids for school. Could a new kind of kids' TV program address this issue? Cooney and Morrisett resolved to find out.

What's notable from today's standpoint is that there was no financial incentive for *Sesame Street*'s founding duo to do what they did. Theirs was not an entrepreneurial undertaking, a start-up in the modern sense of the term. Jon Stone, one of *Sesame Street*'s original producers and its driving creative force in the show's early years, later said of the team that Cooney and Morrisett assembled, "None of us was going to get rich from his labors.... But the challenge of the assignment and the creative freedom granted us to meet that challenge was heady stuff, and we took our responsibility very seriously."

Then in their midthirties, Cooney and Morrisett were exemplars of John F. Kennedy's "Ask not what your country can do for you" ethos, proud to fly the flag of the New Frontier: the late president's slate of programs designed to lead the United States to new heights of greatness and positive influence, be it in the form of anti-poverty initiatives, the Peace Corps, or space exploration. The only wealth that entered into Cooney and Morrisett's considerations was "human wealth"—a coinage of Morrisett's that he used to describe what society was squandering: the untapped potential of disadvantaged children, the contributions that these kids might make to the wider world if only given the chance.

This idealism did not exist in a vacuum. *Sesame Street* was part of a larger movement that saw media professionals and thought leaders leveraging their influence to help children learn and become better citizens. A year and a half before the show's premiere, *Mister Rogers' Neighborhood* had made its national-TV debut, hosted by a gentle ordained Presbyterian minister named Fred Rogers, who had already logged fifteen years in the television industry. And fast on *Sesame Street*'s heels came *Schoolhouse Rock!*, a short-form video series dreamed up by Madison Avenue admen that used music and animation to teach kids times tables, civics, and grammatical rules, and *Free to Be . . . You and Me*, the TV star Marlo Thomas's audacious multipronged campaign (it was first a record album, and then a book and a television special) to instill the concept of gender equality in impressionable young minds.

More broadly, these developments unfolded in an unusually hospitable political climate. For all the polarization that characterized the late sixties and early seventies—as pessimistically described by David Brinkley and epitomized by the anti-war movement and the conservative backlash against it—there was widespread support among the American people and their elected representatives for investing in the country's youngest citizens. The signature achievement of President Lyndon B. Johnson's War on Poverty was the Elementary and Secondary Education Act of 1965, which allocated federal funds to public education on an unprecedented scale, to nearly twenty-seven thousand school districts, and explicitly sought, as *Sesame Street* later would, to close the "achievement gap" between children from lower-income and middle-class households.

Another Johnson administration achievement, the Public Broadcasting Act of 1967, set up the Corporation for Public Broadcasting, a nonprofit entity that distributed federal money to local public television stations, much of it for the purpose of financing educational programming. When, in 1969, a U.S. Senate subcommittee was contemplating cutting the CPB's proposed budget in half, to $10 million, Fred Rogers, already one of public TV's foremost champions and stars, traveled from his home base of Pittsburgh to Washington, D.C., to make his case for keeping the budget in place.

In his customary unhurried pace, Rogers explained to the subcommittee's brusque, skeptical chairman, Senator John Pastore, Democrat of Rhode Island, that his program delivered "an expression of care" to each child viewer, adding, "I feel that if we in public television can only make it clear that feelings are mentionable and manageable, we will have done a great service for mental health." The senator, a self-professed "tough guy" from the mean streets of Providence, softened palpably over the course of the six-plus minutes that Rogers spoke, finally concluding in his Federal Hill accent, "I think it's wondah-ful. *I think it's wondah-ful.* Looks like you've just earned the 20 million dollahs."

— — —

The Rogers-Pastore exchange has become a viral sensation in the YouTube era: a glimpse of a more civil and civic-minded time. But more than that, it represents how transformative this period was for children's culture. "Feelings are mentionable"—this would prove to be a signature sentiment, whether it was expressed, in a marvelous incongruity, by the hulking former NFL defensive line-man Rosey Grier in the *Free to Be . . . You and Me* song "It's Alright to Cry" (because "crying gets the sad out of you") or by *Sesame Street*'s Kermit the Frog as he quietly sang "Bein' Green," which, in less than two minutes, cycled through expressions of insecurity, inadequacy, self-acceptance, and pride. (The song quickly evolved into an American Songbook standard, covered by Frank Sinatra, Lena Horne, and Ray Charles.)

What was new about these shows, relative to the children's programming that had preceded them? They didn't patronize their audiences, and they acknowledged the interior lives of kids. Something similar was happening in children's literature. Mau-rice Sendak's *In the Night Kitchen*, published in 1970, followed the disorienting logic of childhood dreams, as its little-boy protagonist floated in and out of the peril of almost being baked into a cake. Judy Blume, in an extraordinary run of productivity in the early seventies, broke new ground in depicting the emotional turbulence of preteen and teen experience in her young-adult novels, with her characters struggling to make sense of puberty (*Are You There God? It's Me, Margaret*; *Then Again, Maybe I Won't*; *Deenie*); bully-ing (*Blubber*); and divorce (*It's Not the End of the World*).

Far from being derided as squishy or snowflaky, this re-spectful, empathetic approach to engaging children was widely embraced. Blume's books became bestsellers. *Sesame Street* suc-ceeded well beyond its creators' expectations, reaching not only its intended demographic of kids in need but virtually the entirety of preschool America. The songs and stories of *Free to Be . . . You and Me* were incorporated into the curricula of thirty-five of the fifty states.

The further we get from this era, this Age of Enlightenment

Jr., the more remarkable it seems. It came together organically, by accident as much as design, "stalked by good luck," as Cooney put it: with like-minded individuals finding one another just when they needed to. It was shaped, for the most part, by progressive intellectuals, largely from the Northeast—a cultural elite—yet it was received by the public in good faith rather than as an uppity culture-wars provocation.

And it happened to coalesce during a particularly fun, fertile, anything-goes artistic period, in which monsters could be benign and blue (Cookie, Grover) and anthropomorphic traits were routinely ascribed to letters, numerals, and even rolled-up pieces of paper (e.g., the titular star of *Schoolhouse Rock!*'s "I'm Just a Bill").

— — —

I was a part of the first *Sesame Street* generation, three years old at the time of the show's 1969 premiere. My mother, a research scientist, had read newspaper accounts of public television's pending experiment in educational programming for preschoolers, and she dutifully plunked me in front of the TV set on day one of *Sesame Street*'s broadcast existence. My cohort was the first to grow up watching, as a matter of routine, both *Sesame Street* and its sibling program for older children, the reading-oriented *Electric Company*, which came along in 1971. My mother swears that these two shows taught me how to read before I had even entered kindergarten.

Given that this state of affairs was all that I ever knew, it did not register as extraordinary at the time. But as I grew older, I realized that it was, and that the sunny-days era of the late 1960s and 1970s was unique, unprecedented, and amazing. A great confluence of factors—the ongoing rise of television; the backdrop of the anti-war, civil rights, and feminist movements; a political moment in which people in positions of power believed that the federal government could and should play a major role in early-childhood initiatives; and, above all, the emergence of a group of activists and artists animated by a crazily ambitious, optimistic agenda to *do good*—conspired to create an era unlike any before it or since.

These men and women, in counterpoint to the fraught, fractured world that other grown-ups were worrying themselves through, built a world for kids "where the air is sweet" and "where the children run free." (Both of those lyrics—from, respectively, the theme songs of *Sesame Street* and *Free to Be...You and Me*—were by the same writer, Bruce Hart.) It was an era of umber colors and grit, to be sure...but also of sunny days. What follows is an attempt to understand how this era came about, and why it mattered so much.

PART ONE

PART

ONE

How to Get,
How to Get to . . .

Gathered round the set for 'toon time, somewhere in America in the 1950s.

CHAPTER ONE

— — — — —

Putting Down Roots
in the Vast Wasteland

In the spring of 1961, Newton Minow, the newly appointed chairman of the Federal Communications Commission, was gearing up to deliver the keynote speech at the annual convention of the National Association of Broadcasters—addressing the very people he was charged with regulating. He had a lot to say about the state of television, both in a professional capacity and as the father of three young girls growing up in a TV-saturated age.

"My big interest was, from the beginning, children," he later said. "Because I realized that children were spending more time with television than in school. I felt that television was not living up to its potential for kids."

The thirty-five-year-old Minow, a lawyer from Chicago, had come to the attention of the country's forty-three-year-old president, John F. Kennedy, through his friendship with the president's

kid brother and attorney general, Robert F. Kennedy—all of them
the parents of young children. RFK and Minow, born two months
apart, had become close while working on Adlai Stevenson's 1956
campaign for president against Dwight Eisenhower. Even back
then, television had been a frequent topic of conversation between
the two men. "When I was a child," the younger Kennedy told
Minow, "there were three great influences on children: the home,
the school, and the Church. Now I see in my home a fourth great
influence: television."

Indeed, the speed with which TV was transforming America
was troubling to the country's intelligentsia. In 1946, only about
eight thousand homes had television sets. By 1961, that number
had surged to 47 million, accounting for 90 percent of all U.S.
homes. The average American was watching six hours of TV a day.

Minow was no TV prude. To the contrary, he was a dedicated
consumer of it, and, in his capacity as an attorney, represented
one of the medium's earliest national stars, Burr Tillstrom, the creative mastermind behind the Chicago-based breakout hit *Kukla,
Fran and Ollie*. (Though it aired at 6 p.m. and featured puppets,
Tillstrom's wry, mostly improvised show was not expressly aimed
at young children. Among its devoted fans was a gangly teenager
in Maryland named Jim Henson.) But the FCC job was an opportunity for Minow to address TV's growing incursion into American
life, and to make sure it didn't reach a crisis point.

While writing the speech he was to deliver before the NAB,
Minow leaned on another of his friends, a journalist named John
Bartlow Martin, for help. Martin happened to be at work on a series
of articles for the *Saturday Evening Post* about the state of commercial television. As part of his series, Martin had pulled an immer-
sion stunt, watching NBC's Chicago affiliate, WNBQ, for twenty

straight hours. The onslaught of soap operas, game shows, and ads proved stultifying to Martin, leaving him cranky, disillusioned, and resistant to the bandleader Mitch Miller's importunings to sing "By the Light of the Silvery Moon" on the program *Sing Along with Mitch*. ("The author did not join him," Martin dryly noted.)

To Minow, Martin suggested that the FCC chairman refer to television, in his speech, as a "vast wasteland of junk."

The speech that Minow actually delivered to the broadcasters was gentler and more complimentary. He began with some disarming self-deprecation, telling his audience, "I was not picked for this job because I regard myself as the fastest draw on the New Frontier." He proclaimed that he was a fan of *The Twilight Zone* and *CBS Reports* and promised, "I am in Washington to help broadcasting, not to harm it; to strengthen it, not weaken it; to reward it, not to punish it; to encourage it, not threaten it; and to stimulate it, not censor it. Above all, I am here to uphold and protect the public interest."

But Minow, echoing Martin, noted that, at its worst, TV was "a procession of game shows, formula comedies about totally unbelievable families, blood and thunder, mayhem, violence, sadism, murder, Western bad men, Western good men, private eyes, gangsters, more violence, and cartoons." This version of television, he said, was indeed a "vast wasteland."

Nevertheless, Minow believed in TV's potential to be better, and, in his speech, he specifically cited children's television as an area ripe for reinvention. "Is there no room on television to teach, to inform, to uplift, to stretch, to enlarge the capacities of our children?" he asked. "Is there no room for programs deepening their understanding of children in other lands? Is there no room for a children's news show explaining something to them about the world at their level of understanding?"

Minow thought his speech went well. If there was any phrase in it that he expected to resonate with his audience, it was "the public interest." But, to his surprise, the phrase that the broadcasters fixated upon was "vast wasteland"—a term that would enter the lexicon even though he never intended for it to describe the whole of the television landscape. For this coinage, adapted from Martin's words, Minow received not only blowback from the industry—Sherwood Schwartz, the creator of the sitcom *Gilligan's Island*, named the show's shipwrecked charter boat the SS *Minnow* as payback—but also the unwelcome embrace of Luddites and snobs, who, for years thereafter, would proudly announce to him, upon discovering who he was, that they didn't even *own* TV sets.

"To which I would say, 'Well, you're missing something very important in your life,'" Minow said.

— — —

One person who clearly did get the gist of what Minow was trying to say was Joan Ganz. She had moved to New York from her native Phoenix, Arizona, in 1953, when she was twenty-three years old, to pursue a career in television: a still-novel path, especially for a woman. The daughter of a Jewish banker and a Catholic homemaker, Ganz was raised Catholic in a well-to-do household. She harbored dreams of becoming an actress but, facing her father's disapproval, instead took a degree in education at the University of Arizona. Fresh out of college, Ganz became inspired by the teachings of the Christophers, a Catholic group whose progressive leader, Father James Keller, encouraged not only civic engagement but also the embrace of mass media as a means of furthering humanitarian goals. For a time, Keller himself was a TV personality, hosting a syndicated show called *The Christophers* (later renamed *Christopher Closeup*), a benignly low-key, brimstone-free interview program.

In New York, Ganz found a niche as a TV publicist, one of the few options then available to women in the industry. Television in the fifties abounded with highbrow anthology drama series, among them *Playhouse 90*, *Cavalcade of America*, and the one that Ganz worked for, CBS's *The United States Steel Hour*. It was a good job, though it did little to fulfill her interests in social activism, and it wasn't particularly challenging: Ganz tended to finish up her *Steel Hour* work in half the time she was allotted.

Casting about for a way to fill out her schedule and engage herself politically, Ganz volunteered to arrange live events—debates, talks, and the like—for William Phillips, the cofounder of the leftist quarterly the *Partisan Review*. In so doing, she fell in with the city's notoriously argumentative crowd of public intellectuals and literati, among them Lionel and Diana Trilling, Norman Podhoretz, and Norman Mailer.

It was heady stuff for Ganz, if occasionally humiliating. Like the snobs whom Minow encountered, this group had nothing but contempt for the medium that she so believed in. "I became a very looked-down-upon person because not only was I in television but *publicity* of television," she said. "You can't imagine a lower status among the *Partisan Review* crowd. But they had to put up with me because of William Phillips wanting me to help him put on fundraisers. I got to know everybody. I loved Lionel Trilling. Diana was a bitch."

One of the few in the group with whom she developed a genuine friendship was, of all people, Mailer, America's foremost pugilistic man of letters. Mailer embraced Ganz as a platonic confidante, someone he counted on to calm him down in his dark moments. She was, he joked, his "unpaid psychiatrist." Ganz, for her part, found Mailer "very weird and scary, but irresistible."

In 1960, this friendship came close to costing Ganz—and, by extension, the children of the United States—dearly. In the wee hours of November 20, her phone began to ring. "And I knew exactly who would be calling," Ganz said, "because it was the only person who ever called me at four in the morning. I didn't answer it."

Her restraint proved wise. In Greenwich Village, as a party at their home was winding down, an inebriated Mailer had stabbed his wife, Adele Morales, with a penknife. Though Morales would recover physically and choose not to press charges against her husband, the stabbing became a lurid press sensation. Had Ganz taken Mailer's call, she believes, her life might have unfolded differently. "He would have come to me, and I would have had to take him to the police station," she said. "My name probably would have been associated with it. I never would have been chosen to lead *Sesame Street*."

— — —

Fortunately, bad press did not become an issue for Ganz. Indeed, in a decade's time, when she was married and known as Joan Ganz Cooney, she acquired the nickname "Saint Joan" for her tireless, pioneering work in reinventing children's television. But she wasn't the field's only saint. *Sesame Street* was destined to be thought of in tandem with, and occasionally in opposition to, *Mister Rogers' Neighborhood*, the other revolutionary children's program to emerge in the late 1960s. Together, the shows constituted a kind of Big Bang, abruptly shaking up the TV landscape and shaping the sensibilities of at least two generations.

Fred Rogers, as it happened, overlapped with Ganz during her early days in New York City, though the two did not know each other. In some respects, they were quite similar: young altruists who didn't like much of what they saw on TV but were nonetheless excited by the medium's potential. Like Ganz, Rogers had moved to the big city to work in television out of a sense of calling as much as career. In Rogers's case, the religious overtones were even more explicit—he put off attending divinity school in his native western Pennsylvania to give TV a try, going to work for CBS's chief competitor, NBC.

Rogers had attended Dartmouth College for two years before transferring to Rollins College in central Florida, where he majored in music. Home for spring break during his senior year, in 1951, Rogers had his first chance to watch television at length. Like John Bartlow Martin, he was appalled by most of its content, which he found lamentable. But he was fascinated by TV and announced to his parents that he was going to take some time after graduation to live in New York and give the field a try. They were flummoxed by this decision, noting to their son that he knew little about television. "Yes, I know," Rogers later recalled telling them, "but I've seen enough to think that this is something I should do in the world before I go to the cloisters again."

A child of even greater privilege than Ganz, Rogers grew up as a rich kid in Latrobe, Pennsylvania, a factory town where his parents owned the factories. His mother, Nancy McFeely Rogers, came from a family that had made its fortune in bricks; his father, James Hillis Rogers, was an industrialist who owned a die-casting company and assumed the management of his wife's family's firm. His parents were compassionate capitalists, philanthropic and devoted to the arts. Fred grew up a de facto only child, alone until his parents adopted his sister, Nancy Elaine, when he was eleven.

The original expectation had been that Fred would follow in his father's footsteps and take over the family business. But Rogers, asthmatic as a young child and therefore compelled to spend a lot of time indoors, developed a more contemplative, ministerial disposition. His parents, observant Presbyterians, did not object to his seminarian path.

The TV thing, however, was a curveball. His parents had connections at NBC, since one of Nancy's forebears had been an original investor in RCA, the parent company of the network at the time of its founding. At NBC, Fred started out as a gofer and ascended to floor-manager positions on the network's music programs, which abounded in those pre-rock days. He worked on the popular-song showcases *Your Hit Parade* and *The Kate Smith Hour*, and the classical-music-oriented *NBC Opera Theatre* and *The Voice of Firestone*. Among his tasks for the latter, he recalled, was "hiring handsome but mute men for Risë Stevens"—an acclaimed mezzo-soprano—"to smile at while she sang."

With his music background and affable, can-do manner, Rogers proved an adept TV hand, and NBC was happy to have him. He gave little consideration to getting involved in children's television, though, until he was asked to. For NBC's local New York affiliate, WNBT, he was assigned to work on *The Horn and Hardart Children's Hour*, a Sunday-morning variety show that had migrated to television from radio, sponsored by the then thriving Automat chain. The program was devoted entirely to child performers, but Rogers, far from being charmed, was disturbed by the hustling, pushy stage parents and prematurely poised kids. "I think it was then," he later said, "that I decided that children should never entertain children."

He was more disturbed still by Pinky Lee and Soupy Sales, comedians who broke through with programs for kids in the midfifties, on NBC and ABC, respectively. In part, it was a simple clash of sensibilities—Lee (né Pincus Leff), a manic, baggy-pants refugee from vaudeville, and Sales (né Milton Supman), a young, urbane Jewish hipster, were the antithesis of wholesome, Presbyterian Fred. Rogers was especially put off by the violence, as he perceived it, of their signature schticks: in Lee's case, squirting his adversaries in the face with seltzer water, and in Sales's case, receiving a pie in his face. Some kids might have laughed, but others, sharing Rogers's childhood sensitivity, to which he still had ready access as an adult, might have found the wocka-wocka antics downright frightening.

Suffice it to say, the young teetotal Fred Rogers did not travel in the same circles as Joan Ganz. Though he and his new wife, Joanne, a fellow Rollins alum and a trained concert pianist, would not become parents until 1959, children were already on Fred's mind in the early 1950s, intuitively a part of his ministerial calling. "I don't know why," he remembered years later, "but practically every weekend while I was in New York, I took time off to visit day-care centers, orphanages, schools. It was probably some sort of a need to understand who I had been as well as who these kids are." As for children's television, Rogers came to believe that it represented the very worst of what his chosen medium had to offer—but, at the same time, it presented him with an opportunity to do better.

In 1953, Rogers heard that in Pittsburgh, the nearest big city to his hometown of Latrobe, a group of civic-minded educators, activists, and business leaders were starting up the nation's first publicly supported television station. It would be founded explicitly for the purpose of offering educational programming. (There were already four other educational-TV stations in the United States, but they were funded by and affiliated with universities.) The new station's foremost champion, and its first president, was a woman named Dorothy Daniel, a journalist and one-half of a Pittsburgh power couple with Royal Daniel, the managing editor of the *Pittsburgh Sun-Telegraph*. Dorothy Daniel named the station WQED, after the abbreviation for *quod erat demonstrandum* ("thus it has been demonstrated"), the Latin phrase used at the end of mathematical proofs.

For Rogers, the news of WQED's founding was a sign. He moved back to western Pennsylvania, where he eagerly offered up his services to the fledgling station. He had been on a fast track at NBC, and might very well have enjoyed a long career there as a producer or executive—his New York friend Paul Bogart, later to direct such programs as *All in the Family*, told Rogers he was nuts to forfeit his position at the network. But by 1954, Fred and Joanne were living in Pittsburgh.

—   —   —

Ganz, too, was looking for a job in which her dual interests in public service and television would jibe. Her quest took longer, in part because it wasn't until 1962 that New York got its own noncommercial educational-TV station, WNDT, whose call letters stood for "New Dimensions in Television."

Newton Minow played a role in WNDT's getting off the ground. The station that it took over for on the TV dial, WATV, had been an anomaly among New York's seven television channels, in that it was based in Newark, New Jersey. WATV, occupying channel thirteen, was always the poor relation among the New York metro area's commercial stations, and by the beginning of the 1960s, its owners wanted to sell it.

Several big-ticket bidders lined up, including Paramount Pictures and 20th Century Fox. But Minow, keen for the United States' largest media market to have a public television station, set up hearings about channel thirteen's fate. This proved a turnoff to the commercial bidders and opened the way for the Educational Broadcasting Corporation, a nonprofit citizens' group that was partly underwritten by the Ford Foundation, to have its lowball bid of $6.45 million accepted. Though its FCC license still placed it in New Jersey, WNDT—which took to calling itself "Channel Thirteen"—set up offices in New York, beckoning Ganz. In 1963, she finally left CBS, accepting a pay cut to take what she considered her dream job: producing public-affairs shows and short documentaries for Channel Thirteen.

The following year, she married Tim Cooney, a charismatic, well-connected figure in New York's Democratic Party who was then working as the public-relations director for the city's Department of Labor. Drawing public-sector salaries, the Cooneys lived simply in an apartment to the east of Gramercy Park. What they lacked in material wealth they made up for in shared political fervor. Joan's documentaries, whose titles included *Poverty, Anti-Poverty, and the Poor* and *A Chance at the Beginning,* reflected her intensifying focus on alleviating the effects of poverty. The latter film was about an experimental early-childhood educational program in Harlem, founded in 1962, that anticipated Head Start, the Johnson administration's 1965 initiative to better prepare disadvantaged preschoolers for kindergarten—which itself anticipated *Sesame Street.*

— — —

The Cooneys effortlessly fit in with a set of young urbanites and suburbanites who self-identified as New Frontiersmen, fully invested members of the JFK generation. One of the couples with whom the

Cooneys occasionally socialized was Lloyd and Mary Morrisett. Lloyd, a Yale-educated psychologist, had grown up in Los Angeles, where one of his closest childhood friends was a cousin of Joan's named Julian Ganz. When a job opportunity prompted the Morrisetts to move to New York in 1958, Julian suggested to Lloyd that he look up his cousin "Joanie." It took Morrisett until 1961 to do so, but he and Joan quickly established a rapport.

Morrisett regarded education as a sacred duty. His father had been a professor of education at UCLA and, before that, a teacher and principal. But rather than becoming a professor himself, the younger Morrisett was drawn to cognitive psychology. In the aftermath of World War II, when he was in graduate school, psychology was undergoing a boom in popularity—and respectability. Much of this was a consequence of President Franklin D. Roosevelt's establishment, during wartime, of the Office of Strategic Services, the forerunner to the Central Intelligence Agency. The OSS brought together large numbers of psychologists and social scientists for the first time, forging personal and professional connections that would endure after the war.

The OSS used psychologists for a variety of purposes, from creating dark-arts programs to undermine the enemy to developing strategies for optimizing the performance of U.S. soldiers. Two of Morrisett's mentors were psychologists with OSS experience. His favorite professor at Yale, Carl Hovland, specialized in the field of persuasion and attitude change, and had conducted studies on how effective U.S.-made propaganda films were in boosting the morale of servicemen—studies that themselves anticipated the ones that *Sesame Street*'s research team would conduct two decades later on preschoolers. Another OSS alum and psychologist was Morrisett's future boss, John W. Gardner, whose duties as an intelligence officer included assessing potential operatives' fitness to join the agency.

Gardner became the president of the New York–based Carnegie Corporation in 1955 and hired Morrisett four years later. Like his young protégé, Gardner was an evangelist for the power of education, and, though only in his forties, was already considered a wise old head on the subject, an adviser to presidents and universities. (In the late fifties, he coined the phrase "the pursuit of excellence"—a term that, due to its overuse, became almost as much of a millstone for Gardner as "vast wasteland" would be for Minow.)

Morrisett was hired by Gardner to be a program officer at Carnegie in psychology, essentially charged with seeing how new and innovative developments in his field could be applied to further the foundation's aims in education. What made this an especially exciting proposition in the early sixties was that cognitive psychologists were increasingly focusing on early childhood, with new studies indicating that the preschool years were a far more crucial phase of a child's development than had previously been understood. As a result, Carnegie, which had historically invested heavily in programs devoted to higher education, began allocating more of its resources to early-childhood programs.

"We found that too many children were entering school unequipped to benefit from it," Morrisett said. "And the way Carnegie worked is that when we defined an area of concern—early-childhood education, reading—it was the program officer's job to become aware of the good work going on in such a field, how it could be magnified and better used. So that was my job."

— — —

Why weren't 1960s kids getting a leg up on learning in nursery school? Because nursery school barely existed, at least not in the organized, codified form that we know it today. In 1970, just 20 percent of all U.S. three- and four-year-olds were enrolled in a preschool program. Half the country's school districts didn't even offer kindergarten to their five-year-olds.

While the 1950s and 1960s did witness a burgeoning movement of parent-run cooperative nursery schools—accelerated in 1960 by the foundation of a national organization, the American Council of Parent Cooperatives—these existed by and large in privileged communities, serving just a small percentage of the country's pre-K kids. Most American families took an ad hoc approach to managing the days of their preschool-age children. With women still making up only about a third of the labor force—33 percent in 1960, 38 percent in 1970—this hard work generally fell to stay-at-home mothers.

And the more scant a household's resources were, the greater the chance that its children were underprepared for elementary school, relative to their middle-class peers. The studies that Morrisett read determined that a black child from a poor neighborhood in New York was likely, as he recalled, to come to school "a few months behind in first grade and be a year and one-half behind by third grade."

For Carole Demas and Paula Janis, two young women who were teaching kindergarten in the New York City school system in 1962, this sad state of affairs wasn't a theoretical construct but a vivid reality. Friends since their days at Midwood High School in central Brooklyn, they weren't long out of college when they were hired, together, to teach one hundred kids a day—fifty in the morning session and fifty in the afternoon—at P.S. 7, an old redbrick primary school that stood in the shadow of the Brooklyn Bridge. Built in 1882, it had served, in its early decades, the Jewish and Italian children of the families who lived in the neighborhood's nearby tenements, among them an incorrigible troublemaker named Alphonse Capone. By the time Demas and Janis came along, P.S. 7 had fallen into decrepitude, and the tenements were now occupied primarily by black and Latin American families.

Unruliness was seldom a problem in their classroom; intimidation was. "The reality of what we found was children who had never had any schooling. No prekindergarten. No nursery school," Demas said. "Many of them lived in homes that were troubled. They were all terrified. They arrived at this building, which seemed enormous. We worked with them in a huge room, and everything about it was kind of crumbling. When you pulled on the shades, you were in danger of having them land on the floor."

Demas and Janis, both of whom were raised middle-class, discovered that their students needed lessons in such rudimentary skills as how to hold a crayon correctly (with a three-finger grip rather than balled up in the fist) and how to use safety scissors. They smuggled a Christmas tree into their classroom, against city policy and the fire code, because they had learned that few of their kids' families could afford to have a tree at home, let alone presents. Together, the teachers and students trimmed the tree with empty half-pint milk cartons wrapped in colored paper and milkweed pods foraged from a vacant lot across the street. Janis, for her part, went on a few dates with a toy importer she knew but didn't particularly care for, "and conned him out of a hundred toys," she said, "so every kid could have a toy for Christmas."

"Idealism just seemed like a normal part of life" in that era,

Demas said. Hers and Janis's extended beyond the bounds of the classroom, to the point where they scrounged together funds to ensure that each of their students had a coat warm enough for New York's winters. But more important than these acts of kindness was how the two women connected with the children as teachers. Janis was a guitarist and folk singer. Demas was an aspiring actress and trained vocalist. Singing together, the duo performed such classroom standards as "Old MacDonald Had a Farm," along with some Spanish-language songs that Janis had learned on the folkie circuit—and therein lay the breakthrough. The kids started joining in, and soon thereafter began to engage with their teachers in lessons and arts-and-crafts projects.

"They just started to bloom," Demas said. Unwittingly, she and Janis landed upon a formula—integrating the arts and performance into their curriculum—for achieving the supposedly unachievable goal of reaching at-risk young children raised in poverty. It wasn't until a decade later that Demas and Janis were given the opportunity to apply this formula to television. But when they did, with the sweet, low-budget *The Magic Garden*, a local children's program that aired on the New York station WPIX, the two friends became beloved gurus of the preschool set, their instincts ratified by critical acclaim and a twelve-year run in the nation's largest TV market.

In the 1962–63 school year, though, Demas and Janis were marooned in Brooklyn's Navy Yard neighborhood, oblivious to any notion that their methods might be scalable. Lloyd Morrisett, for his part, encountered a similar hurdle: he and Carnegie knew that they were doing good, but the experimental programs they were underwriting reached only so far, aiding children in the hundreds rather than in the millions.

Soon, however, these well-intentioned actors would acquire a powerful ally: the federal government.

— — —

Lyndon B. Johnson, running to retain the office he assumed when John F. Kennedy was assassinated in November 1963, won the 1964 presidential election in a landslide, carrying forty-four of the fifty states. His campaign successfully portrayed his opponent, Senator Barry Goldwater of Arizona, as a nukes-mad, far-right extremist bent on cutting down the social safety net that had been put in place three decades earlier by FDR's New Deal. Johnson, by contrast, was keen to widen the safety net, and now had the political clout to do so; the same election season gave the Democratic Party two-thirds majorities in both houses of Congress.

The result was a storm of progressive legislation and action— Johnson's expansion of and elaboration upon Kennedy's New Frontier vision, which he called "the Great Society." On April 9, 1965, Johnson signed into law the Elementary and Secondary Education Act, whose crucial section, Title I, distributed federal funds to school districts with a high percentage of low-income families, like the one in which Demas and Janis taught. A few weeks later, Johnson's administration launched an eight-week trial version of Head Start, in which educators, during the summertime run-up to the 1965–66 school year, prepped poor children for their entrance into elementary school. (In the late sixties, by which time Head Start had achieved critical mass, Janis ran the Head Start program at P.S. 20 on the Lower East Side of Manhattan, and marveled at the resources at hand relative to her P.S. 7 days: "Fifteen kids in a classroom, with not only a teacher, but an assistant and a parent coordinator. And fantastic lunches. It totally worked.")

More auspiciously for Morrisett, the summer of 1965 saw Johnson tap his boss, John Gardner, to serve in the president's Cabinet as secretary of Health, Education, and Welfare, the federal agency that oversaw U.S. education policy. (Later, in 1979, this agency would be split into two separate agencies, the Department of Education and the Department of Health and Human Services.) For the position of U.S. commissioner of education, the highest-ranking education post after his, Gardner brought in Harold Howe II, who had been his friend and neighbor in the New York City suburb of Scarsdale.

Howe, known as Doc, was a formidable figure in education. One of his grandfathers, Samuel Chapman Armstrong, a Union general during the Civil War, was the founding president of the Hampton Institute in Virginia, established in 1868 as a trade school for freed slaves. (Today it is Hampton University.) Upon joining the Johnson administration in January 1966, Doc Howe took charge of the U.S. government's effort to desegregate public schools in accordance with the Civil Rights Act of 1964. His leverage was the vast amount of federal money that Johnson had set aside for education—in order for school districts to qualify for it, they had to meet the integration goals that he set. In some southern statehouses, Howe was referred to, derisively, as "the Commissioner of Integration."

— — —

This alignment of circumstances—Gardner and Howe in charge of U.S. education policy, the sudden availability of federal money, the advance of cognitive psychology, and the newly heightened interest in early-childhood development—created an ideal environment for grand experiments in education. It was a fortuitous time for the Cooneys to invite the Morrisetts to dinner.

Lloyd Morrisett and his wife, Mary, accepted the invitation from Joan and Tim Cooney. The dinner took place at the Cooneys' apartment in the winter of 1966. Also attending was Lewis Freedman, the station programmer at WNDT and Cooney's boss. For the occasion, Joan made boeuf bourguignon.

A few weeks before the dinner, Morrisett, who had recently been promoted to vice president of the Carnegie Corporation in the wake of Gardner's departure, had experienced a parental episode that piqued his curiosity as a psychologist. Early one Sunday morning, he was awakened by a shrill, high-pitched sound. He followed it into the living room of his house in Irvington, New York, where he found his three-year-old daughter, Sarah, watching the FCC-mandated test pattern that TV stations would broadcast before their regular programming began: a static grid overlaid with concentric circles and an image of an Indian chief's head. Morrisett immediately understood that his daughter was waiting for something—cartoons, probably—to come on. But he was struck by the tractor-beam lock that the TV set had on his daughter: the inherent fascination that the glowing screen itself held.

Over the course of the Cooneys' dinner party, Freedman, echoing Newton Minow, spoke passionately about the unfulfilled potential of TV as an educational medium. His talk bloomed into a conversation, which carried over into the dessert course. Turning to Joan Cooney over coffee, Morrisett, mindful of what he'd witnessed with Sarah, posed a question: "Do you think television could be used to teach young children?"

The young Jim Henson with Sam, Kermit,
and Yorick on the regional TV program Sam and Friends.

CHAPTER

TWO

"The Potential Uses of Television in Preschool Education"

Morrisett left the dinner party at the Cooneys' energized. He wanted to know the answer to the question he had posed, and hit upon the idea of having the Carnegie Corporation underwrite a three-month study on the feasibility of using TV to educate at-risk young children. First, he had to overcome some institutional bias at Carnegie. "A number of our staff members felt television was a black hole," he said—too expensive, too noisy, too much of a vast wasteland.

But Morrisett, now a man on a mission, wangled a $15,000 budget for the study. Shortly after the dinner party, he invited Lewis Freedman and Joan Ganz Cooney to the Carnegie offices to discuss the feasibility study and how it might be executed—perhaps by sending a designated researcher to travel around the country to meet with educators and child-development experts. All through the meeting, Cooney struggled to contain her excitement, inwardly thinking, *I would love to do this. Please, let me do this.* But Freedman, her boss, told Morrisett, "Joan wouldn't be interested. She's a public-affairs producer." Which prompted Cooney to blurt out, "Oh, yes, I would!"

Still, Freedman didn't want to lose Cooney, a valued employee, to Morrisett's project, and dismissed her enthusiastic response, telling Morrisett that he would get back to him with some more suitable candidates for the researcher position. Fortuitously, though, Tim Cooney, who knew of his wife's eagerness to conduct the study, happened to have a lunch on the books with Morrisett just a few days later, on an unrelated matter. Tim Cooney backchanneled word of Joan's interest to Morrisett, who promptly called Freedman and requested Joan by name for the job.

Soon thereafter, Joan Ganz Cooney was on the road, traveling throughout the United States and Canada and conferring with members of the early-childhood educational community on the merits of an explicitly educational, nationally broadcast TV show. "And whether it was Annemarie Roeper in Michigan, who runs a school for gifted children, or Carl Bereiter, who ran the most dramatic of the Head Starts out in Colorado ... all the range of people said, 'Absolutely. Try it. Try a television show. It certainly can't hurt, and it may help,'" Cooney recalled.

Cooney's report on her findings, which she submitted to Morrisett, was entitled *The Potential Uses of Television in Preschool Education.* "The real question behind that title was: Can television teach?" Cooney said. "Well, we knew the answer. I knew the answer right away. Every child in America was singing beer commercials. Now, where had they learned beer commercials?"

— — —

While Cooney and Morrisett were pondering a way forward into children's television, Jon Stone and Tom Whedon were scheming to get out of it. The two men, both in their thirties, had met while working as writers for *Captain Kangaroo*, a mainstay of CBS's daytime schedule since its debut, in 1955. Stone and Whedon became fast friends and writing partners, keen to sell a sitcom to one of the networks and begin life anew in Los Angeles, to which most of the action in TV had shifted by the midsixties.

But they failed to make a sale on any of their pitches. Stuck in New York, the two writers were tossed a lifeline by Fred Silverman, a wunderkind television executive who had been hired by CBS in 1963 when he was only twenty-five to oversee its children's programming. Familiar with their background in kids' TV, Silverman hired Stone and Whedon to develop a new, five-days-a-week daytime series centered around Snow White—the fairy-tale character, not the trademarked Disney princess. To differentiate their Snow White from Disney's, Stone and Whedon decided that their title character would consort with a group of puppet friends rather than with seven dwarfs. They presented this idea to Silverman, who liked it and thought he knew just the right man to realize their vision.

"Friday morning," he told them one day, "we're going to meet with Christ and his dog."

Christ turned out to be Jim Henson, a young puppeteer who had risen to semi-prominence on ABC's *The Jimmy Dean Show*, a weekly variety program hosted by an amiable country singer whose name to this day adorns a popular line of frozen sausages. Dean's sidekick and frequent duetting partner was Rowlf, a brown, floppy-eared dog puppet performed by Henson, who called his creations "Muppets."

Henson, who really did resemble Jesus, was a bearded, lanky, laconic figure who, though he was only thirty years old in 1966, had already amassed a considerable fortune. Born in Leland, Mississippi, where his agronomist father was briefly stationed by the U.S. government, Henson grew up in the Washington, D.C., suburb of Hyattsville, Maryland. While still an undergraduate at the University of Maryland in the late 1950s, he made a name for himself locally with *Sam and Friends*, a five-minute mini program on WRC, Washington's NBC affiliate. WRC aired the show live at 11:25 p.m., as the lead-in to *The Tonight Show* in its Steve Allen and Jack Paar eras—a choice slot that, for WRC's audience, would become a more habit-forming view than the nationally televised main event that followed. *Sam and Friends'* popularity leaped to even further heights when WRC also made it the lead-in, at 6:45 p.m., to another national broadcast: NBC's flagship news show, *The Huntley-Brinkley Report*, then in its infancy.

The Sam on *Sam and Friends* was a little bald man with jug ears and surprised eyes, and he was made of plastic wood. But the characters who really captured the D.C. public's imagination were the pliable, expressive puppets that Henson made out of felt and foam rubber. One of them, Kermit, was fashioned from material salvaged from an old coat belonging to Henson's mother, its color "milky turquoise," in Henson's recollection.

Kermit was not yet green or explicitly a frog. And, given the lateness of the hour at which it was originally broadcast, *Sam and Friends* was not remotely meant for children. But it's remarkable how evolved Henson's sensibility already was, and how well suited it would prove to be, in time, for young viewers. His sense of humor was playful and anarchic, and he had a synesthetic way with letters, words, and songs, seeing them visually as images even as his characters voiced and heard them as sounds.

Long before *Sesame Street*, in a sketch called "Visual Thinking," Kermit and a socklike beatnik Muppet named Harry the Hipster carried out a conversation while animations of their thoughts appeared above their heads. When Kermit remarked "Gee!" to Harry, a letter G appeared. When Harry hummed out five notes of a song he had been practicing on the piano, five quarter notes flashed over him. And when Kermit professed not to dig jazz, a square briefly framed his face—a foreshadowing of how Henson, and *Sesame Street* in general, would engage on two levels, for child viewers and their adult caretakers.

But in 1966, Henson was not particularly disposed toward working in children's entertainment. He had too many ideas, and too much going on. For starters, his career in advertising was going gangbusters. It had begun in the *Sam and Friends* era with a series of eight-second spots for Wilkins Coffee, a local brand, for which Henson had conceived a simple comic premise: a chipper Muppet named Wilkins (vaguely Kermit-like) repeatedly punished a morose Muppet named Wontkins (vaguely Telly Monster–like) for the latter's refusal to try Wilkins Coffee. The spots were savage in their felt-on-felt violence—Wontkins was shot, clubbed, blown up, electrocuted, struck by a falling tree, and run over by a train—but somehow sweet, too; Henson's singsong voice (which he lent to both puppets) and Wilkins and Wontkins's squishy, alien otherness were an endearing combination.

The Wilkins ads became a calling card for Henson. He recreated them for other regional coffee roasters, and was soon engaged by such national brands as Purina, IBM, and La Choy,

America's foremost purveyor of ersatz Chinese food. Henson had also taken to describing himself as an "experimental filmmaker" as much as a puppeteer, and with good reason. A puppet-less short film he made in 1965, *Time Piece*—a fast-paced, surreal wig-out in which Henson himself starred, playing a dying man, a flying man, a man applying a coat of paint to an elephant, and a man whose head appears on a platter as a restaurant entrée—received a nomination for an Academy Award.

With all this going on, the Muppets' popularity kept growing. Henson's original puppeteering partner, dating back to *Sam and Friends* and his University of Maryland days, was a young woman named Jane Nebel. In 1959, Henson and Nebel became husband and wife. By 1966, they were the parents of four children, with a house in Greenwich, Connecticut, and an office for Muppets, Inc., as their company was then known, in a town house in New York City. Jane Henson dialed down her puppeteering activity to look after the children, but, with the Muppets in ever greater demand for such programs as *Today* and *The Ed Sullivan Show*, Jim cultivated a new set of puppeteers who promptly absorbed his sensibility, among them a former actor named Jerry Nelson and a twenty-two-year-old transplant from Oakland, California, named Frank Oznowicz, who would soon shorten his surname to Oz.

So, Henson certainly didn't need to take on Stone and Whedon's project. But, after hearing them out at the meeting that Silverman had arranged, and offering feedback in his quiet, assured way—he advised the writers that abstract "monster" puppets would work better than representational animal puppets—he announced that he was in.

As was Joe Raposo, a young pianist and composer who was

enlisted by Stone and Whedon to write songs for the Snow White program they were doing for CBS. Whedon and Raposo had known each other as undergraduates at Harvard. Stone first met Raposo way back in 1955. Having just received his master's degree from the Yale School of Drama, Stone was directing a summer-stock show in Cape Cod. Raposo, then only eighteen, was also working on the Cape, playing cabaret piano. Stone was impressed by Raposo's work and hired him to play piano over his play's scene changes. Eleven years later, Stone and Whedon were now in a position to give Raposo a proper big break.

But the Snow White program died a quick death. CBS and Silverman pulled a volte-face, deciding they didn't want it. Undeterred, Stone and Whedon, with Henson, reconceived the show around another fairy-tale princess, Cinderella, and successfully pitched this version to ABC as a weekly program, seeing it all the way through to the pilot phase—only for this project, too, to run aground. Though the pilot was well liked, ABC had just acquired rights to televise NCAA football—which would eat up the Saturday slot for which the Cinderella show had been tentatively earmarked. Stone and Whedon's loss was Keith Jackson's gain; the "Whoa, Nellie!" announcer, tapped that year by the network to call college games, would do so for the next four decades.

Though the Cinderella idea would finally see the light of day in early 1969, when the Canadian Broadcasting Corporation aired a one-off special, directed by Henson, entitled *Hey, Cinderella!*, the show's failure to achieve liftoff as a series in 1966 was hard on Stone. Presuming his TV career to be finished, he and his new wife, the former Beverley Owen—an actress who had played Marilyn Munster, the pretty girl in a family of ghouls, in the first season of the CBS sitcom *The Munsters*—began to spend the bulk of their time at their Vermont vacation house, with serious thoughts of re-inventing themselves as innkeepers.

Still, the frustrating experience would reap long-term benefits. Over the course of working on the show, Stone and Henson grew close and earned each other's trust. One thing they had in common was a pronounced *lack* of fretfulness about television's effects on its viewers. Both men came up in the medium rather than happening into it as refugees from other corners of show business. TV made them, and they regarded it as a font of endless possibility, not as a source of furrowed-brow concern. The Cinderella project was also significant in that it marked the first time that Stone, Henson, Raposo, Oz, and Nelson collectively worked together. It would not be the last.

Bob Keeshan, not yet out of his twenties,
as Captain Kangaroo in the 1950s.

CHAPTER

THREE

The *Captain Kangaroo* Finishing School for Children's-TV Professionals

Jon Stone, just a little younger than Joan Ganz Cooney and Fred Rogers, was yet another well-born kid who found his way to New York and the TV industry while just barely out of college. Like Cooney, he began his career at CBS. Unlike Cooney, he was a man—with an MFA from Yale, no less—and was therefore quickly admitted into the network's directors training program. The trainees started on the lowest rung of the corporate ladder, in clerical and mail-room positions, but if they showed intelligence and initiative, as Stone did, they were quickly elevated, first to production assistants, then stage managers, and then associate directors.

Stone's path to television was not blazed with moral righteousness, as Cooney's and Rogers's were. He was, initially at least, just a driven guy who wanted to make it in show business as an actor or director; early on in his time in New York, he landed some small parts in plays and on soap operas. He was, by and large, apolitical, leaning, if anything, slightly to the right. He had grown up in New Haven, Connecticut, the son of an obstetrician, and attended the Pomfret School, a posh boarding school in the northeast corner of the state. He voted for Richard Nixon over John F. Kennedy in the 1960 presidential election. In his bachelorhood, he tooled around the city in a Triumph TR3 convertible that he had splashed out on with his earnings.

But Stone was a headstrong young man and a bit of a rebel in his own family, where his artistic temperament stood out. At Williams College, where he earned his undergraduate degree, he majored in music, directed and starred in plays, and became friendly with Stephen Sondheim, who was two years ahead of him.

Children's television was something that Stone more or less fell into, when his first year at CBS coincided with the launch of *Captain Kangaroo*, a low-budget, low-key children's program that served as shrewd counterprogramming to the time slot's unassailable ratings leader, NBC's *Today*. *Captain Kangaroo*'s title character was played by Bob Keeshan, who also created and produced the show. Though only twenty-eight at the time of the program's premiere, Keeshan fashioned himself as a benevolent, grandfatherly figure, performing in a powdery wig and false mustache. (The "Kangaroo" part of his name derived from the conductor's jacket that he wore, which was adorned with oversize patch pockets.)

Captain Kangaroo aired live in its early years, six days a week, schooling Stone in the rigors and nuances of TV production. When his rotation through the CBS directors training program was over, he accepted an offer to work for Robert Keeshan Associates, the independent production company that packaged the show, and gradually took on greater responsibilities as a writer and producer. Keeshan was good at spotting and nurturing talent.

Among Stone's contemporaries were two future *Sesame Street* colleagues—Dave Connell, who rose through the ranks to become *Captain Kangaroo*'s executive producer, and Sam Gibbon, with whom Stone shared an Upper West Side apartment—as well as Tom Whedon and Elaine Laron, later to write for *Sesame Street*'s sibling program for older kids, *The Electric Company*.

By the midsixties, Stone had wearied of Keeshan, chafing at a management style that he perceived to be egomaniacal and autocratic. But even after they parted ways, Stone acknowledged that Keeshan was one of the good guys in the business—a man who had the compassion and insight, he recalled, to "address the child at home like a thinking, reasoning person."

— — —

In the frenetic, product-hustling world of 1950s and early-1960s children's TV, this approach was still an anomaly. Keeshan's sensibility was more closely aligned with that of the period's foremost editor of children's books, Ursula Nordstrom. Since 1940, the year she turned thirty, Nordstrom had run the Department of Books for Boys and Girls at Harper & Brothers, later to become Harper & Row. In this capacity, she cultivated authors who took seriously the interior lives of children, bucking the cornball, *Fun with Dick and Jane* mind-set that kids' books were obligated to model good behavior and talk down to their readers.

A game changer in her field, Nordstrom shepherded to publication such titles as E. B. White's *Stuart Little* (1945) and *Charlotte's Web* (1952); Maurice Sendak's *Where the Wild Things Are* (1963); Shel Silverstein's *The Giving Tree* (1964); and Louise Fitzhugh's *Harriet the Spy* (1964). Her mischievous credo was that, while the rest of the industry was publishing "bad books for good children," she was publishing "good books for bad children."

More to the point, Nordstrom, like Keeshan, simply wanted to give children credit for their innate intelligence. Her authors never dumbed down their storytelling nor shied away from portraying childhood as messy, anarchic, and, at times, melancholy. As Sendak, Nordstrom's most notable protégé, later commented, "My great curiosity is about childhood as a state of being, how all children manage to get through childhood from one day to the next, how they defeat boredom, fear, pain, and anxiety, and find joy."

But children's TV lagged significantly behind children's literature in this regard. Keeshan, like Fred Rogers, was appalled by what his adopted industry was offering to kids, and he was keen to save children's television from itself.

In Keeshan's case, he had experienced its flaws firsthand. He had been a regular on NBC's first blockbuster kids' program, *Howdy Doody*, which dated all the way back to 1947. Though it shall forever be held in warm regard by baby boomers, for whom it remains, like the Davy Crockett coonskin hat, a totem of childhood innocence and postwar prosperity, *Howdy Doody*, whose title character was a freckled man-boy marionette, was an abomination that managed to be simultaneously anodyne and terrifying. The show's buckskin-clad host, Buffalo Bob Smith, addressed his viewing audience with a forced merriment that bordered on belligerence, and shilled his sponsors' products to the small, captive children assembled in the studio's "peanut gallery." Keeshan was the first actor to play one of Smith's main foils, Clarabell the Clown, a mute, nightmarishly made-up Pierrot whose recurring bit was—shades of Pinky Lee—to spray seltzer in Buffalo Bob's face.

Captain Kangaroo was consciously conceived as a refuge from *Doody*-ish cacophony. Keeshan spoke in dulcet tones and performed in a loose, conversational manner, as if in a John Cassavetes movie for children. He chose as his chief sidekick a tall, thin, droll non-actor named Hugh "Lumpy" Brannum, by trade a bass player, most recently in the TV bandleader Fred Waring's orchestra. Brannum's character, Mr. Green Jeans, wore green bib overalls and presided over the garden outside of the Captain's house, introducing Keeshan to the various farm and zoo animals that CBS had wrangled for the program. ("This is a baby coatimundi, you see him? Strange-looking animal. Why don't you tell us where he comes from, Mr. Green Jeans?" "He comes from Central America, Captain. Sometimes he gets up to North America. To Texas, for example.")

Keeshan's show was not strictly educational and had no curricular adviser, but it was, in spirit and practice, on the side of kids rather than of CBS's sponsors and executives—sometimes to its peril. Keeshan refused to let commercials for toy weapons air during his show, and in the early sixties, *Captain Kangaroo* nearly fell victim to a standoff between its creator and the network over an ad buy by Deluxe Reading, the manufacturer of a product called Johnny Seven O.M.A. The three letters stood for One Man Army, and the toy was a remarkably realistic multifunction weapon that served as, among other things, a tommy gun, a grenade launcher, and an anti-tank rocket launcher. Though CBS threatened Keeshan with cancellation if he didn't accept the ad, he stood his ground, threatening to take the matter to the press. He prevailed, and the show ran on CBS, in the slot opposite the eight o'clock hour of *Today*, until 1981.

Stone was inspired by Keeshan's sense of principle and would carry it with him for the rest of his career. As he later recounted, "Where the signposts clearly pointed out a choice between the 'Be Smart, Save Yourself a Lot of Trouble Road' and the 'Speak Out for Your Principles and Really Piss People Off Road,' I always took the Speak Out Road."

*Josie Carey and Fred Rogers up in the attic of
WQED's The Children's Corner.*

CHAPTER
FOUR

"God's Program" and *Early Childhood Television Program*: Fred Rogers and Joan Ganz Cooney Chart Their TV Destinies

Keeping a close eye on *Captain Kangaroo* was Fred Rogers, by 1955 a dedicated employee of WQED in Pittsburgh. Keeshan's gentle, direct-address monologues to the camera, which tracked him slowly as he wandered the soundstage, struck Rogers as just the right approach. In later years, when both men were nationally known figures, they considered themselves kindred spirits, and appeared on each other's programs.

Rogers had only recently made his own television debut, though not as an on-camera performer. WQED, operating on a shoestring budget out of a converted Presbyterian rectory—apt, given Rogers's religious background—needed whatever programming it could get, and Rogers and a young woman named Josie Carey put together a live, daily hour-long program, *The Children's Corner*, which made its debut in April 1954. Carey, born Josephine Vicari, was only twenty-three years old to Rogers's twenty-six, but she was a natural in front of the camera—effervescent and kindly, with dark, curly hair, her pep more genuine than Pinky Lee's hopped-up Benzedrine menace.

Carey, an original employee of WQED, was working there as a secretary when she and Rogers hatched their show. The original concept was for Carey, as host, and Rogers, operating different hand puppets, to perform interstitial bits between screenings of short films made for children. But the delicate film clips kept breaking, and, rather quickly, *The Children's Corner* developed into the Josie and Fred show, with Carey committing fully to sincere conversations with the various puppets who popped out through doors in a gray canvas "wall," as if in an Advent calendar.

Rogers's puppets were the same ones who would later become familiar on *Mister Rogers' Neighborhood*: Daniel Striped Tiger, King Friday XIII, Lady Elaine Fairchilde, Henrietta Pussycat, and X the Owl. They arrived on television pretty much fully formed, with Rogers assigning Daniel a tender falsetto indicating his role as a proxy for small, curious kids watching at home, and King Friday a basso that could sound paternal or imperious, depending on his mood. The puppets, unlike Henson's creations, were simple hand puppets, store-bought and incapable of changing their facial expressions. Rogers brought many from home, and Daniel had been a gift from his namesake, Dorothy Daniel, WQED's cofounder and general manager.

It must be noted that Rogers's capacity for conjuring an ethereal, uniquely out-there atmosphere was already evident. In one episode, Daniel Striped Tiger needed a moment to sort out his feelings of confusion and mild melancholy when Josie appeared before him wearing a wig, therefore looking different than she normally did. In another, Josie and Daniel passed some time speculating on how nylon is made. And *The Children's Corner* was not without its utterly loopy elements of make-believe. An "attic" segment featured Rogers and Carey voicing a family of talking plants, Phil O. Dendron, Rhoda Dendron, and Baby Dendron, as well as a proto–*Pee-wee's Playhouse* array of talking inanimate objects, including Lydia Lamp, Lawrence Light, and Gramma Phone, an old phonograph cabinet that spoke by wiggling its speaker louvers.

The two performers' chemistry and goodwill made up for *The Children's Corner*'s lack of production values, and effectively put WQED on the map. It wasn't just children watching, either. A British-born traveling lecturer on poetry, Emilie Jacobson, caught an episode of the program while visiting Pittsburgh and was so taken with it that she sent WQED a fan letter. Jacobson was invited on to give a talk to Carey and the puppets about poetry, opening the floodgates for all manner of grown-ups to visit the studio and explain their passions or jobs to young home viewers. Most of these visitors were local—like the navy lieutenant who explained how semaphore and Morse code worked, and various musicians from the Pittsburgh Symphony Orchestra—but as favorable word of the program spread over the course of the fifties, some higher-profile guests presented themselves. Among them were the concert pianist Van Cliburn, *Peanuts* cartoonist Charles Schulz, and Johnny Carson in his pre–*Tonight Show* days.

By 1955, *The Children's Corner* had acquired enough momentum for Rogers's old employer, NBC, to take notice. The network invited Rogers and Carey to New York to produce a few half-hour episodes of the show while one of its regular Saturday-morning programs, *The Paul Winchell Show*, a vehicle for a then popular

ventriloquist, was on summer hiatus. Viewer response was beyond
expectation, with the duo's very first broadcast bringing in twenty-
five thousand fan letters.

Writing to his parents from the Hotel Pierre that summer, Rogers
exulted in his choice to work in television. "I'm more convinced than
ever that 'Children's Corner' is God's program," he wrote. "There's
no doubt about it now in my mind that we are being well guided:
whatever happens from now on I know will be for the best. Just too
many factors have come together today for it to be 'man-planned.'"

NBC brought back *The Children's Corner* for another twenty-
three weeks the following year, with Rogers and Carey shuttling
between Pittsburgh and New York to fulfill their obligations to the
local and national versions of their show. The membership in Daniel Striped Tiger's fan club, the Tame Tiger Torganization, swelled
to 125,000 members. (Torganization members, Rogers explained,
earned their stripes "not by buying things, but by doing things—
like learning a song or helping a parent or making a sandwich
or proving that they could count or say the days of the week in
French.") Once again, Rogers appeared to be on the cusp of a long
career in network television.

In the end, though, *The Children's Corner* just couldn't muster
the commercial sponsors needed to sustain it as an NBC program.
It remained a beloved staple of WQED in Pittsburgh, where it aired
through 1961. But the show was just too eccentric, too cerebral, and
too appreciative of high culture (all those classical musicians!) for
network TV. It was too PBS-like, when there wasn't yet a PBS.

— — —

The upshot of Joan Ganz Cooney's feasibility study for the Carnegie Corporation was that, yes, by all means, there was room

on television for a daily educational program for preschoolers. Cooney specifically noted the efficacy with which TV commercials insinuated their jingles and pitches into children's heads and suggested that similar techniques could be used to teach letters and numbers. She distilled her findings into a proposal for a brand-new program "to promote the intellectual and cultural growth of preschoolers, particularly disadvantaged preschoolers."

This show, she wrote, would serve "not only to teach a certain amount of specific information (letters, numbers, language tools, etc.)" but also, as one of Cooney's interviewees, the Harvard psychologist Jerome Kagan, summed up, "to teach the children *how* to think, not *what* to think."

Cooney's ardent advocacy for such a program was particularly noteworthy because it was a product of her ideals rather than any personal experience she'd had with kids. She did not have children of her own, and never would; she and Tim Cooney divorced in 1975, their marriage falling victim to the latter's alcoholism-related physical and mental decline. Likewise, Fred Rogers was not yet a father during the run of *The Children's Corner*, and Ursula Nordstrom never became a mother, living a quiet private life with her longtime companion, Mary Griffith, in a time when the prudent course for gay people was to keep their sexuality under wraps. Cooney, Rogers, and Nordstrom were children's advocates because they had high regard for children, believing them capable of intellectual and emotional engagement, and of seeing through cutesy artifice.

Cooney's friend and sponsor, Morrisett, saw no reason to doubt her conclusions about the potential for a totally new kind of children's program. After reviewing and circulating Cooney's feasibility study, he got the Carnegie Corporation to grant $1 million toward the development of the proposed show, whose stopgap title was *Early Childhood Television Program*. But he was unable to persuade his counterparts at the Ford Foundation to buy in; they, like some of Morrisett's own colleagues, remained skeptical of television's ability to do anything good for children.

Still, there was the convenient fact that Morrisett had friends in high places in the Johnson administration, where his former boss, John Gardner, was running the Department of Health, Education, and Welfare, and Gardner's friend Doc Howe was serving as the department's commissioner of education. Morrisett mailed a copy of Cooney's proposal to Howe. It included a broad outline of the program's goals and a detailed breakdown of how it would be managed, personnel-wise: there would be departments devoted to research, production, community outreach, and public relations.

Howe proved more than amenable to the proposal, and beckoned Morrisett and Cooney to Washington for a meeting in June 1967. As Cooney later recalled, Howe's various deputies were arrayed around a large conference table, each shaking his head and saying, "This isn't for us." Blithely ignoring them, Howe declared, "The ayes have it." The U.S. government, via Howe's office, would supply half the money—a sum that eventually totaled $4 million—for the development of a model children's TV program.

Morrisett and Cooney spent the better part of 1967 and 1968 raising further funds and mapping out the steps they needed to take to put together the show that they envisioned, a show whose budget, for an initial, experimental season of 130 episodes, would run to about $8 million. The Ford Foundation reconsidered its stance and joined in as an underwriter of the project. In March 1968, the Carnegie Corporation, the Ford Foundation, and the U.S. Office of Education held a joint press conference at the Waldorf-

Astoria announcing the creation of the production entity that would oversee the labor-intensive process of creating the new program: the Children's Television Workshop. Its chairman of the board was Morrisett, and its executive director was Cooney.

— — —

Just two months earlier, a new, quasi-psychedelic comedy-sketch show called *Rowan & Martin's Laugh-In* had premiered on NBC, exploding into the public consciousness. In its first two seasons, *Laugh-In* was the number one show on television. Cooney was taken with its zippiness—how it jumped with alacrity from one bit to another, never allowing the viewer to get bored. *Laugh-In*, with its innuendo-laden jokes and undulating, body-painted go-go girls, was the antithesis of educational and child-friendly programming, but to Cooney, it was a useful model for how to keep kids engaged without their eyes glazing over: with a rapid succession of sketches, songs, cartoons, and short films. Here, her attitude toward children and television differed from Fred Rogers's: she believed that kids born in the 1960s, her viewing demographic, were media-literate as no generation before them had ever been and wouldn't be discomfited or emotionally undone by a fast pace.

To this end, Cooney knew that, for all the various education and child-psychology professionals she needed to hire, she also needed some seasoned TV-production pros who were, plainly and simply, good at entertainment.

— — —

Jon Stone, out of work and with time on his hands, had kept busy during his period of unemployment by building an addition to his house in Vermont and taking care of his first child, Polly, who was born in 1967. One day in the spring of 1968, the phone rang and Beverley Stone took the call. It was a woman she had never heard of, named Joan Ganz Cooney, asking to speak to her husband. Jon came to the phone. Cooney told him, "I'm putting together a children's show, and many people have told me that I need to talk to you."

*Jon Stone directs Kermit in one of the frog's
many "brick wall" sequences.*

CHAPTER
FIVE

Geniuses Produce in Abundance: Putting Together the *Sesame Street* Team

The Jon Stone who reluctantly drove down from Vermont in early 1968 to meet with Joan Ganz Cooney was a different man from the fellow who'd earned his stripes as a writer and producer at *Captain Kangaroo*. Gone were the neckties and crisply creased trousers of his CBS years; he now avoided business dress, preferring rumpled sweaters, Nehru-collared shirts, and baggy corduroys, and he had grown a bushy beard that he would keep for the rest of his life.

Beyond the cosmetic changes, the theretofore apolitical Stone was undergoing a political awakening. In Vermont, he and his wife, Beverley, had become active in protests against the Vietnam War. Some of this anti-war sentiment found its way into a TV film that he worked on with Jim Henson that winter and spring, *Youth 68: Everything's Changing . . . or Maybe It Isn't.*

An hour-long stand-alone entry in an NBC anthology series devoted to experimental films—prosaically entitled *NBC Experiment in Television*—*Youth 68* was more Henson's project than Stone's, but the former brought in the latter for his acumen as a director and creative thinker. Broadly speaking, *Youth 68* was a documentary, mainly a collage of interviews with young people—some of them famous, like Jefferson Airplane's Grace Slick and Marty Balin, and many more of them ordinary kids on college campuses and in hippie enclaves. They were invited to express their thoughts on the war, drugs, youth culture, and the general state of the country. Like Henson's *Time Piece*, the film was unmoored from the conventions of linear storytelling, with quick cuts, split screens, and sequences in which newsreel footage was projected onto the white leotard dresses of dancing young models.

But *Youth 68* had little of *Time Piece*'s whimsy. Though it was made shortly before the assassinations of Martin Luther King Jr. and Robert F. Kennedy, it bore the already heavy weight of the times. Balin said of his fellow twentysomethings, "They're the generation who's gonna really have to, you know, do an Oedipus on their fathers and just take over." While Henson was not a political beast, and regarded *Youth 68* more as a reflection of the Zeitgeist than of his own opinions, Stone embraced the film as an opportunity to editorialize. He was particularly proud of a segment that juxtaposed footage of wounded American soldiers being carried to rescue helicopters with a hired actor's spirited reading of a U.S. Army recruitment pamphlet: "It offers travel, challenging opportunities, and a chance to participate in the newsmaking events of our day!"

Youth 68, which aired on April 19, 1968, offers a glimpse of the directions in which Stone's and Henson's careers might have gone had Cooney not intervened. Neither man was particularly disposed toward creating content for young children. Stone was contemplating a return to TV as a producer of historical dramas; he had tried to option Laura Ingalls Wilder's *Little House* series of books, but the actor Michael Landon had beaten him to it. As for Henson, the Muppets were but a part of his ever-expanding portfolio of projects and interests, which at one point included plans for a high-tech, sensorially immersive nightclub called Cyclia—there very well could have been less felt in his future.

But as Stone would later recall, his meeting with Cooney changed everything. "The indifference with which I had agreed to meeting with Joan disappeared within moments of my entering her office," he said. Cooney's pitch worked precisely because it was simpatico with Stone's expanding social consciousness. The TV show that she envisioned, she said, "was not aimed solely at minority or inner-city children and rural, impoverished children. But that was to be the bull's-eye of the target, no question: inner-city, poor four-year-olds."

Stone was electrified by the idea. "I had never heard anyone involved in children's television speak of it with such fire, not even Bob Keeshan, whose commitment to the betterment of the medium was famous," he said. "Joan spoke earnestly of the good this program might do in righting some of the inequities in our society, in closing some of the grievous gaps which existed in the education system."

Among those who had tipped off Cooney to Stone's talents was Sam Gibbon, his old roommate and fellow *Captain Kangaroo* alumnus. In Cooney's recollection, Gibbon described Stone as "probably the best children's-material writer in the United States." Cooney had actually tried to hire Gibbon first, and whiffed. Like

Stone, Gibbon felt that he had served his time in children's TV, and he was trying to break into the movie business. Happy nonetheless to advise Cooney, he recommended two other former *Captain Kangaroo* people: Stone and their old boss, Dave Connell, who had recently left Keeshan's show after serving for years as its executive producer.

Cooney swiftly hired Connell to serve in the same capacity for her program. The straitlaced Connell and the temperamental Stone had butted heads at *Captain Kangaroo*, but, at Cooney's urging, the two men put aside their differences for the good of the program. Stone was now aboard as a producer, reporting to Connell.

Soon enough, Cooney also had Gibbon in the fold. Martin Luther King Jr.'s assassination on April 4, 1968, caused him to rethink his earlier resistance to Cooney's entreaties. As he and his wife, Carol, were leaving a memorial held for King in New York's Central Park, Gibbon recalled, "I said, 'I feel as though I should do something more than just stand at a memorial service.' And Carol said, 'Well, why don't you go talk to Joan Cooney again, and do something for inner-city kids in his honor?' At that point, doing anything that could use your talents and experience for a larger cause seemed like it was obligatory."

The three *Captain Kangaroo* alums were joined in due time by a fourth producer, Matt Robinson, late of the Philadelphia TV station WCAU, and the only African American of the group. For WCAU, Robinson had written documentary films and created and hosted *Opportunity Line*, a public affairs show that alerted black viewers to promising job openings. He also produced the local variety programs *The Discophonic Scene* and *Black Book*.

The four producers divided up responsibilities according to their personal areas of expertise. Connell, beyond being the boss of bosses, had worked for an animation company in his post-*Kangaroo*, pre-CTW interregnum, and took charge of commissioning animated shorts. Gibbon, a Rhodes scholar and graduate of Princeton University, fell naturally into the role of chief intermediary between the production staff and the show's curricular advisers. Robinson oversaw the production of the show's live-action shorts. And Stone took on, in his words, "what was left: the shape of the show to come." In practical terms, this meant that he would be the primary talent wrangler and conceptualizer in chief, responsible for casting, hiring writers, and establishing the tone and atmosphere of the new program.

It's telling that all of these men were seasoned TV pros and had at least some experience as performers. Stone had been a music major in college and briefly worked as an actor in New York. Connell and Gibbon had acted in repertory-theater productions while serving in the air force and the army, respectively. Robinson was an on-camera presence at WCAU and a playwright as well; one of his teleplays, *Rained All Night*, about a slave revolt, was produced by CBS in 1962.

Cooney, too, had trod the boards, performing in school plays and aspiring, in her teen years, to act professionally. As dedicated as she now was to using the medium of television to educate children, she never lost sight of the fact that she was putting on a *show*.

This, in Stone's view, was Cooney's masterstroke, the thing that she figured out that no one before her had. The fundamental mistake of earlier educational TV programs, he said, "was in the assumption that a teacher, even an inspired one, could suddenly become a seasoned television performer, aware of pacing, camera angles, comedy timing, technical special effects, and the thousands of other tricks of the trade. Joan recognized this problem and solved it by reversing the emphasis. Rather than find teachers and teach them how to be television professionals, Joan went looking for television professionals with the intention of turning them into teachers."

— — —

Cooney knew that she wanted puppetry in her program, and she knew of Jim Henson by reputation, but she considered him out of reach—too busy and successful to devote his time to an experimental public-TV project. But Stone was adamant that Henson was the only person worthy of the job, and their preexisting friendship sealed the deal—that, and some hardline negotiations by Henson's management team, who established that Henson would work for the show as an independent contractor, never as a CTW employee.

Henson's trust in Stone wasn't his only reason for joining the project, though. By 1968, he was the father of four young children under the age of nine: Lisa, Cheryl, Brian, and John. He had cast them in short films that presaged the live-action clips that would later air between the "street" segments of *Sesame Street*. A 1965 short, "Run, Run," featured Lisa and Cheryl running hand in hand through an autumn wood. A 1967 short, "Wheels That Go," featuring an ambient soundtrack by the electronic-music pioneer Raymond Scott, juxtaposed scenes of Brian playing intently with a wooden toy car with scenes of him observing full-size cars and trucks moving along on highways and bridges.

Play fascinated Henson, and drove him as well. "I think he had the same sense of play that Albert Einstein had, of using it to instigate ideas," said Frank Oz, Henson's protégé and frequent performing partner. Cheryl Henson recalls that her father liked to get down on the floor with his children and commence play activities on his own. He did this, she said, both because he enjoyed it and because it was a way of modeling creative behavior without giving orders: "It was like 'Hmmm, here are a bunch of blocks. I'm going to paint this block. Hmmm, there's some paints, and there's *another* block.'"

This gentle, participatory approach dovetailed with that of the Mead School, a new progressive elementary school that was soon to open in the Henson family's adopted hometown of Greenwich, Connecticut. The school's founder, Dr. Elaine de Beauport, espoused a philosophy of experiential learning, in which children learned by partaking in stimulating activities rather than by dutifully sitting at desks and observing a teacher at a blackboard.

Both the Mead School and Cooney's educational TV show came along at a fortuitous time for Jim and Jane Henson. Their fourth child, John, was born in 1965. Unlike his three older siblings, he was late to learn to speak and struggled to identify the letters of the alphabet; he was later diagnosed as dyslexic. John's learning issues marked an inflection point in the Hensons' life. "Both of my parents became very, very committed to 'What is learning? How do you help kids learn?'" said Cheryl.

This made them open to new ideas in early education. Jim and Jane became charter parents at the Mead School, pulling their primary-school-age children from the public school they had been attending and enrolling them at Mead in 1969, its debut year. Ultimately, all of the Henson kids—a fifth, Heather, was born in 1970—would attend the school.

More consequentially for the nation's twelve million children aged three to five, Jim dove headlong into the new public-TV show. In doing so, he forsook the lucrative advertising career that had enriched him and raised his national profile. While he never became an expressly political person, as Stone increasingly would, Henson did become, in his quiet way, a children's advocate, vigilant in controlling how his Muppets were used. With a few exceptions—a soda ad made solely for the Mexican market and two early-1980s campaigns for Polaroid and American Express that were targeted at adults and used non-*Sesame* Muppets—Henson never did TV commercials again.

In early 1969, he filmed the last of a series of spots for Munchos, a brand of Frito-Lay potato crisps, and then called it a day. At that point, quite a few of the Muppets from Henson's myriad advertising jobs were in the process of being repurposed for the benefit of young viewers. One of them, voiced and operated by Oz, was a furry monster, pinkish purple rather than blue, who, in the recent past, had demonstrated such a passion for Munchos that he ate them by the bagful while exultantly shouting "Munchos!"

It would not be long before the Munchos monster switched his allegiance from savory treats to sweet ones.

— — —

Getting Henson on board early in *Sesame Street*'s developmental process was a coup. The Muppets conferred upon the nascent show a visual and spiritual identity that would set it apart from other children's programming: furrier, featherier, weirder, cleverer. "I think, somehow, Jim Henson knew in his soul what the educators and psychologists talked about in detail, but they talked about it *intellectually*," said Norton Wright, who oversaw the production of *Sesame Street*'s international editions in the early seventies. "Jim knew that deep within kids who are three to five years old, what they want to do is destroy something. So, if you are going to have Kermit explain the geometric form of the rectangle"—as he did in the seventeenth episode of *Sesame Street*'s first season—"at the end, Cookie Monster is going to show up, smash it, and say, 'It's a wreck, and a tangle!'"

Indeed, much of what we think of as the *Sesame Street* sensibility was present in the Muppets even before their energies were channeled toward young viewers. Monsters were not scary beasts but agents of comedy and catharsis. Kermit the Frog already exuded sunny-days cheer and wonder. Stone recalled visiting Henson's Manhattan workshop in the pre-*Sesame* days and regarding it with the awe of a child. One wall, he said, "was filled floor-to-ceiling with drawers, each labeled with a sign describing its contents" by Don Sahlin, the Muppets' chief designer and builder. "And on those signs were words like 'SCRUFFIES,' 'ZORKS,' 'FUZZIES & WUFFLES,' and 'PLOOPS.'"

The sheer otherness of Henson World—fantastical but self-assured, powered by its own internal logic—sparked Stone's imagination. He took to visiting the puppet shop regularly in the early days of *Sesame Street*, browsing through Sahlin's drawers in search of inspiration for comedy sketches. Henson was innately an agent of imaginative thought, and, to boot, a born teacher and mentor: ideal qualities for a children's television program.

"I joined Jim when I was nineteen, and I never realized that what we had was a unique thing," said Frank Oz. "I thought this was how everybody works—that people work together really hard and collaborate happily, with no politics or backstabbing. The difference is that we had a man who led us that way. By being pure. Being honest. Being caring."

So telepathically tight was Henson's crew that it operated as a sort of gestalt. For starters, nearly all of *Sesame*'s founding puppet team—chief among them Henson, Oz, Sahlin, Jerry Nelson, and Caroll Spinney—shared a look, sporting prodigious facial hair and counterculturist threads. Loretta Long, in her first day on set as Susan, was struck by the sight of this group advancing assuredly through the studio in a flying wedge, "like geese," with Henson at the fulcrum. "It was like this *breeze* coming through," Long said. "From the direction of Hooper's Store comes this man with shoulder-length brown hair and a benevolent look on his face, like Jesus. The others are on either side of him, tunics and ponchos flapping. They all just moved like one big force field."

Stone's other key early recruit was his friend Joe Raposo, the songwriter, who would serve as *Sesame Street*'s first musical director. Like Henson, Raposo had an outsize influence on the show's sensibility, not only composing "Bein' Green" and such other standards as "Sing," "C Is for Cookie," "Somebody Come and Play," "One of These Things" (as in "...is not like the other"), and "I've Got Two" (as in "I've got two eyes: one, two"), but also scoring the show in its entirety in its early years—handling cues, incidental music, and the melody and arrangement of the theme song.

For his house band, Raposo brought in such crack jazz musicians as Jim Mitchell, a seasoned session-pro guitarist, and Bob Cranshaw, the bassist in the saxophonist Sonny Rollins's band, versatile guys who could pull off whatever sound Raposo was after in the moment: "Schmaltz, 1920s, oompah Bavarian, you name it," Stone recalled. In an even bigger coup, Raposo got the world's foremost jazz harmonica player, the Belgian-born Toots Thielemans, to play lead on the show's closing theme, delivering a soulful, melismatic variation on the opening theme's sung melody.

The result was a musical atmosphere unique for children's television: chill, fluid, and freewheeling, worlds away from the scary toy-town jollity and noisy faux–Sousa brass that under-scored earlier kids' programming. Stone called the distinctive Raposo sound "his most under-recognized contribution to *Sesame Street*." It was inviting and unsquare, and anticipated the similarly jazzy, virtuosic house-band sound that *Saturday Night Live* would introduce to late-night TV a few years later. (As a matter of fact, Cranshaw would go on to be the *SNL* band's bassist for that show's first five seasons.)

Cooney rated both Raposo and Henson as bona fide geniuses, and observed years later, "Most geniuses, I have found, produce in abundance. They don't just do something once in a while. And Joe was always producing music in abundance, so that it was just *sailing* in, for all kinds of purposes." Raposo's and Henson's prolificacy was particularly crucial in *Sesame Street*'s early days, when the show was racing to realize its insanely ambitious goal of producing 130 one-hour episodes for its first season.

But Raposo and Henson did not get to work on the program in earnest until 1969. In 1968, Cooney, Stone, and their colleagues at the Children's Television Workshop were still figuring things out—the show's shape, its curricular aims, and how it would deliver on its promise. The period from when Cooney hired Stone to when *Sesame Street* went on the air spanned eighteen months. "I am positive," Stone said, "that no program in history was more meticulously constructed."

— — —

Sesame Street's meticulous construction began with a series of seminars held in the summer of 1968 that were presided over by Gerald Lesser, the chairman of CTW's new board of advisers. Lesser was yet another member of the Lloyd Morrisett network;

the two men had been classmates while pursuing their PhDs in psychology at Yale. Personal connections aside, Lesser was eminently qualified for the task—he was a professor at Harvard University's Graduate School of Education who was keenly interested in the effects of television on children.

Each of the five seminars, which lasted three days apiece and took place either at Harvard or at the Waldorf-Astoria in New York, was centered around a specific area of learning: language and reading; mathematical and numerical skills; social, moral, and affective development; reason and problem-solving; and perception. Lesser and Cooney convened an array of professionals from various fields to meet with the producers: educators, scholars, child psychologists, advertising executives, the children's-book editor Ursula Nordstrom, and a sprinkling of starrier figures, such as the animation auteur Chuck Jones (of Warner Bros. cartoon fame), the design guru Charles Eames, and the children's-book authors Maurice Sendak, Ezra Jack Keats, and Betty Miles.

Also in attendance was Henson, whose physical appearance aroused Cooney's suspicion; though she held his work in high esteem, she had never met the puppeteer. "Dave Connell and I were sitting up front, and there was this man sitting at the back of the room with long hair and a leather vest and beads," she said. "I whispered, 'How do we know that man back there isn't going to kill us?' Dave said, 'Not likely. That's Jim Henson.'"

To some degree, the seminars were an exercise in seeing how creative people and academics would get along when placed in the same room and tasked with achieving a common goal. It was a bit of a process; Lesser, who had invited seven of his Harvard colleagues to participate, noted that the creatives bristled at the academics' analytical approach to content creation, contending "that any creative product must be conceived intuitively and lov-ingly, with the creator drawing freely upon his own fantasies and feelings."

To the creatives, Lesser recalled, the academics' use of such terms as "symbolic representations," "cognitive processes," and "self-concept" represented nothing less than "the mutilation of the child through analysis." Cooney recalls the normally serene Sam Gibbon growing frustrated early on, pleading with the professors, "Will you guys please speak English?"

For Sendak, a lone wolf, the meetings were not his thing—too much like being back at school. Stone, for his own amusement, made a point of grabbing a seat next to the author and illustrator to see what Sendak was doodling on his notepad to pass the time.

"The drawings were incisive, the perfect scalpel to cut right to the heart of the sometimes unbearably stuffy discussions," Stone remembered. "My favorite, I guess, he titled 'One Minute of Educa-tional TV,' and it showed a normal-looking child watching televi-sion, then yawning, then sticking his tongue out at the screen. The child grew more and more ferocious, hitting the set with his fist, then attacking it with a hatchet, reducing it to a smoldering pile of wires and plastic, and finally taking out his tiny penis and peeing on the whole thing."

But Gerry Lesser proved an adept referee, de-escalating con-flicts and, over time, getting the participants from various camps to engage with one another in good faith, to productive ends. Cooney said that Lesser himself underwent a change over the course of the seminars, moving from skepticism about the project to a be-lief that "maybe, just maybe, television could help rather than be a hindrance to children learning." (And Sendak wasn't a total spoilsport. He collaborated with Henson on two animated shorts that would air in *Sesame Street*'s first seasons, "Bumble Ardy" and "Seven Monsters." He also provided the illustrations for a promotional brochure that CTW put out in advance of *Sesame Street*'s premiere, as well as for Lesser's 1974 memoir of the show's first five years, *Children and Television: Lessons from Sesame Street*.)

Above all, the seminars helped produce, by the end of 1968, concrete curricular goals for what at the time was still thought of as the program's single, experimental season. The goals fell broadly into four main categories: symbolic representation, which included learning shapes, the numbers 1 to 10, and the letters of the alphabet; cognitive processes, which included understanding relational concepts such as size, shape, position, and distance; reasoning and problem-solving; and "the child and his world," which included teaching the concepts of the self, social units, and natural environments versus man-made ones.

CTW also established a research division, headed up by Dr. Edward L. Palmer, an academic psychologist. In his previous job, at the state of Oregon's Department of Education, Palmer had already conducted a study of preschool children's responses to television—determining, among other things, that children particularly enjoyed watching footage of animals and of other children, and were bored by talking adults. In his new job at CTW, he set out to learn two things: how well a specific TV segment held a child's attention, and how effective the segment was in teaching its intended lesson.

For this first goal, Palmer rigged up an invention he called a "distracter," which was a rear-screen-projection unit arranged at a right angle to a television set. Every eight seconds, a different image was projected on the screen. Palmer's researchers carefully observed their child subjects as they watched CTW's test material on the television, noting the frequency with which a child's eyes left the TV screen to look at the projected slide image, and the duration of each look away.

Over the course of *Sesame Street*'s development period, the distracter helped the producers determine, in quantifiable terms, how absorbing, and therefore effective, their material was. One particularly consequential Palmer discovery, made in mid-1969, by which time CTW had created some test episodes, was that young viewers' attention wandered during the "live" segments of the show: the street-based material featuring the adult characters. This prompted the integration of Henson's Muppets into the street scenes—most prominently the two characters performed by Caroll Spinney: Big Bird and Oscar the Grouch.

With hindsight, it's easy to regard Palmer's conclusions as obvious, and to envision how CTW's dry curricular directives would manifest themselves as entertaining bits. Of *course* the perspective and behaviors of a person with a different point of view could be represented by an irritable hair ball who lives in a trash can! Of *course* a child will readily learn the alphabet if the "ABC" song is set to a funky groove and sung by Lena Horne and six jiving Muppets!

But there was no template in 1968 for what the Workshop had set out to do, and with $8 million at stake and a set of quantifiable goals to be met, building *Sesame Street* was a painstaking, laborious process.

*Chef Brockett, Mr. McFeely, Lady Aberlin, Mister Rogers,
and Handyman Negri gather in the Neighborhood.*

CHAPTER SIX

Mister Rogers Develops
His Neighborhood

F red Rogers, by contrast, was ready to go: his *Mister Rogers' Neighborhood* program went national in February of 1968. His first kids' show, *The Children's Corner*, with Josie Carey, had run its course by 1961. In the intervening years, Rogers had finally been ordained as a minister—"with a very special ordination," he noted, "to work with families through mass media"—and had refined his thoughts on how best to use TV to help children.

He had been encouraged by an early-sixties stint living in Toronto, during which, under the aegis of the Canadian Broadcasting Corporation, he created and starred in a fifteen-minute daily program called *Misterogers*, his first experience in front of the camera. *Misterogers* was very much a proto-version of the *Neighborhood* program that American children would come to cherish, with an extended segment set in the Neighborhood of Make-Believe (already anchored by the crenellated castle in which King Friday resided) that was bookended by shorter sequences in which Mr. Rogers himself appeared—gently cradling a live goose, for example, and serenading it with "I Like You As You Are," a Rogers-Carey cowrite that served as a sort of prequel to Rogers's more famous song of affirmation "It's You I Like."

Validated by the Canadian program's positive reception, Rogers returned to Pittsburgh on a mission. Late in 1964, he and WQED put together a fund-raising proposal for a new program for children ages four to nine. In its ambition and prescient long-term vision, the document was a testament to Rogers's steely resolve—gentle a man as he was, Fred Rogers was not soft. "I am anxious to make a *lasting* contribution to the field of children's television," he wrote. "The past ten years have been excellent experience. I have produced almost four thousand hours of programming. Now I want to do something which can be used over and over as new children come to their television sets needing constructive ideas for their growing bodies and feelings."

Mr. Rogers would function "as the child's adult friend and the personification of the child's loving super-ego," and "would introduce *experiences* of all kinds—some as mundane as getting a haircut, some as fanciful as King Friday's giving away the moon." The proposal envisioned an eventual library of 650 half-hour episodes and included an itemized budget of $150,000 for the first hundred.

The first incarnation of *Misterogers' Neighborhood* (as the program's title was spelled until 1970) debuted in 1966 and was distributed by the Eastern Educational Network, a cooperative of public stations in the Northeast whose members (which included

WQED, Boston's WGBH, and New York's WNDT) shared their original programming. The show found popularity, but precisely how much popularity didn't become evident until the spring of 1967, when its funding ran out and Rogers was forced, temporarily, to cease production.

This interruption coincided with a public appearance by Rogers at an open house held by WGBH. The station had expected around five hundred people, but more than ten thousand parents and children showed up, standing in line for hours to get in. This event, coupled with outcries from anguished parents in other cities where *Misterogers' Neighborhood* aired, prompted the Sears-Roebuck Foundation and National Educational Television (NET), the precursor to PBS, to partner to fund the show and distribute it nationally. In short order, millions of viewers became familiar with the words "It's a beautiful day in this neighborhood" and the unusually peaceable man who sang them.

— — —

For all the conspicuous differences between *Mister Rogers' Neighborhood* and what was to become *Sesame Street*—slow pace versus fast, small cast versus large, low production values versus high—the two shows shared some crucial traits that reflected how much of a sea change they represented. Both programs, for example, bore the imprint of the social sciences. Though it may have seemed like Rogers was simply following his muse, acting on his own peculiar if well-honed instincts, he in fact had crucial help in the form of Dr. Margaret McFarland, a professor of pediatric psychology at the University of Pittsburgh School of Medicine.

McFarland, a slight woman twenty-three years Rogers's senior, was no ordinary child psychologist. She was an expert in early-childhood development and the director of the Arsenal Family and Children's Center, an experimental Pittsburgh nursery school that she had cofounded in the 1950s with Dr. Benjamin Spock, the dean of American pediatricians, and Erik Erikson, the developmental psychologist who coined the term "identity crisis."

Rogers met McFarland when, after receiving his degree from the Pittsburgh Theological Seminary in 1963, he decided to take some graduate-level courses in child development at the University of Pittsburgh. He was assigned McFarland as an adviser, a fortuitous pairing. As part of his studies, Rogers, under McFarland's guidance, worked with children at Arsenal. "I got so many ideas on how to approach things from that," he said.

When Rogers got his show, he asked McFarland to serve as its psychological consultant, and they conferred on a weekly basis until the end of her life, in 1988. This arrangement, while small-time in comparison with the Children's Television Workshop's battleship-size apparatus of curricular advisers and researchers, played an important role in shaping *Mister Rogers' Neighborhood*.

McFarland essentially imparted a method to Rogers's mellowness. So many of the program's signature moments served developmental purposes. Rogers's entrance, singing "Won't You Be My Neighbor?," deliberately found him walking from screen left to screen right, the way a child's eyes would track when learning to read. The show's transitional moments, such as when Rogers swapped out his coat and shoes for a cardigan and sneakers, or when the toy trolley journeyed from his living room to the Neighborhood of Make-Believe, were there to help children navigate daily transitions in their own lives.

Sometimes, Rogers's developmental goals were less evident to parents than they were to his young viewers, who grasped them intuitively. He was particularly proud of a series of episodes from May 1968 that dealt with water and plumbing—with a visit to a farm to show how water pumps work, and a day of small crises that were remedied by the character Handyman Negri: a leaky faucet and faulty toilet in Mr. Rogers's house, and a broken fountain in the Neighborhood of Make-Believe. The point of this exercise, Rogers explained in an interview, was to acknowledge how obsessed children are with their own bodily fluids, and their control of them or lack thereof.

Going even deeper into developmental theory, Rogers followed up the water episodes with an arc in which the Neighborhood's rocking-chair factory, run by the puppet character Corney, caught fire and burned down. "We know children's fantasies and dreams about fire often have as their root the control of urine," Rogers said. When a concerned father in Boston called Rogers to complain that the factory fire had scared off his daughter from further watching the program, Rogers asked the father if the girl had experienced difficulties with toilet training. The father, surprised, confirmed this to be the case. "We talked two or three times thereafter, and that child, after a few weeks, with that family's added understanding about her fluid, came back to watching the *Neighborhood* again," Rogers said.

— — —

Like *Sesame Street, Mister Rogers' Neighborhood* had an unmistakable sound, recognizable to children even when they were out of viewing range of the TV set. Rogers, a gifted pianist himself, was friendly with a lot of musicians—including the show's "handyman," played by Joe Negri, in real life a professional jazz guitarist, and its "policeman," played by François Clemmons, in real life a singer—and he asked the jazz pianist Johnny Costa to be the program's musical director. Costa initially protested that he was no fan of children's television, which he described as an onslaught of "clowns and cartoons and too much noise." But he was swayed by Rogers's vision for the show, and the promise of artistic freedom.

Working from his bank of keyboards, Costa created the stampeding piano theme music for the trolley (with a celeste providing its ding-ding chimes) and, via an early synthesizer, the fife-like descending phrases that accompanied the sprinkling of fish food into the aquarium. For Rogers's original songs, Costa and his jazz-trained house musicians, Bobby Rawsthorne on drums and Michael Taylor or Carl McVicker Jr. on bass, stuck to predetermined arrangements. But, over the course of a typical episode, Costa, his eyes fixed on a monitor, improvised his way through Rogers's physical movements and interactions with other characters—"I'm not completely sure what it will sound like until I play it," he said.

As a result, the Neighborhood had a rather sophisticated sonic palette, with the music serving as a running commentary on the episode: twinkly and easy-swingin' most of the time, but dissonant and (mildly) ominous when it had to be. The saxophonist John Ellis, who in 2012 released an album largely composed of Fred Rogers's songs entitled *It's You I Like*, observed of Rogers in his liner notes, "He wrote kid songs, but they feel like part of the American jazz tradition, with quirky forms. Early on, he sang them live, playing the piano and looking to the side at the camera, the way you'd see Nat Cole do it on his show; towards the end, you'd hear

Johnny Costa improvise. Mr. Rogers was exposing an American audience to jazz."

Jazz suited the new, inclusive breed of children's TV shows because it was itself inclusive: collaborative, playful, welcoming of all races—values that *Mister Rogers' Neighborhood* and *Sesame Street* were trying to celebrate. It was also idiomatic and variable enough for its composers and players to put their own authorial stamp on the programs to which they contributed. Like Joe Raposo's work, Costa's was enveloping and transportive, impressing upon children the feeling that they weren't so much watching television as they were entering a *world*.

— — —

Rogers, this world's creator, would prove irresistible to parodists as his popularity grew. In a loud, fast, cynical time, he was dulcet, unhurried, and beatifically calm: through an adult lens, a total weirdo. Though Eddie Murphy's and Johnny Carson's takeoffs were more famous, the most nuanced and cutting was Christopher Guest's on the *National Lampoon* 1977 comedy album *That's Not Funny, That's Sick*, which sent up Rogers's frequent sit-downs with musicians. Bill Murray, playing a strung-out jazz bassist visiting the Neighborhood, described a violin as "a little wimpy thing" compared with his bass. "I like the way you say that! Did you know that?" asked Guest. "I do *now*," replied Murray. "The hell? You easily amused, aren't you?"

But Rogers was quite the opposite of the wimp portrayed in such send-ups. Rather, he was a man of iron will and uncommon principle, fearless in taking his program to places where children's television had not previously ventured. Themed episodes about bodily fluids weren't the half of it. Just days after Robert F. Kennedy's murder, in June 1968, Rogers rushed an episode to air in which the puppet Daniel Striped Tiger turned to the character Lady Aberlin (the actress Betty Aberlin) and said, "There's something I want to ask you. What does 'assassination' mean?" In convincingly stunned, halting tones, Lady Aberlin responded, "Well . . . it means somebody . . . getting killed. In a sort of surprise way."

What this moment represented, Rogers said, was "a plea not to leave the children isolated and at the mercy of their own fantasies of loss and destruction." The program also allied itself with the civil-rights movement. In 1968, the year the show's distribution went national, *Mister Rogers' Neighborhood* incorporated two black regulars: Joey Hollingsworth, a tap dancer who featured in the Neighborhood of Make-Believe as Mr. Hollingsworth, Corney's sales representative for the rocking-chair factory, and Clemmons, whom Rogers pointedly cast as Officer Clemmons, the Neighborhood's friendly beat cop.

In an episode that aired in May 1969, in an era when hotels and recreational centers still regularly forbade black people from using their swimming pools, Officer Clemmons happened by Mr. Rogers's place while the latter was sitting by a plastic kiddie pool, his trousers rolled up, cooling his feet with the spray from a garden hose. Rogers beseeched the police officer to join him and take a moment to cool *his* feet.

"That looks awfully enjoyable, but I don't have a towel or anything," Officer Clemmons said. "Oh, you share mine!," Rogers responded. Then the camera cut to the pool, and the image of two bare brown feet next to two bare white feet. Rogers didn't need to add anything more than the cheerful observation "Cool water on a hot day!"

Looking back many years later on the fraught era in which her show and Rogers's show were born, Joan Ganz Cooney observed, "Every night, the TV set brought you bad news.... And finally, it was as if the public was saying 'So *do* something!' to the TV set. And one day, they turned on the TV set, and the TV set did something."

The original cast of The Me Nobody Knows, *1970, including, upper right, Northern Calloway, soon to be of* Sesame Street, *and, lower right, Irene Cara, soon to be of* The Electric Company, *and, later, of* Fame.

CHAPTER
SEVEN

Give a Damn:
The Children's-Auteur
Romance with the Inner City

The urge to *do something*, particularly where children of color were concerned, wasn't limited to well-intentioned TV professionals. The period during which *Sesame Street* was being developed saw a wave of memoirs by teachers who documented their struggles to make a difference in inner-city public-school systems ravaged by white flight and institutional neglect.

Foremost among these were Herbert Kohl's *36 Children*, Jonathan Kozol's *Death at an Early Age*, and James Herndon's *The Way It Spozed to Be*, all published to widespread shock and acclaim. The shock came from the books' revelations of how cruelly and indifferently large urban school systems (New York's in Kohl's case, Boston's in Kozol's, Greater Los Angeles's in Herndon's) treated their pupils, essentially regarding black children as destined for failure and therefore not worthy of a proper education, or even of individual attention. Here were the fifth and sixth graders for whom salvation would never come, for whom Lloyd Morrisett's push to give poor kids a big nudge in early childhood had arrived too late. (Kozol, pulling no punches, subtitled his book *The Destruction of the Hearts and Minds of Negro Children in the Boston Public Schools*.)

None of these men posited himself as a white savior who magically got through to his students and transformed their lives. "It is one thing to be liberal and talk," Kohl wrote, "another to face something and learn that you're afraid." But the teachers scored some small victories, and one common to them all was that they got their students to write. Often, they did so by assuring the students that they would not be graded for their efforts. Writing freely— about their lives, where they lived, what their fantasies were—was validating to the kids, giving them a sense, at least for a moment, of accomplishment.

Steve Joseph, a New York City schoolteacher himself, read these books avidly. Inspired by them, he compiled one of his own, *The Me Nobody Knows*, whose influence, while not on a *Sesame Street* or *Mister Rogers* order of magnitude, would prove significant.

Joseph had felt the calling to teach in 1967, having spent the previous few years working for the Metropolitan Life Insurance Company as a public-relations man. "It was the easiest job in the world, in that beautiful building on Madison Square," he said. "They had a gymnasium and high-quality food and all these nice things to keep their employees close. I remember once looking into that big boardroom and imagining myself there."

But there was a problem: Joseph found the job to be dull and soul-crushing, to the point where he took to chronically showing up late, daring his employer to terminate him. Once Joseph got his wish, his girlfriend and future wife, Barbara Randall, encouraged him to go back to what he had been doing before the MetLife job: teaching in New York City public schools.

Joseph and Randall were an unusual couple: he, a Jewish kid from Far Rockaway, in Queens, and she, a black woman with Shinnecock Indian blood who had grown up on Long Island in a fervently leftist family. Randall's father had served for a time as a bodyguard to Paul Robeson, the actor, singer, and activist who was blacklisted in the 1950s for being a member of the Communist Party.

"Barbara was a true socialist, and after I got myself fired, she said, 'Come back to teaching; you're not happy with where you are,'" Joseph said. "And she was right."

An indifferent teacher his first time around, Joseph threw himself into his work in his second teaching stint, albeit in unorthodox fashion: a restless soul, he chose to be a roving substitute, teaching in every borough of New York except Staten Island. Like Carole Demas and Paula Janis, the future stars of *The Magic Garden*, he found a system in disarray, with black and Puerto Rican children ill-served by doctrinaire administrators, defeatist teachers, and crumbling facilities.

But Joseph, steeped in the books he had read, came equipped with a strategy. Whether he was subbing at a school for just a couple of days or for more than a week, he asked his students to write. Their reflexive reaction, he quickly learned, was to complain. Writing, in their experience, was a punitive exercise, in which their teachers chided them for poor spelling and sloppy penmanship.

Joseph impressed upon his students that writing was akin to talking or singing: a means of self-expression. Given that most of the kids enjoyed talking, why, he asked them, wouldn't they enjoy writing? When the students began to rattle off their reasons, he told the kids to write them down instead.

It was a modestly successful gambit, pinched from Kohl's book. But Joseph was still operating in a vacuum, relying on his instincts rather than any training, with no awareness of whether anyone else in the city's schools was actively pursuing a similar course. Then someone tipped him off about a woman named Naomi Levinson, who was teaching writing at one of the city's most hopeless and poorly performing schools, Edgar G. Shimer Junior High, in South Jamaica, Queens. He went to observe her in action.

Levinson was not a warm and fuzzy peddler of uplift. She was the product of a turbulent upbringing, having fled Nazi-occupied France in 1942, when she was fourteen years old, with her mother, a French-Ukrainian philosopher of some renown named Rachel Bespaloff. Bespaloff became a professor at Mount Holyoke College in Massachusetts but committed suicide just seven years into her and Naomi's new life in America. Levinson, after taking degrees at Mount Holyoke and Radcliffe College, bounced around the New York City school system as a teacher, struggling with an addiction to amphetamines. Like Ursula Nordstrom, who reveled in creating "good books for bad children," Levinson preferred teaching the city's "bad" kids, she recalled, "because I actually related to them."

"The good kids never made any mistakes," she said. "The bad kids couldn't spell if you paid them, but they had *feelings*."

Joseph watched Levinson take command of her class by writing a single-word prompt on the blackboard—"angry," say, or "scared," or "death"—and inviting her students to write whatever came to mind. In Joseph's recollection, Levinson was "a totalitarian in the classroom, stern, bossy," but she was clear about her expectations, and her students took to her with affection. Levinson gave them three choices. They could write something, sign their name to it, and read it aloud to the class; write something and turn it in unsigned, and have Levinson read it aloud; or write a page but neither sign it nor turn it in. Plus, they could use whatever words came readily to them, including curse words.

Joseph more or less appropriated Levinson's approach for the remainder of the 1967–68 school year, albeit with a gentler touch, and was amazed at the results. Teaching kids from ages seven to eighteen, with some of the eldest living under lock and key at juvenile-detention centers, he found boys and girls eager, once liberated from the pressure of a graded assignment, to express themselves through writing.

And the material they produced was often stunning. One sixteen-year-old wrote unblinkingly of the junkies, prostitutes, and hustlers in his neighborhood, and of "the preacher who on Sunday is so 'yes Lord' and just as high from a bag on Saturday night." Another sixteen-year-old wrote a stark poem called "Black," a proto-rap that began with the lines "Black we die / Black you cry / Black I cry / Does White they cry / Cause Black we die?" and posed the question "What of the soul that yearns to be free?"

A second grader lamented the death of Martin Luther King Jr., writing, "I bet he wanted to stop the War in Vietnam after he was finished with his other work to." A fifteen-year-old wrote lyrically of nighttime—"the stars are little children playing on a blanket of black coals"—and of the dawn that follows: "Father and mother gets up and it's the sun. A new day is born. No more darkness. Light sings all over the world."

As the school year progressed, Joseph became aware of other teachers besides Levinson and himself who were engaging in inner-city experiments in freewriting. Two of them, Spenser Jameson and Ed Grady, taught at the Spofford Juvenile Center, in the Bronx, a detention home for boys. Another, Elaine Avedon, taught at James Fenimore Cooper Junior High School, in Harlem, and had started a literary magazine with her students called *What's Happening?* Still another middle-school teacher in Harlem, Susan Rosen, asked her students to write about what they would do with a million dollars, with funny and poignant results. One sixteen-year-old wrote, "I'll buy myself three lions two bears and a gorilla. I'll have 130343097 wives. The rest for College." Another answered, "I would buy me a 1943 military amphibian Jeep. And I will buy me a cashmere coat and a pair of gators at the shop and I will run for President. And I will be the first Black President."

A light bulb went off above Joseph's head: What if he compiled the work of these teachers' students and his own into an anthology? Keen to reach as wide an audience as possible, Joseph struck a deal with Avon, a paperback-book publisher that he admired for having recently scored a massive best seller with a reissue of Henry Roth's thirty-year-old novel, *Call It Sleep.*

In early 1969, Avon published the book, whose full title was *The Me Nobody Knows: Children's Voices from the Ghetto.* It quickly became a critical and commercial success, eventually selling more than half a million copies. Writing for the *New York Times Book Review*, Julius Lester, a prominent black author and academic, praised the anthology as "a book for teachers, children, and for all who do not know that the children of the ghetto are 'something special.'" Soon, through circumstances that Joseph did not anticipate, the book would benefit from a whole new wave of attention.

— — —

Among progressive intellectuals, "the ghetto" increasingly held fascination as both a concern and a canvas—a place in need of intervention and an anthropologically fascinating world worthy of artistic exploration. As 1968 turned into 1969, Jon Stone, under the gun, was desperately looking for inspiration to turn the Children's Television Workshop's abstract goals into an actual television show, with a setting and a cast of characters. Watching TV at home one night, he was struck by a commercial produced by the New York Urban Coalition, an advocacy group, that opened with a title card that read, "Send your kid to a ghetto for the summer."

The spot then cut to a black actor sitting on a stoop, caustically describing his neighborhood's luxury "amenities": "Want to see the pool? C'mon. The kids clog up the sewer with garbage, open a hydrant." Onward he continued in this vein, describing cramped tenements as "camp cabins" and busy streets as "ball fields," until the actor looked into the camera and said, "You don't want your kids to play *here* this summer? Then don't expect *ours* to." The ad closed with a voice-over artist intoning the Urban Coalition's slogan: "Give jobs. Give money. Give a damn."

Stone was moved to action by the ad, though not in quite the way that the Urban Coalition intended. "For a pre-school Harlem child," he later wrote, "the street is where the action is. As often as not, she is housebound all day while her mother works, and from the vantage point of her apartment, the sidewalk outside must look like Utopia. Kids hollering, jumping double Dutch, running through open hydrants, playing stickball. Our set had to be an inner-city street, and more particularly, it had to feature a brownstone so the cast and kids could 'stoop' in the age-old New York tradition."

The next day, Stone happened to meet up with Charlie Rosen, an old friend from his Yale days and a well-regarded production designer. Rosen was working on a film for which he had created a convincingly timeworn jazz club, its interior covered in graffiti and multiple layers of peeling paint. Impressed by Rosen's handiwork, Stone told the designer about his idea to situate the new kids' program on an inner-city street, and asked Rosen if he was up to building such a set. Rosen, a dab hand at scuzzy atmospherics—he was later the art director for Martin Scorsese's *Taxi Driver*—was happy to oblige.

Convincing Joan Cooney to go along with this vision was another matter. Stone set up a meeting with Cooney to pitch his visual concept. "She listened intently, and I thought I perceived just a hint of the color draining from her face as she absorbed the idea of her show looking like a production of *Dead End* or *Angels with Dirty Faces*," he said. "But when I finished my pitch and sat there waiting for her response, God bless her, she remained true to her laissez-faire approach to leadership and, as I recall, said something to the effect that we were the people she chose to create the program, and if that's how I saw it, so be it."

Stone's view of "the street," as a wonderland of vibrancy and freedom, was absurdly romantic, the antithesis of the picture that the Urban Coalition was trying to paint. But his instincts for what would make the show visually unique and appealing to children were on point. Rosen's huge, built-to-scale set, a mélange of faded brownstones, gray, litter-strewn sidewalks, dented trash cans, clotheslines hung with laundry, and brick walls covered in street art, felt real and inviting. It may have been a sanitized version of "the ghetto," but it wasn't antiseptic—and the famous stoop, in its centrality and cramped intimacy, would be a convivial staging ground for sing-alongs of Joe Raposo tunes and dialogues with Ernie, Bert, Big Bird, and Oscar the Grouch.

Furthermore, Stone's brain bolt about the show's set was followed by a torrent of thoughts about who its occupants might be. Ultimately, he decided that the brownstone to which the stoop was attached would be owned by a black couple. Stone named them Gordon and Susan, for, respectively, the filmmaker and photographer Gordon Parks and the black Broadway actress Susan Watson, a friend of Stone's. Gordon and Susan would have a white neighbor named Bobby, a good singer who could shoulder much of the show's musical load. And there would be an older man, a shopkeeper—implicitly Jewish, in Stone's imagining—named Mr. Hooper.

"I was determined that our neighborhood present a positive image of interracial harmony and a community united through its pride and sense of responsibility," Stone said.

—   —   —

As sales of *The Me Nobody Knows* took off, the book acquired a following of well-intentioned white readers who, like Jon Stone, saw the ghetto as a place not to be avoided but celebrated and *heard from*. One especially fervent fan was Herb Schapiro, the head of the theater department at Mercer County Community College, in central New Jersey. A part-time playwright and an activist who believed, in his son Mark's words, "that you could solve all the problems in the world by making people come together through the arts," Schapiro was inspired by Joseph's book to put his beliefs to the test in the poorest neighborhoods of nearby Trenton, whose residents were predominantly African American.

In the summer of 1969, Schapiro rounded up some jazz-musician friends and a few students from his theater program and staged a series of spoken-word happenings on the sidewalks of Trenton.

While the musicians laid down a groove, Schapiro and his troupe either freestyled over the music or read aloud passages from *The Me Nobody Knows*. Somehow, no one told this group of interlopers to go away. The locals, in fact, warmly embraced the happenings and participated in them, with adults and children alike volunteering to join in the performances.

Invigorated by the success of this street-theater experiment, Schapiro decided to take his idea a step further: to turn *The Me Nobody Knows* into a proper show for the stage. His aim, he said, was no less than to create, in his words, "a ghetto *Under Milk Wood*." Dylan Thomas's classic multicharacter, multiperspective play was set in a Welsh fishing village. Now it was Harlem's turn.

Schapiro reached out to his friend Gary William Friedman, a composer with whom he had collaborated on another musical project. Friedman, like Schapiro, was the product of a Brooklyn Jewish family. He considered himself primarily a jazz musician at the time, a saxophonist who played in an avant-garde group called the Freeform Improvisation Ensemble. But Friedman, too, was a socially minded fellow, having put in time as a schoolteacher and participated in a pilot program in Bedford-Stuyvesant—another predominantly black neighborhood, in Brooklyn—in which students stayed in school until five o'clock. Scrounging up loaner instruments, Friedman used the extra two hours allotted to him in the school day to teach his students how to play songs and be a band: a sort of *School of Rock* analog to the freewriting experiments that Joseph and his peers were conducting.

Conversant in multiple genres—in college, he had studied classical and electronic music—Friedman proved adept at turning the passages that Schapiro had selected from Joseph's book into infectious pop-soul. "Black," the poem, became a pulsing, Curtis

Mayfield–like expression of anger and pride. "If I had a million dollars" and "Light sings all over the world" became the lyrical hooks for songs that recalled the more euphoric moments in *Hair*, the rock musical that had opened on Broadway in 1968.

The initial work on *The Me Nobody Knows*, the musical, was done without Steve Joseph's knowledge or consent, and he reacted with proprietary annoyance when he first learned of the project's existence. But after meeting with Schapiro, in whom he recognized a kindred spirit, he gave the project his blessing. From there, with remarkable speed for a musical—normally one of the slowest-gestating of all art forms—the stage version of *The Me Nobody Knows* snowballed into a proper show. Schapiro and Friedman were soon joined by a director, Robert Livingston, and the professional lyricist Will Holt, author of the folk standard "Lemon Tree," who augmented the passages from Joseph's book with additional lyrics.

The team constructed a framework for the show: it would progress from morning to noon to night, with twelve children of various ages addressing the audience directly in monologue and song. When the musical opened Off Broadway, on May 18, 1970, in the Orpheum Theatre in downtown New York, it had a multiracial cast and a stark set of cold, unforgiving surfaces—concrete and brick—onto which were projected photographs of ghetto streetscapes.

And it was a surprise hit. "I loved it. I loved its understanding and compassion, and I felt its pain and yet also its unsentimental determination for hope," wrote the *New York Times*' lead theater critic, Clive Barnes. The audience, Barnes noted, was left cheering, "and it was not cheering gloom, but the victory of the human spirit over circumstances. For the slums these kids find themselves in may have been squalid, but the kids are beautiful."

Even the notoriously dyspeptic reviewer John Simon was a believer, writing in the *Hudson Review*, enthusiastically if patronizingly, "*The Me Nobody Knows* gets it all across with the directness, illiterate poetry, touching unadornment, flashes of extraordinary originality, spontaneity even in banality, which make the writings of children, like the drawings of cavemen, what the sight of dawn is to eyes accustomed to sleep till noon."

The show went on to win that year's Obie Award for Best Musical, the highest honor for an Off Broadway production, and later in 1970 moved to Broadway, where it proceeded to run for 385 performances. None of this escaped the notice of the Children's Television Workshop, which raided four members of *The Me Nobody Knows*'s cast: Northern Calloway, who joined *Sesame Street* as the character David in 1971; and the show's three youngest performers, Melanie Henderson, Douglas Grant, and Irene Cara, who became founding members of *The Electric Company*'s kid band, the Short Circus. (A fifth member of *The Me*'s cast, Hattie Winston, would join *The Electric Company* in 1973.)

Of arguably greater importance than the initial success of *The Me Nobody Knows* was its enduring afterlife. Over the course of the 1970s, it became part of the repertoire of musicals staged regularly by high schools and colleges, offering young people in the suburbs the chance to hear, or even channel, the "children's voices of the ghetto." In a sense, the show developed into a sort of advanced-placement successor to *Sesame Street* and *The Electric Company* for children of the seventies, wherein they learned about heavier subjects—such as poverty, drug use, and racial identity—via an effective mix of music, good writing, and a charismatic, mixed-race ensemble of performers.

While today this might be construed as cultural tourism or appropriation, *The Me Nobody Knows* received little blowback over the course of its Off Broadway and Broadway runs. Steve Joseph recalled that his wife's brother, a black man, "was one of the few people who raised the idea, in a sardonic way, that it may have been exploitative." But this notion never crossed the minds of Joseph and the show's creative team. They were sincere in their belief that they were doing good—giving a damn.

Tuning in to Sesame Street *in an inner-city preschool day camp.*

CHAPTER

EIGHT

The Street Gets Real

Joan Ganz Cooney made no bones about identifying "the inner-city ghetto" as *Sesame Street*'s "chosen area of concentration." But getting its children to actually watch a new, unfamiliar show proved to be an ambitious and daunting undertaking. Anticipating this, in 1969, CTW established its Department of Utilization, a division devoted to community outreach. Evelyn Payne Davis, formerly the director of community relations for the New York Urban League, came aboard to run it. Nominally, "utilization" described the follow-through process of helping parents, teachers, and caregivers use *Sesame Street* to pursue further educational activities with children. But in practical terms, the department's first job was simply to create awareness in inner-city neighborhoods that the show existed.

Davis brought to CTW a knowledge of African American community dynamics that the Workshop's mostly white, mostly middle-class staff otherwise lacked. During *Sesame Street*'s first season, she focused heavily on her home turf, New York City, and the black neighborhoods of Harlem and Bedford-Stuyvesant in particular. Much of her work entailed ensuring that children were able to watch the show in the first place; many households in these neighborhoods lacked TVs, or had outdated, unreliable sets. Davis petitioned churches, community centers, nursery schools, day-care facilities, and libraries to create space for "*Sesame Street* centers," where families could view the show. She persuaded RCA, the electronics company, and Bergdorf Goodman, the upscale department store, to donate new color televisions to be used in these centers, and convinced the *Daily News* and WNDT, New York's public television station, to issue appeals for further donations of TV sets.

In the run-up to the show's November 1969 premiere, Davis and her deputy, James McConnell, spearheaded the TV-show equivalent of a get-out-the-vote campaign, tirelessly holding workshops and orientation meetings with teachers, Head Start leaders, church groups, and parent associations about the show's aims and attributes. A small army of volunteers—from organizations such as the Urban League, the National Council of Negro Women, the National Council of Jewish Women, the Boy Scouts, and the Girl Scouts—canvassed door-to-door, distributing promotional literature.

Davis also got Consolidated Edison, the utility company, to donate four trucks that functioned as literal promotional vehicles, equipped with projectors and demonstration reels of *Sesame*

Street material. She astutely recognized the promotional potential of a football game between Morgan State and Grambling State, two historically black colleges, that was being played that fall at Yankee Stadium. She enlisted about fifty teenagers, paying them a dollar apiece, to pass out *Sesame Street* flyers both at the game and at a parade that followed the next day. "We didn't find many being thrown away," Davis said. "We were surprised. We gave away at least two hundred thousand."

In Washington, D.C., the utilization effort was bolstered by the Howard University chapter of the Alpha Phi Omega fraternity, whose members were spreading word of *Sesame Street* as their public-service project. Viewing centers were established in seventy-five locations, many of them in the city's high-rise public-housing complexes, and even at a 7-Eleven store in Washington's impoverished Ward 8. In D.C., the need for viewing centers and new TVs was more acute than in New York, since the public station on which *Sesame Street* would air, WETA, was on a hard-to-receive UHF (ultra-high frequency) channel, and most older sets didn't have UHF capability. The Watergate Hotel, not yet infamous, happened to be upgrading its TVs, and donated its lightly used old ones to the effort.

Within a year, the Department of Utilization was renamed the Community Relations Department, and Davis was promoted to the level of vice president at CTW, overseeing offices in twelve different cities. Effectively, she was running her own social-services agency out of the Workshop rather than out of the U.S. government, with field coordinators from all over the country reporting to her. Most of them were African American and leaders within their communities. When Davis was looking for a Los Angeles coordinator, George Broadfield, an intellectual man-about-town in Harlem, tipped her off to Sandra Lindsey, a woman he described as "the Czarina of Watts."

"It took quite a bit of convincing from Evelyn to get me to do it," said Lindsey, who was at the time a young community organizer, activist, and mother, leading boycotts of subpar supermarkets in South Los Angeles. "I didn't know about the Children's Television Workshop," she said. "You have to remember, it didn't have the reputation or the public awareness back then." Lindsey went on to work for CTW for thirteen years, eventually overseeing its entire West Coast utilization operation.

The coordinator for the Deep South was Dr. Ollye Brown Shirley, of Jackson, Mississippi, an educator and one-half of a powerhouse couple of the civil rights movement; her husband, Dr. Aaron Shirley, was the state's first (and, for a time, only) black pediatrician, known statewide for providing medical care to the underprivileged. The Dallas utilization operation was run by Mary Dodd Greene, one of the few white coordinators, though she, too, was a formidable civil-rights and anti-poverty activist, plucked from the Dallas chapter of the Urban League, where she was the education director.

Sesame Street's development had been closely followed by the press from the moment that the Children's Television Workshop held its inaugural press conference at the Waldorf-Astoria. Part of this was attributable to the high-stakes nature of the project, given its backers and the mediagenic presence of Cooney, whom the press nicknamed "Saint Joan" well before the show made it to air. And part of this was a matter of the Workshop's own dogged efforts; it had hired Bob Hatch, formerly the director of public information for the Peace Corps, as its full-time PR man. But Davis's operation gave the show something that no amount of mainstream press coverage could give it: street cred.

— — —

Sesame Street's interracial cast offered another reason for black viewers to tune in: to see themselves represented on-screen. In the late 1960s, appearances by African American actors on television were still sufficiently infrequent that *Jet*, a weekly magazine for black readers, ran a page in the back of each issue highlighting which programs would be featuring black performers in the coming week ("Nichelle Nichols on *Star Trek*; Ivan Dixon on *Hogan's Heroes*; Greg Morris on *Mission Impossible ...*"). As Gordon and Susan, Matt Robinson and Loretta Long created a whole new paradigm—not only were they program regulars; they were regulars whose program aired five days a week.

Curiously, Jon Stone, in most respects so thoroughgoing in his planning, took a surprisingly last-minute approach to casting. Long auditioned before Stone had landed upon the idea of having Gordon and Susan be a couple. In Long's recollection, Susan was not even necessarily black at that point; most of Long's fellow auditioners were, she said, "Joan Baez types, folk-playing women with long hair and guitars. I showed up in a short skirt, with big hair and a bunch of show tunes. They asked me, 'Where's your guitar?'"

Long had come to audition for *Sesame Street* by way of Charlie Rosen, the set designer. He happened to be friends with both Stone and Long's then husband, Pete Long, a concert promoter and artists' manager who, at the time, handled much of the programming for the Apollo Theater in Harlem. Loretta, who aspired to a career as a singer, was working by day as a substitute teacher and had gained a foothold in show business as the cohost of *Soul!*, a variety-and-interview show on WNDT that featured such black performers as Patti LaBelle, Sam and Dave, Redd Foxx, and the Last Poets. Rosen also did the sets for *Soul!*, and passed along word to Long that she would be a good fit for the new educational program he was working on.

Long was the outlier of her group of auditioners and was treated as such; she didn't have a guitar, and every other aspiring Susan was called in before her. But her a cappella audition, performed in a state of exasperation—"I had spent $15 getting there by cab, trying to keep my Afro together, and thank God I channeled my negative energy into determination," she said—was the one that made an impression.

She performed "I'm a Little Teapot," playing directly to the camera and imploring her audience to hop to its feet and mimic her movements—much to the bemusement of the salty Brooklynite camera operator, who mockingly obliged. The audition, which was taped, ended up testing better than any of the others with real preschoolers. Ed Palmer, CTW's research chief, noted that the kids watching got to their feet and followed Long's instructions. "He told me, 'Loretta, you made us understand that if we invite the children in a very direct way, they will participate,'" she said. "Because the producers were getting a lot of flak that they were going to turn kids into zombies, just sitting there, letting the show wash over them."

Casting Gordon proved more problematic. Garrett Saunders, a stage actor, was the initial winner of the role, and he played Gordon in the test episodes that CTW produced in mid-1969. Saunders's presence was benign enough, but he lacked a certain *je ne sais quoi* and didn't test well in Palmer's focus-group screenings. Stone kept saying that what he really wanted was "a Matt Robinson type," referring to his writer-producer colleague. Finally, the *Sesame Street* brass convinced Robinson, a non-actor, to audition for the role, and he was just what they were looking for: slim and muttonchopped, with a dignified air befitting Gordon's role as a science teacher and the show's unofficial dad figure. With some reluctance, Robinson accepted the part, and Gordon and Susan, both African American, became husband and wife.

Bob McGrath, too, was a non-actor who came to the show by an unusual route. A child singing prodigy from rural Ottawa, Illinois, he had attended the University of Michigan, majoring in music. In the early 1960s, his limber high tenor won him a featured spot on NBC's variety show *Sing Along with Mitch*, the very program whose corniness had been bemoaned by John Bartlow Martin in the article that helped inspire Newton Minow's "vast wasteland" speech. Nevertheless, McGrath and Mitch Miller were a good fit. When Miller took the show on the road to Japan, McGrath, though already in his thirties, proved to be immensely popular with teenagers, who responded to his affability and scrubbed good looks as much as to his voice.

One day early in 1969, McGrath was waiting for a bus in front of Carnegie Hall when he was spotted from across the street by an old fraternity brother from Michigan: Dave Connell, *Sesame Street*'s executive producer. Connell approached McGrath, explained what he was up to, and noted that the part of Bobby had not yet been cast. Would McGrath be interested? His answer was instantaneous: "Not in the least." In contemplating the next phase of his career, McGrath envisioned himself as an heir to Perry Como and Andy Williams, keeping the flame of easy listening alight in the rock era. The matter was dropped in that moment.

But Connell persisted in his pursuit, and a few months later McGrath received a call asking him to formally audition. He assented and, while visiting CTW's offices, was blown away by the sample footage of the show that was screened for him. As the father of five children, including a newborn, McGrath recognized that *Sesame Street* was going to be important. "I felt immediately that this was where I wanted to be," he said, and he accepted the role of Bobby "on the condition that they drop the *B-Y*."

Midwestern, of Irish descent, and late of Mitch Miller's prerock world, McGrath was about as white a person as *Sesame Street*'s producers could have found. Indeed, he had not interacted with many black people up to that point in his life. "I never had a whole lot of exposure to multiculturalism until *Sesame Street*," he said. "There were only two African American boys in my grade school, the King brothers. Their father was a foot surgeon." But his sweetness and sincere embrace of the show's mission made him the perfect man to model positive Caucasian-adult behavior.

The only true actor among *Sesame Street*'s four original cast members was the Brooklyn-born Will Lee, né Lubovsky, who was sixty-one when he became Mr. Hooper. A veteran of the socially conscious Workers Laboratory Theatre of the 1930s, Lee had lost several years of his acting career to the Hollywood blacklist, having refused to name names when he was called to testify before the House Un-American Activities Committee in 1948. But over time, he steadily rebuilt his life as a character actor and teacher.

On the set, he was generous with advice, serving as the other performers' de facto acting coach.

For 1969, this was a groundbreaking cast, its adult hosts supplemented by a mix of black and white child visitors. Cooney, reviewing the show's progress a year later, wrote that "a strong black image for the program was deliberately sought" from the get-go, and noted that *Sesame Street* had welcomed such guests as James Earl Jones, Harry Belafonte, and Bill Cosby. In its first season, at least, *Sesame Street* was the blackest show on national television; the debuts of *Soul Train* and *The Flip Wilson Show* were still a year away.

The integrated nature of the cast was so novel that, in the early days, it actually presented technical challenges. "Big Bird had to be totally re-dyed, because he was so light," Long recalled. "The light bounced off of him and the iris of the lenses would go down, and then they'd shoot Matt and me, and all you'd see were eyes and teeth. We had a lighting designer win an award for learning how to light interracial groups of people."

— — —

A year into *Sesame Street*'s on-air existence, the Workshop's research team validated Cooney's faith in the power of a "strong black image." Naomi Foner, who joined the CTW staff as a young production assistant in 1968, recalled, "When we first tested four-year-old black children and asked them if they wanted a black doll or a white doll, they wanted a white doll. But after a year of watching people like themselves on television, they wanted the black doll. That was an undeniable effect."

CTW's surveys of teachers in *Sesame Street* viewing centers bore out these test results. The testimonials were powerful. One Head Start teacher reported, "The black children in my class feel very good about seeing so many black children on the show." A day-care-center aide said, "One of my boys said, 'Look at the black boy, he knows all the right answers!' Some children seemed surprised that the black children know as much as the white children on *Sesame Street*."

While these children didn't yet have the words to convey how emotionally and psychologically impactful *Sesame Street*'s look and cast were, Sonia Manzano did. When the program hit the airwaves, Manzano, two years away from joining it as the character Maria, was a nineteen-year-old college student at Carnegie Mellon University, in Pittsburgh, enrolled in its prestigious acting program. But her background was very much akin to that of Cooney's target viewer. She had grown up in the South Bronx, in a Puerto Rican neighborhood poorly served by its inferior public schools, and in a household troubled by domestic violence; her father beat her mother. Manzano's talent as a performer provided her with a pathway out—she had received a full scholarship from Carnegie Mellon.

But acclimating to her bourgeois collegiate surroundings was difficult, and Manzano frequently found herself in a state of anger, simultaneously bearing the weight of her tumultuous upbringing and the sense that she didn't fit in. One day, she ducked into the school's student union, her foul mood exacerbated by cold, rainy weather, to get a cup of coffee. By chance, *Sesame Street* was playing on a television: her first sight of it.

"It was just such a shocking image, to see James Earl Jones reciting the alphabet, and then this beautiful black couple, and this inner-city scene, the stoop and everything." In the moment, *Sesame*

Street seemed more real to Manzano than her campus did. "I was from the Bronx, very provincial," she said, "and here I was in this environment that was about speech and diction and acting—all this stuff that was out of my reach, that I thought was jive. I wasn't going to get parts. No one was going to ask me to play Juliet. But this show was so compelling and smart. I stopped and watched it for a bit. I thought, *I actually could do this.*"

Newly minted kids'-TV stars Mr. Hooper, Susan, Gordon, Bob, and Big Bird command the stage in Baltimore, autumn 1970.

CHAPTER
NINE

"A Street Where Neat Stuff Happens": *Sesame Street* Is Released into the Wild

Sesame Street's title, like its cast, fell into place at a relatively late stage. Bob Hatch, the Workshop's PR chief, had scheduled a press preview for May 1969 in which a "pitch reel" of highlights of the program-in-development would be screened for reporters. Jon Stone and Jim Henson had already come up with a narrative conceit for the reel, in which the Muppets Rowlf and Kermit would describe the goals, format, and content of the new program, with an occasional cut to a boardroom full of corporate Muppets in suits (and a couple of corporate monsters), who were vigorously debating what the show should be called:

MUPPET IN SUIT: Hey. These kids can't read or write, can they?
GROUP: Mm-mm. No. Nah. Nuh-uh.

MUPPET IN SUIT: Then howza 'bout we call the show "Hey, Stupid!"

But the bit lacked its kicker: the reveal of the title. Stone wanted to call the show *123 Avenue B*, which suggested both an educational purpose and the urban grit he so cherished. But his colleagues at CTW found the title too cumbersome and New York–specific. Finally, the Workshop compiled its staff's suggestions into a master list. "Sesame Street" was but one suggestion on the list, submitted by Virginia Schone, a writer on the show. Stone didn't like the name, worrying that children would read the first word as "see-same"; others worried that the title's sibilance would make it difficult to pronounce for preschoolers, especially those who had lisps or didn't yet have all their teeth.

Yet no one could think of anything better, and, essentially by default, up against a deadline, *Sesame Street* was decreed the final choice. Stone wrote an addendum to the pitch-reel script in which Rowlf, in a Muppets-imitating-life moment, despaired of ever coming up with a good title. Then Kermit had an epiphany: "Hey, Rowlf? Why don't you call your show *Sesame Street*? . . . You know, like 'Open Sesame'? It kind of gives the idea of a street where neat stuff happens."

— — —

The Stone-Henson naughtiness aside (in today's climate, the "Hey, Stupid!" joke would have cost the show its federal funding), the twenty-six-minute pitch reel was conscientiously assembled. It was bookended by segments in which Joan Ganz Cooney, in a red blazer and with a potted ficus tree behind her, patiently explained the program's methodology. "You'll note in one or two of the animated sequences in this film ...that the short, simple sixty-second form used by TV advertisers in commercials to sell products is used here to teach numbers and letters," she said. "As teachers and parents know, young children learn through repetition. And so, as with television ads, this material will be repeated many times during the 130 hours of original programming in our first season."

Gerald Lesser, the chairman of the board of advisers, gamely appeared with Kermit and Rowlf to walk the viewer through *Sesame Street*'s preparatory process. He explained everything from the 1968 seminars to the multiple steps taken to produce an animated clip about the letter *J*: the writing, the storyboarding, the consultation with educators and child psychologists, the making of the short film, and the postproduction research conducted by Ed Palmer to determine the cartoon's educational efficacy.

The *J* clip, produced by the animation shop Ken Snyder Enterprises (where executive producer Dave Connell had worked immediately prior to joining *Sesame Street*) featured two boys, one black and one white, learning about the letter via a poem recited to a shuffle beat. The poem was about a man named Joe who jammed a June bug in a jar, incurring the wrath of a judge and then serving an hour in the city jail. The moral? As one of the boys put it, "Don't jive a judge by jamming a June bug."

In retrospect, it's easy to see how it was all coming together: the production side's irreverence and the educational side's earnestness and rigor. But while most reporters were impressed by what they viewed, or at the very least willing to give *Sesame Street* the benefit of the doubt, some simply couldn't make sense of the show. For Terrence O'Flaherty, the longtime TV critic for the *San Francisco Chronicle*, the material he saw was antithetical to what educational television was supposed to look and sound like.

"The excerpts shown were foolish grotesques deeply larded with ungrammatical Madison Avenue jargon," he wrote. Misperceiving Kermit and Rowlf to be the show's future hosts (and misidentifying them as "Moppits"), he described them as "two formless puppets whose characters are totally lacking in the affectionate qualities of either man or beast and whose attitude is that of a wise-guy pitchman in a cartoon commercial." O'Flaherty then suggested his own j-words for *Sesame Street*: "junk, jargon, and jabberwocky."

At any rate, the program had the nation's attention. *Sesame Street*'s debut, on Monday, November 10, 1969, drew a lot of eyeballs, reaching roughly two million households.

What viewers saw was gloriously radical. The show announced its intent in the very first scene of its opening credits: three boys playing on a jungle gym while public-housing towers loomed behind them. The words "sweepin' the clouds away" were accompanied by footage of children energetically running down concrete steps and past a graffiti-tagged concrete wall—a real one, not a Charlie Rosen creation. Most of the kids in the opening credits were of color: black, Hispanic, Asian.

The through line of Episode 0001 was that Sally, a girl new to the neighborhood, was being introduced to all of the show's characters. As the vocal version of "Can You Tell Me How to Get to Sesame Street?" segued into Toots Thielemans's harmonica version, the action proper began with Sally being guided through Rosen's urban set by Matt Robinson's Gordon. "Sally," he said, "you've never seen a street like Sesame Street. Everything happens here!" Very efficiently, within the first five minutes, Sally became acquainted with Bob, Mr. Hooper, Susan, Big Bird, Ernie, and Bert. Her introductions to Oscar and Kermit came slightly later.

The episode was, as Will Lee announced over its closing credits, "brought to you today by the letters *W*, *S*, and *E*, and by the numbers *2* and *3*." It encompassed forty segments in its fifty-eight minutes, counting on-set "street" scenes, Muppet inserts, cartoons, films, and live-action sketches. It included *Sesame Street*'s first celebrity cameo (by Carol Burnett, saying, "Wow, Wanda the Witch is weird!") and two of the ten "Numerosity" live-action shorts that Jim Henson filmed in June 1969, each of which focused on a number from one to ten and culminated with a scene in which a baker, perilously balancing a tray bearing the relevant number of desserts, sang out what he was holding ("Two! Chocolate cream! Pies!") and promptly pratfell down a flight of stairs.

There were kinks yet to be worked out. Susan was too subserviently wifely; her first actions on the show were to take Gordon's briefcase and invite Sally over for milk and cookies. (By season's end, after the program received complaints from feminist groups and individual viewers, Susan had resumed her pre-marriage career as a nurse.) Oscar the Grouch was orange rather than moss green. Big Bird looked raggedy, his plumage uneven and his head squished, not yet configured as a sunburst of yellow feathers. And Caroll Spinney, the puppeteer who played him, hadn't quite cracked the character—the bird was more vaudevillian-dopey than sweetly childlike, as he would later be.

But the program was a marvel. The best thing about the first episode was that the end product bore no obvious traces of all the various CTW departments that had contributed to it—which is to say it was wholly entertaining to children. This would hold true for the entire season to come, and the one after it, and the one after that. Renata Adler, writing about *Sesame Street* for the *New Yorker* in 1972, observed, "A lot of what the programs create is really art—which is extraordinary, considering that the ideology here, the catechism, the product, is just letters, geometric forms, decency, and numbers."

Indeed, for anyone lucky enough to have been a small American child as the sixties turned into the seventies, watching early *Sesame Street* was a nurturing, mesmerizing experience, the opposite of the passive, zombie-breeding scenario that detractors and even some supporters had feared. So effectively "sticky" were the show's repeat-play educational sketches, songs, and films that the best of them made impressions that were not just lasting—meaning, useful as *Sesame Street*–watchers entered kindergarten and primary school—but *indelible*, carried into adulthood and forevermore exerting a primeval tug. Such *Sesame*-hatched terms and phrases as "rubber duckie" and "one of these things is not like the other" entered the American lexicon, and an entire generation associated the riddle "Which came first, the chicken or the egg?" with the ersatz-hoedown song that Joe Raposo made out of the question. *Sesame Street*'s songs, the composer and actor Lin-Manuel Miranda later observed, "are the closest thing we have to a shared childhood songbook."

The show was both joyful and mysterious. Raposo's bright, poppy "I've Got Two Eyes" was made brighter and poppier by the chemistry between Bob McGrath, looking a little like Paul McCartney as his hair grew out, and Loretta Long—both of them in vivid period colors, he in a Tang-colored cardigan, she in a canary-yellow blouse worn underneath a navy jumper dress. Jim Henson's voice was everywhere: in Kermit's melancholy "Bein' Green," in Ernie's buoyant "Rubber Duckie," in the sung exclamations of the pratfalling baker (who was played on-camera by a stuntman), in "Mah Nah Ma Nah," an absurdist nonverbal song sung by a hairy freak and two female sidekicks, and in the stop-motion animated short "King of 8," in which a crowned little figurine proto-rapped "I'm the King of Eight / And I'm here to state / That everything here has to total eight!"

Celebrities featured prominently in the program from the beginning. Between CTW's shrewd advance-PR efforts and the federal government's imprimatur, *Sesame Street* had no problem drawing guests from show business and public life, on a level previously unheard of for a children's program. Jackie Robinson, gray-haired and stoic, turned up to recite the alphabet. James Earl Jones, in a black mock turtleneck, Method-counted from one to ten. The R&B crooner Lou Rawls spiffed up the street in a smart peak-lapel striped suit and led five kids in an R&B reinterpretation of the alphabet song. Grace Slick, Jefferson Airplane's female vocalist, was heard but not seen, singing atonally over acid-rock jamming in a series of animated counting shorts.

Other animations were accompanied by gentle psychedelic music. One, a floaty, blissed-out short by the Oscar-winning husband-and-wife animation team of John and Faith Hubley, told the fable of "the queen on her knee under a tree by the sea" over a sitar-and-violin duet. Another, from Season Three, depicted a cross-legged Indian guru counting to twenty on his fingers over a trancey raga; when the guru got to eleven, he mind-blowingly sprouted a second pair of arms. A hippie strum-along called "I in the Sky," written and performed by a young singer-songwriter named Steve Zuckerman, accompanied a minute-long vignette of three elf-like fellows who lived inside of a capital *I*. Both the song's incantatory delivery and its trippy words ("We all live in a capital *I*, in the center of the desert, in the middle of the sky") lent it a mesmerizing elusiveness, as if it held a secret higher meaning.

In 1975, six years after *Sesame Street*'s debut, Steve Martin, then an ascendant comic, tuned in to the premiere episode of *Saturday Night Live* and, with a mixture of admiration and envy, thought to himself, "Fuck, they did it." What he meant, he later explained in his memoir, *Born Standing Up*, was that the show's writers and cast, at that point still strangers to him, had captured the insurrectionist, underground spirit of baby-boomer humor and figured out a way to present it on television to a mass audience. *Sesame Street* was a similar watershed. Its peewee viewers had no idea that it was the program they had been waiting for, but there was something so ineffably *right* about it; it was on their wavelength more than that of their parents or their older siblings. In its quick pacing, visual audacity, and musical genre–hopping, the show both mirrored and expanded upon the sensory intake of these children's short, TV-literate lives. And, without their even realizing it, these kids were learning how to learn.

— — —

One unintended consequence of *Sesame Street*'s sui generis cool was that the program acquired a substantial viewership among adults, even those who weren't raising small children. Orson Welles, appearing on *The Dick Cavett Show*, pronounced it "the greatest thing that ever happened to television." Another devotee, George Plimpton, told the *Wall Street Journal* that his habit of watching the show "destroyed God knows how much writing I could have done."

In "Hold On," the second song on his debut solo album from 1970, *John Lennon/Plastic Ono Band*, John Lennon gutturally croaked "Cookie!" during an instrumental break. And "Rubber Duckie," issued as a single the same year, was a surprise chart hit, making it to No.16 on the *Billboard* Hot 100. That the song was written by Jeff Moss, *Sesame Street*'s head writer, rather than Raposo, and that its success stoked their ego-driven rivalry—Moss also wrote such staples of the show as "I Love Trash," "The People in Your Neighborhood," and "Five People in My Family"—was immaterial to its delighted listeners.

Captain Kangaroo's Bob Keeshan tuned in to *Sesame Street* with some apprehension, concerned that his program, long the gold standard for children's television of integrity, was about to become passé. Cooney, out of deference to and respect for Keeshan, whose show aired at 8 a.m., didn't want her show to be seen as competition, and lobbied local public TV stations to broadcast *Sesame Street* at 9 or 10 a.m. (Oddly, one of the few stations not to accede to her request was the one she used to work at, WNDT. In its first year, *Sesame Street* aired in the New York market at 9 a.m. on channel 11, the commercial station WPIX, and was rebroadcast on WNDT at 11:30 a.m. and 4:30 p.m.) Nonetheless, Keeshan and his staff couldn't help but feel threatened.

Norton Wright was still working for Keeshan, and two years away from joining the production team of *Sesame Street*, when the newer show premiered. "We watched it at Keeshan's shop," Wright said, "and, as I recall, Bob simply said, 'Well, it sure is *fast.*' We all knew that we'd seen something very, very different. Whereas *Captain Kangaroo* was a gentle, kind show with generalities, we saw that the way things were probably going to go was this sort of high-powered cognitive curriculum packaged in wonderful show business."

Fred Rogers, too, was wary. Publicly, he was diplomatic about *Sesame Street*, but the show was, quite literally, not his speed. He found it too fast-paced and expressed concern that its zingy density didn't suit the developmental needs of preschool children. He also didn't care for some of its humor. Without naming names, Rogers expressed distaste for Henson's pratfalling baker, saying in a 1977 interview, "Adults falling down stairs and dropping things is not funny to kids. They may laugh, but they laugh in a very anxious way because it hasn't been too long since they learned to walk upright themselves." (He may have had a point; CTW received many letters from parents complaining that the baker's noisy tumbles upset their children, and the segments were eventually pulled from *Sesame Street*'s rotation.)

In the early years, some CTW-ers regarded *Mister Rogers' Neighborhood* with an air of condescension, or at least a belief that they were the cool kids to Fred's Squaresville dork. Frank Oz, a Rogers admirer now, has sheepishly confessed to having derided the *Neighborhood* as "unhip" when *Sesame Street* was the fresh upstart. "We made fun of him and his private life and things like that," said Sonia Manzano, who joined *Sesame Street*'s cast in its third season. "He was so straight, and I do think that he was authentic and sincere, but we were the drug generation and the smart alecks."

Jon Stone's friend and former writing partner Tom Whedon, who came to CTW in 1971 to write for *The Electric Company*, the Workshop's new reading program for grade-schoolers, recalled that he and Jim Thurman, a fellow *Electric Company* writer, had a daily ritual of watching Rogers's show for laughs—"The puppet part, with King Friday the XIII, was so bad; that was what we waited for," he said—and for the opportunity to ogle Betty Aberlin. Still, Whedon said, he and Thurman weren't totally hate-watching. "We kind of *liked* the show," he said. "And Joan was furious, because she thought that it was just awful."

Cooney maintains that this wasn't the case, though she acknowledges that Rogers's program never was her cup of tea. "I certainly knew about and had watched Fred Rogers. I watched him for ten minutes or whatever, and I understood why kids liked him," she said. "But it was not my kind of show or my kind of talent." Eventually, CTW and Rogers reached a détente. In 1975, Rita Moreno, one of the stars of *The Electric Company*, appeared on *Mister Rogers' Neighborhood* with her husband, Leonard Gordon, and their young daughter, Fernanda. Gordon, a cardiologist, took Rogers's blood pressure on-camera, and Moreno took the lead on one of Rogers's signature songs, "It's You I Like."

"Fred did something so spectacular," said Moreno. "Fernanda was painfully shy at the time, and she didn't say a word the whole time, but she was a big fan. When we said our goodbyes, Fred turned to the camera, and he said, 'Did you notice that Fernanda is very shy? But did you also notice that her mommy and daddy love her anyway?'"

Six years later, in a cross-promotional gesture of goodwill, Spinney, as Big Bird, made an appearance in the Neighborhood of Make-Believe, and Rogers reciprocated by visiting *Sesame Street*, where, McGrath recalled, his manner completely disarmed the cast. "I was in the makeup room talking to somebody," McGrath said, "and suddenly I heard this voice say very slowly and gently to me, 'Now, *there's* a voice I've wanted to meet for a long, long time.' We ended up having a wonderful time together."

— — —

More important for *Sesame Street*'s fortunes, children took to it immediately. Leaving nothing to chance, CTW reached out to executives at NBC, who, in the spirit of public service, agreed to carry, two nights before the show's premiere, a half-hour sneak preview for parents—an unprecedented instance of a commercial network's running a promo for another network's show.

Written by Stone and hosted by Ernie and Bert, the preview, entitled *This Way to Sesame Street*, included clips from Episode 0001 and a brief address from the then U.S. commissioner of education, Dr. James E. Allen Jr., who effectively plugged *Sesame Street* on behalf of the federal government. "There never has been before a nationwide TV program designed especially to help prepare young children for school. Next week, there will be," he said. "And I hope you will help your child find this exciting new way to learn by tuning to your local educational station each day at *Sesame Street* time."

With an eager audience thus teed up and ready to go, *Sesame Street* was an instant hit. By the end of its first season, it was reaching an estimated seven million of the U.S.'s twelve million preschoolers, a number that would climb to nine million by 1975. It would win the Emmy Award for Outstanding Achievement for Children's Programming in each of its first four seasons. Most important of all from CTW's point of view, the show was doing its job educationally.

The Workshop commissioned the Educational Testing Service, of Princeton, New Jersey, to perform a summative study of the first season of *Sesame Street*. ETS's report confirmed what Cooney and Lloyd Morrisett had suspected all along: that TV was, in fact, an effective medium for teaching small children. *Sesame Street*–watchers could better identify letters, numbers, and body parts than the control group of non-watchers. Disadvantaged children who watched the program regularly made greater gains than middle-class kids who watched infrequently. And, strikingly, three-year-olds who watched the program showed greater gains than four- and five-year-olds.

"This finding has important implications for education in general," the ETS report said, "for it suggests that 3-year-olds are able to learn many skills that have traditionally been introduced at later ages." Four years after Cooney and Morrisett had begun their working partnership, pushing past the doubts and derision of skeptical peers, their television experiment was succeeding beyond their expectations.

Indeed, in the early 1970s, as the first crop of *Sesame* "graduates" entered the school system, kindergarten and first-grade teachers noticed a palpable difference in how knowledgeable their newest pupils were. Some teachers even complained that their lesson plans had been upset by their students' unforeseen preparedness. Most, however, were grateful. As one Cleveland teacher told *Nation's Schools* magazine in 1971, "Besides the knowledge about letters and numbers, the kids seem to have a different attitude about school—as if they've already learned what school is for and what to do there."

Sesame Street *director-producer Jon Stone readies Reverend Jesse Jackson for his recitation of "I Am—Somebody," 1972.*

CHAPTER
TEN

In Search of the
Urban Audience

For all its early success and acclaim, *Sesame Street* struggled in some markets to connect with its principal intended audience: disadvantaged children. Public television, to that point, had been oriented toward a white, middle-class viewership. While this demographic was crucial in making *Sesame Street* an instant cultural phenomenon, the Workshop wasn't content to stand pat, mindful of Cooney's "bull's-eye" target of inner-city poor kids. In a study commissioned by CTW, the analytical firm of Daniel Yankelovich, Inc., determined that while the show was performing well in the New York neighborhoods of Bedford-Stuyvesant and East Harlem, where Evelyn Davis had concentrated much of her early community outreach—with penetration rates of 91 and 78 percent, respectively, in terms of reaching low-income homes with preschool-age viewers—Washington, D.C., with its UHF-only public television station, lagged far behind, with a penetration rate of only 32 percent.

Ed Palmer, the research chief, went so far as to describe Washington, Detroit, and Los Angeles—all cities where *Sesame Street* was broadcast over UHF—as "disaster areas" in terms of inner-city reach. Davis recognized that she had to redouble her department's efforts to connect with low-income viewers. One prong of her strategy was to organize a fifteen-city cast tour that took place in the run-up to *Sesame Street*'s second season, in September 1970. Washington, Detroit, and Los Angeles were all on the itinerary.

The tour, featuring Long, Robinson, McGrath, and Lee, along with Caroll Spinney as Big Bird, was specifically targeted at disadvantaged children. Tickets were free. The Workshop coordinated with the National Urban League, local public TV stations, and such organizations and agencies as the NAACP, Head Start, and the Council of Mexican-American Affairs to arrange sponsors for each show.

More than one hundred thousand people attended the shows, and, per CTW's internal report, 62 percent of this collective audience was black, 23 percent white, and 13 percent Hispanic. Though the tour's primary purpose was to bring new viewers to *Sesame Street*, the cast members came to realize, as they had not before, that they were rock stars to every child who had already seen the TV program. "When Big Bird came out, there was just a whole response from children in the audience who had never seen him in color. You could hear it: 'Big Bird is *yellow*!,'" said Sandra Lindsey, the utilization director for Los Angeles. "This really highlighted where these children were coming from, from homes that didn't have color televisions. It let us know that what we were doing was really super important."

McGrath recalled that the children erupted into hollers and applause at the mere sight of the cast. "In Los Angeles, we had two or three thousand kids on a big lawn in a park, and Matt went out to warm up the crowd," he said. "He came backstage smiling and said, 'God, it's like Woodstock out there! I think I'm going to go out there and say, 'Kids, there's some bad gum going around. If you have to, just do half a stick.'"

In Chicago, *Sesame Street* found an admirer in the Reverend Jesse Jackson, in 1970 the twenty-nine-year-old director of Operation Breadbasket, the economic-empowerment arm of the Southern Christian Leadership Conference. While Operation Breadbasket's mandate was to foster the creation of black-owned businesses and better job opportunities for African Americans, Jackson had also assigned it a social role, "to further the meaning of black family life and to defend the integrity of the black community," as his organization's literature put it.

Jackson and Evelyn Davis became acquainted via an introduction by Cecil Hollingsworth, one of the cofounders of *Essence*, a brand-new monthly magazine for black women. (In its early issues, *Essence* carried CTW's "Parent's Guide to *Sesame Street*.") As Christmas approached in 1970, Jackson invited the *Sesame Street* cast to perform two more live shows, to take place just before the holiday in Chicago's Capitol Theatre, under the aegis of Operation Breadbasket.

But there was a conflict: the Workshop had also received an invitation from Pat Nixon, the First Lady, for the cast to be the entertainment at the White House's Christmas party for the children of Washington's international diplomatic corps. "We were very anti-Nixon at that point, all of us," said McGrath. "We said to our bosses, 'If you don't mind, we'd really rather pass on this one.'

But we were reminded, 'Look, we're still getting a chunk of change from the government.'"

Grudgingly, McGrath, Robinson, Long, Lee, and Spinney flew down to Washington, D.C., at the crack of dawn on December 20, a day before the Chicago shows. Lee was especially reluctant to participate in the White House show, as his security clearance had been delayed by the vetting team's discovery of his blacklist past. But the cast forged on, rehearsing in the White House before their performance, and then, since they had yet to eat anything that day, requesting some food during their break. The First Lady's assistant looked at her clipboard and informed them that breakfast was not on the schedule, and that no food had been prepared for their visit. After some protestation—Spinney put on his Oscar puppet and, in the character's voice, demanded, "I wanna speak with President Nixon!"—the White House finally ordered in: "Cold burgers from a Walgreens," in Long's recollection.

The cast was so incensed by their treatment that after performing for the diplomats' children, its members actively avoided being corralled for a group shot with the First Lady, excusing themselves to a bathroom or a hallway. But Spinney, in his cumbersome Big Bird getup, was too conspicuous to escape—and so Pat Nixon got her one-bird, no-humans photo op.

The following day, after completing their rehearsal at the Capitol Theatre, the cast was greeted by Jackson, who asked them if they were hungry for lunch. "We followed him outside, walked a couple of doors down the street, and up a very long, creaky flight of wooden stairs that opened onto a hall, and there was just this *line* of soul food," said McGrath.

"All the old ladies had been cooking for days," said Long. "Will Lee said, 'This is more like it. Give me more of that peach cobbler!'"

The *Sesame Street* team had found its people, and, soon enough, the people found *Sesame Street*, as the live shows and public-outreach campaigns in America's inner cities reaped their desired result. By the end of the show's second season, the Yankelovich firm reported that Washington, D.C.'s inner-city penetration rate had climbed from 32 to 59 percent, and that, in Chicago, the number was "near saturation," at 95 percent. By 1973, a third Yankelovich report described *Sesame Street* as "virtually an institution with ghetto children."

— — —

Jon Stone got to know Jesse Jackson through Pete Long, Loretta's husband, the Apollo Theater impresario and all-around connector in African American power circles. When, in 1971, Jackson broke with the Southern Christian Leadership Conference after a falling-out with its leader, Ralph Abernathy, he invited Long to serve on the board of his new organization, People United to Save Humanity, better known as Operation PUSH.

Pete Long invited Stone to join him at various Operation PUSH functions and other events at which Jackson was present. One was a benefit jazz concert for Daytop Village, a drug-rehabilitation center where Jackie Robinson's namesake son had been treated for heroin addiction and later became a counselor. Tragically, the younger Robinson had died in a car accident just days before the benefit, which he had planned with Long's help. But Jackie and Rachel Robinson carried on nevertheless with the concert, which featured the pianist Billy Taylor and the singer Roberta Flack.

It also included Jackson leading the audience in his trademark call-and-response recitation, "I Am—Somebody," which he had adapted from a poem by William Holmes Borders Sr., a Baptist minister and radio preacher in Atlanta. While Borders's original was a celebration of African American achievement, namechecking such figures as W. E. B. Du Bois, George Washington Carver, and Harriet Tubman, Jackson's version was more of an affirmation of strength and self-belief in the face of adversity: "I may be poor. But I am somebody. I may be on welfare. But I am somebody . . ."

Stone, recalled his former wife, Beverley (they split in the mid-1970s), "was changed, radicalized, by the objective of *Sesame Street*." And as he grew ever more passionate about the show's mission to help underprivileged black children, he became besotted with black culture. Never a fan of suits and ties, he took to wearing dashikis at awards ceremonies. He also developed something of a man crush on Pete Long, regarding him as a no-nonsense sounding board and a crucial conduit to the program's black constituency.

"Here's this Ivy League white boy, and Pete didn't cut him any slack," said Loretta Long. "But Jon appreciated Pete's candor. And Pete appreciated that these were people who had privilege and were willing to lay it down for those who didn't have any. That was big. They all respected each other."

In its early seasons, *Sesame Street* featured a number of musical performances by Listen My Brother, a vocal ensemble that Pete Long had assembled at the Apollo to nurture and showcase local New York City talent. Its young members, resplendent in brightly colored shirts and dresses, included Luther Vandross, for whom *Sesame Street* represented his first national exposure, and the future session singer Robin Clark, whose husband, the guitarist Carlos Alomar, accompanied the group on a stonking, Billy Taylor–composed gospel rave-up from Season Two called "Count to 20." Within five years, Vandross, Clark, and Alomar were collaborating with David Bowie on his album *Young Americans*.

Taylor, too, was a Long connection, a jazz polymath who led his own trio, served as a DJ and program director for WLIB, one of New York's few black-owned radio stations, and had invested himself in civic outreach well before *Sesame Street* existed. In 1964, he cofounded Jazzmobile, a nonprofit program devoted to acquainting inner-city children (and their parents) with live jazz, using a float donated from a beer company as a mobile stage. For *Sesame Street* (and, later, *The Electric Company*), he became a musical contributor of remarkable versatility, not only writing songs for Listen My Brother but also scoring animated segments; it was he who composed the haunting raga of the four-armed counting guru.

But the most memorable result of the Jon Stone–Pete Long alliance was Jackson's appearance on *Sesame Street* during its third season, in which the reverend, using the set's stoop as his pulpit, led a large, multiracial group of children in a junior version of "I Am—Somebody" ("I may be small. But I am . . ."). This scene—of a black man with an Afro, casually attired in a purple crewneck, a large medallion of Martin Luther King Jr. hanging from his neck, presiding over a rainbow coalition of kids who followed his lead in declaiming, "I am somebody"—was as explicit as *Sesame Street* ever got in promoting its vision of inclusivity.

"There was no sense in which Jesse Jackson's leading the children was controversial," wrote Renata Adler in her *New Yorker* article, published a few weeks after Jackson's appearance. "But, for much of the country, the performance, and the integrated life on *Sesame Street* in general, may have been maddening. Nothing but the once apparently token but now vital appearance of black performers on network television would have put many adults in the frame of mind to stand it."

Some of the maddened did write in. One mother sent a letter

to CTW complaining that "*Sesame Street* is changing its aim from teaching children basics in learning and living with others to some sort of mini protest movement." Another wrote to denounce "the blatant Communism shown on this program" and likened Jackson to a "slim Negro Chairman Mao." A father described his two-and-a-half-year-old growing agitated as the boy watched the segment, yelling "No!," "I don't like you!," and "I hate you!" at Jackson. The man took pains to say that his issue was not so much with the segment's content as it was with the manner of its delivery, which, he theorized, his son took to be "violent."

This sort of feedback wasn't entirely new to the Workshop. The folk legend Pete Seeger paid a few visits to the street in the show's early seasons, just a few years after CBS had cut his performance of the anti-war song "Waist Deep in the Big Muddy" from an episode of *The Smothers Brothers Comedy Hour*, deeming it too inflammatory to air. On *Sesame Street*, Seeger stuck to such child-friendly standards as "Skip to My Lou" and "Michael, Row the Boat Ashore," but his very presence rubbed some adult viewers the wrong way. A few protested the show's embrace of a "Communist," and one even took issue with Seeger's flat cap, which, evidently, was "after the style of Lenin."

But these little tempests simply blew over, never growing into proper controversies. As "radicalized" as Stone may have become, and as stocked as the Workshop was with unabashed liberals, *Sesame Street* was accepted by most parents at face value, as an educational experiment that was delivering on its promise—so much so that, in 1971, Max Gunther, a writer for *TV Guide*, could credibly assert, "*Sesame Street* has enjoyed what may be the most astonishing success of any show in the whole history of American television. It has ceased to be merely a show. It has become a cause."

Midway through the show's first season, President Richard Nixon himself wrote to Cooney, "This administration is enthusiastically committed to opening up opportunities for every youngster, particularly during his first five years of life, and is pleased to be among the sponsors of your distinguished program."

— — —

Which is not to say that the Nixon administration and CTW enjoyed the easiest of rapports—as the *Sesame Street* cast's near revolt at the White House demonstrated. Cooney and Morrisett couldn't afford to be flippant toward the president, given how dependent *Sesame Street* was on federal funding. When Nixon succeeded Lyndon Johnson in 1969, they cultivated friendly relationships with members of the new administration. Cooney and Morrisett found willing partners in James Allen, Nixon's first education commissioner, who had lent his presence and gravitas to the promotional film *This Way to Sesame Street*, and Allen's successor, Sidney Marland, with whom Morrisett was already friendly.

When Nixon, in 1970, designated the seventies as the Right to Read decade, in which America would lick illiteracy through a combination of public and private initiatives, Morrisett recognized an opportunity to secure federal funds for a second CTW show, this one devoted to teaching reading to primary-school-age children. Marland was all for it, and Morrisett's idea quickly evolved into *The Electric Company*.

But CTW was very much the product of Lyndon Johnson–era ideals of big-government largesse and progressivism, and its honeymoon with the Nixon administration was not to last. Outside the Office of Education, Nixon's people regarded public TV in general with suspicion. By 1972, word got back to Cooney and Morrisett that the president did not believe that the federal government should be in the business of underwriting original programming.

Fortunately, *Sesame Street* was already developing a significant revenue stream from what the Workshop called "nonbroadcast materials," meaning *Sesame Street*–branded record albums, toys, licensed Muppet products, and books. (Stone wrote the Workshop's first instant classic, 1971's *There's a Monster at the End of This Book*, a meta-narrative in which Grover, the protagonist, is terrified to reach the book's end for fear of the monster who awaits—only to discover on the last page that the monster is *him*.) As the seventies progressed, product income would cover an ever larger percentage of CTW's operating costs. But in the short term, Cooney and Morrisett couldn't be sure of this. As Cooney told the *Sesame Street* historian Michael Davis, "Suddenly, we had enemies, all these powerful forces were against us and wanted to see us curbed. I couldn't believe it. It disoriented me."

And in the context of Nixon's growing paranoia, as the Watergate scandal closed in on him, Cooney and Morrisett's interactions with the White House grew ever stranger. In March 1972, they were notified by the National Science Foundation, a federal agency, that they were to be among seven recipients of a new award: the Presidential Prize for Innovation. The other five winners—among them Willem Kolff, the Dutch-born inventor of the dialysis machine, and John W. Backus, the creator of the computer language Fortran— were to receive $50,000 apiece, while Cooney and Morrisett, as cowinners, would each receive $25,000. But later that year, before the awards were distributed, the honorees received calls from the White House trying to suss out if they were "willing" to accept their prizes from the increasingly embattled president, as opposed to snubbing the honor and causing Nixon political embarrassment.

Cooney and Morrisett heard nothing further on the matter until early 1974, when the head of the National Science Foundation declared the prize program dead—much to the Workshop's founders' chagrin. "We would have accepted the prize," said Morrisett. "At that time, our future seemed very fragile, and the prize would have been, we thought, valuable recognition and credibility."

"It was heartbreaking to me to lose that money," said Cooney. "I was as poor as a church mouse, married to someone who wasn't working and was an alcoholic. I supported us. Twenty-five thousand dollars was a fortune to me. It would have helped me for years. I would have been able to spend $5,000 a year for five years on my expenses."

— — —

Stranger still was the discovery that "Lloyd N. Morrisett" was among the names on the extended version of Nixon's infamous "Enemies List," a secret White House memorandum enumerating the president's perceived political opponents, the existence of which came to light when Nixon's former counsel, John Dean, mentioned it in his testimony before the Senate Watergate Committee in the summer of 1973. Some confusion remains to this day over whether the Morrisett in question was the CTW chair or his namesake father, a distinguished professor of education at UCLA. "My father did not like Nixon at all, so it could have been either one of us, but I think it was probably me," said Morrisett. "It's more likely that I would have been considered a political opponent, because of my connections with Carnegie, John Gardner, Lyndon Johnson, and so forth."

Whereas some more famous names on the list, such as Paul Newman and the journalist Daniel Schorr, considered their inclusion a badge of honor, "it wasn't a laugh at the time," said Morrisett.

"It created a lot of anxiety, because you don't know how that could be used in determining or not determining the kind of support that *Sesame Street* needed."

It was in this period that Cooney and Morrisett paid a visit to the office of Caspar Weinberger, who was then the secretary of Health, Education, and Welfare, under whose umbrella the Office of Education fell. The goal was to secure more funding for CTW. The meeting did not go well; Weinberger was standoffish and noncommittal.

But once again, CTW found itself, to use Cooney's phrase, stalked by good luck. Newton Minow, the FCC chairman under John F. Kennedy, had become a big fan of *Sesame Street*, which was precisely the kind of programming he had hoped for at the time of his "vast wasteland" speech. Though he was based in Chicago, Minow was on the board of PBS, and, while in New York for a board meeting, he met Cooney and learned of her struggles to get the funding she needed. Next up on Minow's schedule was a trip to Washington to meet with then FCC chairman Dean Burch. Though Burch was working for Nixon and had served as the chair of the Republican National Committee during Barry Goldwater's 1964 presidential campaign, he and Minow, in those days of bipartisan comity, held similar ideas about improving the quality of children's television and had become good friends.

Minow mentioned Cooney's situation to Burch. Burch, it transpired, had known Cooney when they were both students at the University of Arizona. (Minow recalled Burch saying, "I asked her to marry me!" Cooney denied that any such proposal occurred.) Burch recognized that Goldwater, who had rejoined the U.S. Senate in 1969, could be of help to Cooney, and set up a meeting between the two. Goldwater, too, was an Arizonan, and though he and Cooney had never met, their families went way back—his father, Baron, and her grandfather Emil Ganz had both been prominent and civically active Phoenix merchants (the latter serving two terms as the city's mayor) when Arizona was still a territory, not yet a state.

"Barry was happy to see me when Dean asked him to," Cooney said. "He recounted knowing my father, and I told him how we would gradually be able to support ourselves by selling merchandise, and I told him the numbers. He didn't take a single note. He said, 'I know I'm considered anti-federal on many things, but not on education. I'll write Cappy.' And then he wrote a letter recounting our meeting exactly right to Cappy Weinberger, and we got an infusion of money."

It speaks volumes of both the period and the power of *Sesame Street* that Barry Goldwater, the political bogeyman of 1964—considered to be so dangerous an archconservative that more than a thousand psychiatrists polled by *Fact* magazine deemed him psychologically unfit to be president—was happy to lend his support in the early seventies to Cooney and her hairy, gritty, funky, righteous educational TV show. For all the political enmity associated with Nixon and the Watergate era, Washington was a more collegial place back then, with less predictably dug-in partisan stances. It was on Nixon's watch that the Environmental Protection Agency was established with overwhelming bipartisan support, and that the Equal Rights Amendment was approved by huge margins in both the House and the Senate, coming up short of ratification only because not enough state legislatures would approve it.

Sesame Street was both the product and beneficiary of an uncommonly progressive-skewing time—so progressive, in fact, that most of the political blowback that the program received in its early years came not from the right but the left.

*Joan Ganz Cooney, getting it done with
Sesame Street executive producer Dave Connell.*

CHAPTER ELEVEN

These Are the People in Your Neighborhood: Diversity on the Street

I n early 1972, the Children's Television Workshop was the target of a coordinated letter-writing campaign by the National Organization for Women. From all over the country, members of the feminist advocacy group, which had been founded six years earlier, wrote in to express their displeasure with how women were represented, and underrepresented, on *Sesame Street*.

"Why do you persist on picturing women as simple-minded, do-nothing creatures?" wrote Sonja Sorkin, the president of NOW's Central New York chapter, based in Syracuse. Sorkin intimated that there was some hypocrisy to CTW's self-image as a paragon of inclusivity. "If you want children to grow up with more tolerance and understanding of all people," she wrote, "it is time that you extended this to women."

The precipitating incident for this letter, and the others like it, was an excoriating opinion piece by a writer named Jane Bergman that ran in the *New York Times* in January of that year under the headline "Are Little Girls Being Harmed by 'Sesame Street'?" Bergman noted that the program's cast was disproportionately male, as were the characters who populated its animated segments and Muppet inserts. She also commented upon the Susan character's subservience to Gordon and the writers' apparent abandonment of Susan's nursing career.

These were fair points; *Sesame Street* had plenty of work to do in terms of achieving gender parity. The show's mostly male creative team held on to some retrograde notions about women in the workplace. Matt Robinson had only grudgingly gone along with the story line of Susan's return to nursing—a reflection, said Dolores Robinson, his wife at the time, of his personal views on the subject matter. "He felt that a woman's place was in the home," she said. "It was all about ego. If you were a successful black man, your wife didn't work. I went along with it because in the family I was raised in, you always had an elder woman—your mother, your grandmother—who said, 'Well, hon, that's what men are like.'"

Fran Brill, who joined *Sesame Street* partway through its second season, was for years the program's only full-time female puppeteer. (Jane Henson performed occasionally on the show in its early seasons.) Both Jon Stone and Jim Henson attributed this circumstance to a simple lack of qualified female puppeteering candidates, either ignoring or not realizing that they held the power to cultivate talented women—though Henson, at least, changed his tune as time went on, taking a more proactive role in bringing women into the fold.

The Bergman piece ran midway through Season Three, at a time when one of the new female characters who had been introduced to redress *Sesame Street*'s gender imbalance, a letter carrier named Molly, had already fizzled out as a regular. (Molly was played by Charlotte Rae, later of *Diff'rent Strokes* and *Facts of Life* fame.) The only compliment that Bergman paid *Sesame Street* was about the show's other new female character, Sonia Manzano's Maria, a bright young woman who worked part-time at the local library and was "much better integrated into the life of the program."

But, otherwise, Bergman's piece was a take-no-prisoners condemnation that undermined its good arguments with rhetorical overkill, demeaning Long's Susan for always having "this highly inappropriate smile on her face," accusing *Sesame Street* of "pervasive anti-feminism," and expressing revulsion that Grover, the scrawny blue monster Muppet voiced by Frank Oz, had a crush on Maria: "Grover is ingenuously explicit about the cause of his passion: 'OHHH, she is so pret-ty.' So much for Maria, the ex-person."

Bergman did passingly acknowledge the show's founding impetus, writing, "I have the impression that originally the program was put together in part with an eye toward upgrading the image of men for the benefit of black children who have had small opportunity to see brothers or fathers functioning in the world with autonomy and self-respect." Still, she concluded, "even if this be true, there can be no justification for the creation of a program for black and white boys and girls full of such vicious, relentless sexism."

Joan Cooney was taken aback by how adversarially NOW and Bergman had positioned themselves vis-à-vis *Sesame Street*; at one point, NOW's New York City chapter even threatened a boycott of General Foods, the maker of Alpha-Bits and Raisin Bran, for underwriting weekend rebroadcasts of the program. Writing to

NOW's president, Wilma Scott Heide, in response to the letters she had received from various chapters, Cooney faulted the organization for picking a fight with a natural ally.

"While I certainly don't object to having our faults pointed out to us (and God knows, everyone is doing it), I wonder if NOW is really performing a service by concentrating so much public attention and energy on one of the few really decent programs for young children on television," Cooney wrote. "Perhaps you are not aware that preschool children watch up to eight hours a day and that the number of badly sexist commercials and situation comedies they are exposed to during that time is not to be believed."

Cooney further noted that one letter writer had complained that "the program has shown greater responsiveness to the needs of blacks than women." This pitting of one group's agenda against another's incensed her. Though the term "intersectionality" was not yet in common usage, Cooney essentially invoked it, asking Heide to be mindful that the show was addressing multiple, overlapping needs. "We acknowledge that we can and should change our portrayal of women and girls on *Sesame Street*, but we don't like to see the issue cast in racial terms nor compared with the nightmare of racism and poverty," she wrote. "And certainly, our Black staff—men and women—harbor resentments against the feminist movement when it speaks in such terms, making it more difficult for us to achieve our mutual aims."

Still, Cooney and CTW took measures to address the issues that NOW had raised. Over the course of the 1970s, more women were added to *Sesame Street*'s cast, among them the deaf actress Linda Bove, who joined in 1972, the Native American (though Canadian by nationality) singer-songwriter Buffy Sainte-Marie, who joined in 1975, and the actress and singer Alaina Reed, who joined in 1976 and played Gordon's sister, Olivia, a professional photographer. The program also started portraying women in more non–traditionally female occupations, as when Sonia Manzano's Maria, in the mid-1970s, took a job working on a construction site.

This story line prompted some damned-if-you-do letters from anti-feminists. A Texas mother wrote to CTW that she changed the channel when she saw Maria in her hard hat and boilersuit, on the grounds that "the woman's place is in the home, or at least in a feminine position in the business world." A Missouri mother interpreted Maria's new job to be propaganda for the Equal Rights Amendment, expressing alarm that *Sesame Street* "seems to be backing the new fad E.R.A." and that "the Libbers are running things into the ground." She admonished CTW for bending to the will of "a few he-women in our nation with mixed up personalities."

— — —

But the Workshop forged onward. Particularly in its early years, CTW continued to regard *Sesame Street* as an experiment rather than as a finished product, which afforded the producers a nimbleness to make big changes to the show from one season to the next. In its second season, the program added "bilingual skills" to its listed curricular goals and half-heartedly introduced a new character, Miguel, who was played by the Puerto Rican–born actor Jaime Sanchez. Miguel, like Molly the mail lady, didn't take, and the show's lip-service commitment to its purported new goal wasn't lost on Latin American viewers.

A coalition of leaders from the Hispanic community demanded a meeting with Cooney and issued a press release denouncing "the racist attitude" of the Workshop, and, furthermore, of "this nation towards its Spanish-speaking people." As she had been with NOW,

Cooney was surprised to be cast as a villain rather than as an ally. But she agreed to the meeting. Though it was not without its contentious moments, it produced results. For two years, the Workshop worked with a committee of Latin American advisers on its bilingual and bicultural material. And *Sesame Street*'s third season introduced three new Latin American cast members: Sonia Manzano, Emilio Delgado, and Raul Julia.

To Manzano, who was only twenty-one when she was hired to play Maria but stayed with the program for forty-four years, Cooney's willingness to engage with her critics was crucial to *Sesame Street*'s evolution. "That's a remarkable thing that Joan did," Manzano said. "White people do not listen. Or they listen and then they give it back to you in their terms. It has to be *their* kind of understanding. Most people in power, CEOs, they don't want to hear anything that they don't already know. Except for the people at *Sesame Street*. They really listened."

Manzano's path to *Sesame Street* was not a straight line from her "I actually could do this" epiphany in the Carnegie Mellon student union. In 1970, while still in college, she was cast in a new, student-developed musical in which her self-perceived unsuitability for the traditional theater canon didn't matter. It was an oddball show, a series of parables from the New Testament as performed by hippie clowns, and it was called *Godspell*. The show quickly grew into something bigger than a campus production, moving first to La Mama, an experimental theater in New York's East Village, and then, in revamped form, to bigger Off Broadway theaters. Manzano quickly went from an uneasy student actor to an original cast member of what would turn out to be one of the most enduring musicals in American theater history.

All the while, she kept an eye on *Sesame Street*, catching it occasionally on TV, fascinated, she said, by "the live, Sid Caesar–type sensibility to it" and the way its animations and film shorts summoned memories of her own childhood. "There was something about the show that spoke to me," she said. "Like, when I was a girl, I would find shapes in the cracks of the ceiling of my room. And *Sesame Street* was doing films where it was 'What shapes do you see in this?' That's exactly how my mind used to work when I was in the South Bronx."

When her time in *Godspell* came to an end, Manzano was a qualified acting professional, but the parts available to her were unappealing: mostly stereotypical Puerto Rican tough-chick roles. Then, through her agent, she got an audition for *Sesame Street*—a possibility that she had never seriously entertained, despite her affinity for the show.

The audition turned out to be simply a one-on-one meeting with Jon Stone in his office. Stone asked her to tell him a scary story as if he were a child. Manzano unspooled a narrative based on one of her own childhood nightmares, in which a little girl was pursued by a giant, tubular, periscope-like eye. In the version she told to Stone, the girl finally vanquished the eye by eating it. Stone was amused, and, just like that, she was anointed Maria.

Whereas Manzano considered herself mostly apolitical at the time—"I just wanted to be a funny actress," she said—Delgado, a resident of Los Angeles, was a committed activist in the Chicano Movement, the L.A.-based Mexican American civil rights movement that encompassed everything from Cesar Chavez's supermarket boycotts on behalf of farmworkers to the Chicano Moratorium, which mobilized protests against the Vietnam War and the disproportionate number of Latin Americans serving in it while affluent and well-connected white kids stayed home.

Delgado, who had put in several years in the California National Guard, managed to avoid being shipped off to Vietnam, but his two younger brothers, one an enlisted Marine and the other a draftee, weren't so fortunate. In August 1970, the thirty-year-old Delgado, with his wife and toddler son, participated in the Chicano Moratorium's anti-war march through East Los Angeles. They narrowly escaped the march's violent conclusion, in which the police came down on the protesters with tear gas and billy clubs, and the *Los Angeles Times* journalist Ruben Salazar was killed by a gas canister thrown by an L.A. County sheriff's deputy.

Delgado's most active role in the Chicano Movement was as an agitator, alongside such fellow Angelenos as the actor Edward James Olmos and the film producer Moctesuma Esparza, for greater opportunities for actors of Hispanic descent. "At the time, the only parts that were available for young men like me were as gang members and drug addicts. And for young women, it was prostitutes and maids," said Delgado.

Still, for all his efforts, Delgado found little in the way of decent acting work besides a stint on a bilingual children's television show, *Angie's Garage*, that aired Sunday mornings on the local station KABC. He was unaware that the Children's Television Workshop was on a West Coast talent search, looking for a young Mexican American actor who could sing. Delgado was exactly that: he had grown up in the California border city of Calexico, routinely and casually crossing over into Mexico to visit his grandparents. "On the Mexican side, there was music all over the place," he said. "I would go into bars to shine shoes, and there were mariachis. And there were Mexican trios singing romantic songs, and big bands playing in the breweries." Delgado soaked it all in, and, equally inspired by the advent of rock 'n' roll on the American side of the border, he learned to play guitar.

In the summer of 1971, just as his unemployment benefits were running out, Delgado received a call out of the blue from a casting agent, who asked if he was willing to meet with Dave Connell, *Sesame Street*'s executive producer, while Connell was in Los Angeles. Delgado was unfamiliar with the program, but he took the meeting. Though it went pleasantly enough, Delgado heard nothing for a few weeks and assumed he hadn't made the cut. Then the same casting agent called him again, asking Delgado if he could meet with Jon Stone at the Beverly Wilshire Hotel. Like Manzano, Delgado discovered that his audition was a simple one-on-one conversation with Stone. "He was very nice. I didn't have to sing, I didn't have to dance, I didn't read anything," Delgado said. "He just asked questions about me, where I was from, my family. And after about twenty minutes, he said, 'Well, Emilio, if you want to work for us, be in New York on October 11.'"

Delgado was so surprised by the casual nature of Stone's offer that he wasn't sure if it *was* an offer. But he confirmed that it was for real, and that autumn moved to New York to take on the role of Luis. In the course of Season Three, Luis opened the street's Fix-It Shop with another new bilingual character, Rafael, who was played by the most accomplished of *Sesame Street*'s new recruits: the actor Raul Julia, who already had a successful stage career.

Stone was characteristically passionate about the show's redoubled mission to reach young Hispanic viewers. "The first year we did nothing," he said in an interview in the middle of *Sesame Street*'s third season. "The second year, we did some token materials that were worse than nothing, I think. This year we're doing whole blocks of the show in Spanish, with no translation, no apology, no anything, in order to draw the Spanish-speaking, bilingual children into the show, involve them with the characters, and turn them on, not only to the Spanish, which would relate to them, but hopefully also to the 95 percent of the show which is in English, the language they are ultimately going to exist in."

Stone recognized that this cast expansion would serve social and educational purposes for non-Hispanic children as well. "That kid out in Iowa hasn't seen anybody Spanish except the 'Frito Bandito' on television," he said, alluding to an animated, sombrero-wearing stickup artist that Frito-Lay used to sell corn chips in the 1960s. "Suddenly," Stone said, "he realizes these aren't all comic bandits that come down out of the hills. These are real people who care about kids, and each other."

Manzano and Delgado credit Cooney with creating a workplace culture in which the creatives were responsive to the cast's concerns. The *Sesame Street* writing staff, which was then mostly white, heeded the actors' advice on the show's Spanish-language segments, since there existed significant idiomatic differences between Manzano's Nuyorican Spanish, Delgado's Chicano Spanish, and the Spanish of Florida's Cuban Americans. "Things would come up like they wanted to have a character say, 'I like those mangoes,' and you can't have that, because for Cubans, 'mangoes' also means a woman's breasts," Delgado said.

By the same token, many of the actors' suggestions were incorporated into the program. "After I had been on the show for a year, I saw Big Bird walk in, and I said, 'Hey, *pájaro*,' which means 'bird,'" said Delgado. "And it stuck. I called him *pájaro* ever after." Manzano would go on to actually join *Sesame Street*'s writing staff in the 1980s, even as she continued to perform on the show.

Raul Julia, though, was an uneasy fit. He didn't test well with

Ed Palmer's focus groups of children (the chunky aviator glasses he wore at the time did him no favors), and the character of Rafael was dropped after a single season. Stone blamed himself for this outcome. "We did not write a strong, delineated character for him," he later said, "and he was left on his own to try to find a way to communicate." Julia would console himself in later years with Broadway and film stardom.

But Maria and Luis established themselves almost immediately as stalwarts of *Sesame Street*, essentially completing what would be, for more than four decades, the program's core cast of characters. Delgado recalls that their chemistry as a troupe became evident when Stone, normally a stickler for the actors' sticking to the script, began to indulge their improvisations and embellishments. "Except for Bob, who was always right on it, we were like a bunch of rowdy kids, man," Delgado said. "And it became kind of a fun group activity to try to make a scene better, each of us by bringing our own personalities. We knew we were making it come alive when we saw Jon cracking up in the corner. That's when we knew we were doing something good."

What's more, Luis, Maria, Susan, Gordon, Mr. Hooper, Bob, Linda (Bove's character used her real name), and Northern Calloway's David, a black man from a younger generation than Gordon and Susan's, comprised a lineup whose diversity was unmatched on television, yet worn lightly. Whereas Norman Lear's socially conscious sitcoms of the period, such as *All in the Family* and *Sanford and Son*, brought characters of different races together precisely so that sparks would fly—both for the viewers' entertainment and their edification—*Sesame Street* was modeling a world for children in which difference was noticeable but unremarkable. These were the people in your neighborhood.

Roosevelt Franklin (center) bonds with his creator, Matt Robinson,
while Ernie, Bert, Prairie Dawn, and Loretta Long look on.

CHAPTER

TWELVE

Backlash, Controversy, and the Complicated Saga of Roosevelt Franklin

Sesame Street's unprecedented diversity did not inoculate it from criticism from black viewers, the audience that CTW had targeted most assiduously. In his 1974 book, *Children and Television: Lessons from Sesame Street*, which was essentially a review of the program's progress at its five-year mark, Gerry Lesser, the Harvard child psychologist and head of CTW's board of advisers, took note of the flak the show had received for its diversity efforts.

"Although *Sesame Street*'s racial integration generally was commended, the program was accused of both racism and reverse racism," he wrote. "Most complaints were of reverse racism, that *Sesame Street* is *too* black, *too* integrated, or that black adults and children are shown as better and smarter than others. On the other hand, it was also observed that *Sesame Street* displays racism by not being black enough or by sugar-coating the realities of the ghetto, teaching minority-group children to accept quietly middle-class America's corrupt demands to subjugate themselves."

In their flagrancy, the claims of reverse racism are more jarring to revisit today. In May 1970, Mississippi's State Commission for Educational Television, whose members were appointed by Governor John Bell Williams, voted to ban *Sesame Street* from its public TV stations because, as a commission member said, "some of the members of the commission were very much opposed to showing the series because it uses a highly integrated cast of children. Mainly, the commission members felt that Mississippi was not yet ready for it."

The commission reversed its position after news of the ban went national, causing the state embarrassment, but the attitudes underpinning the ban were persistent. The following year, when *The Electric Company* premiered, CTW's tireless utilization coordinator for Appalachia, Paul Elkins—who was based in St. Paul, Virginia, but traveled all over the rural South to spread word of the Workshop's programs—reported back to New York that some of the teachers he had met with complained vociferously of "too many black people" on the new show. (By contrast, Gene Hazzard, the utilization coordinator for Oakland, California, reported, "Everybody is really making positive comments about Easy Reader," the suede-clad groovester, played by Morgan Freeman, who took an almost orgasmic pleasure in reading street signs and soda-pop labels.)

But, at the time, the accusations of racism were more troubling to the Workshop. An April 1971 hit piece in *New York* magazine by Linda Francke did its best to burst the bubble of goodwill that surrounded *Sesame Street*, leveling the sort of accusation that wounded Cooney the most: that the program was both detrimental to and disliked by black people. Francke, herself a white woman, portrayed CTW as a clique of privileged elitists who squeezed millions out of the federal government for a program that overpromised and under-delivered. It was a success story, she wrote, built "more on faith than on evidence."

Noting that *Sesame Street* was reaching far more middle-class viewers than poor ones, given the higher likelihood of those in the former group to own a television set and tune in to public TV, Francke suggested that CTW had abandoned its original goal of uplifting inner-city children, and, what's more, was posing a threat to Head Start. Given the widespread perception that *Sesame Street*, with its $8 million budget, was an efficient means of preparing disadvantaged children for school, wouldn't it seem to be a better deal for taxpayers than the $360 million that was allotted that year to Head Start?

This argument ignored the fact that the Workshop had never regarded Head Start as a competitor, and, indeed, had positioned itself as a complement to the federal program. CTW made this explicit in the promotional materials that it published at the time of *Sesame Street*'s launch: "Perhaps the most valuable, exciting use of the program will be as a supplement to Head Start and other nursery school classes. The child watching the program may find in it a vital reinforcement of what he has learned in the classroom."

But Francke did offer one provable criticism of *Sesame Street*: that it was not closing the "achievement gap" between advantaged and disadvantaged children. Kids in both categories benefited from watching the program, but, given that they were starting from different baselines, the gap remained largely the same at the point when these children entered grade school.

Cooney came to regret the "closing the gap" rhetoric of CTW's early days, as it was a setup for failure, judged on its own terms. (In the Workshop's first promotional brochure, she had written, "The intellectual achievement gap between the disadvantaged and middle-class child can be substantially narrowed if we begin teaching children early enough.") But as Morrisett pointed out many years later, the problem with critiques like Francke's "is that any generally distributed social good has that same characteristic. Social Security, which is a generally distributed social good ... the people who don't need it get the same amount as the people who do, and you could say you haven't diminished the gap." The bottom line, he said, was that "we knew from the beginning that we were trying to help all children. We hoped disadvantaged children would be helped significantly, if they watched, and that turned out to be true."

Nevertheless, Francke did not seem particularly impressed by the Workshop's good intentions. She mocked Evelyn Davis's utilization operation as an attempt to "flush out non-viewing ghetto children and lead them to *Sesame Street*," and described the Workshop's plans for overseas versions of the program as an exercise in "ghetto-hopping, presumably, around Europe using local filmmakers on the Rue de Sesame, Via Sesame, and Sesame Strasse."

Most damningly, Francke went to Harlem to interview "a cross-section of the black community—educators, social workers, mothers and fathers, a minister—*all* of whom, at the mention of *Sesame Street*, had a good deal to say, almost none of it complimentary." This avalanche of backlash didn't square with the feedback that CTW was receiving, or with the personal experiences of the cast, but Francke was industrious in finding black adults eager to bash the show. A theater producer denounced it as "plastic programming for white, middle-class America." A daycare supervisor complained that the show presented too idealistic a depiction of an inner-city neighborhood. "So unreal it doesn't relate to the children," the woman said. "As far as *Sesame Street* is concerned, there are no drunks, there are no dope addicts. It doesn't half make sense."

In *Sesame Street*'s formative period, Gerry Lesser recounted in his book, CTW had seriously considered presenting a picture of the inner city that was truer to the "harsh realities," as he put it, in which its children were growing up. "Our judgment, however," he wrote, "was that in order to depict reality, *Sesame Street* should not add more stridency and bitterness to the harshness already present in the child's environment."

Most of Francke's article could be dismissed as selective negativity in the service of a journalistic whack. But when Francke met face-to-face with Cooney, she managed to genuinely fluster the CTW head by telling her that some of the people she had interviewed in Harlem regarded Oscar the Grouch as an offensive depiction of an inner-city dweller. An unnamed minister was quoted in the article as saying, "*Sesame Street* is telling a black kid that it's perfectly normal for you to live in a garbage can if you keep it clean. The Man is perpetrating the idea that that's where you're going to live and you ought to be happy living there."

Cooney, thrown off balance, went silent for a moment before replying, "It hurts me to hear that blacks think that. It tells me so much about the damage that 300 years have done that they think they're Oscar. We don't think they are Oscar."

— — —

As it happened, by the time the *New York* article was published, there actually was a Muppet on the program who had been explicitly conceived as an inner-city black child: Roosevelt Franklin, a little purplish guy outfitted with googly eyes, a yellow-and-red-striped turtleneck, and a shock of dark hair.

Unusually for a *Sesame Street* Muppet, Roosevelt was not an invention of Jim Henson, Frank Oz, or any other member of Henson's troupe. Rather, he was the creation of Matt Robinson, the show's Gordon, who was among a chorus of voices at CTW calling for a Muppet character of color. Though Henson preferred to think of the Muppets as existing in a world outside of race, the default setting for them behaviorally and verbally was white, given that that's what all of the program's original puppeteers were.

Robinson shared some of the skepticism of Francke's interviewees about *Sesame Street*'s goals, offering a surprisingly blunt assessment to *Ebony* magazine in its January 1970 issue. "This aim to reach the disadvantaged child just won't be realized, I'm afraid," he said. "These kids need less fantasy and ... more realism in black-oriented problems."

Roosevelt, who made his TV debut a month later, was an attempt by Robinson to forge a closer connection with black viewers, bringing some African American realness to the street, even if in felt form. He first appeared in a counting song with his mother, a look-alike in female garb, voiced by Long. The song, a catchy R&B number with music by Joe Raposo and words by Robinson, left no ambiguity about the characters' race. Roosevelt's first words on TV were not words but a scat that sounded something like "Skibbi-dibbi-dip-dip-dip." Robinson, making no attempt to do a high-pitched child's voice, responded in a funky basso to Roosevelt's mother's questions about what he would do on each birthday leading up to his tenth:

ROOSEVELT'S MOTHER: Young Mr. Franklin, what about six?
ROOSEVELT: Get my first job, haulin' bricks.
ROOSEVELT'S MOTHER: Roosevelt, what about when you get eight?
ROOSEVELT: I'm gonna eat all the collard greens off my plate.

Long recalls that Henson, who operated the puppet to which she gave voice, took her advice on how to authentically convey Roosevelt's mother's body language in this song and its companion number, in which Roosevelt recited the alphabet. "I said, 'Jim, when I say, "Hmm, Roosevelt Franklin knows his alphabet!," her hand should be on her hip,'" said Long. "He stopped the tape and rewired that Muppet so that she could put her hand on that hip."

Roosevelt quickly evolved into a full-on series regular, his ebullience and funky dance moves making his segments dynamic even by Muppet-insert standards. In 1971, he became the first *Sesame Street* character to have an entire record album devoted to him, *The Year of Roosevelt Franklin—Gordon's Friend from Sesame Street.* (The album is better known today under the title of its 1974 reissue, *My Name Is Roosevelt Franklin.*)

The LP, again with lyrics by Robinson and music by Raposo, is a twelve-song platter of infectious soul-pop that would have sat comfortably alongside the latest from Eddie Floyd and Rufus

Thomas in that year's Stax Records catalogue. The actress and singer Rosalind Cash took over Long's role as Roosevelt's mother, while Robinson expanded Roosevelt's circle to include a little brother, Baby Ray; a sister, Mary Frances (also voiced by Cash); a friend named Mobity Mosely; and a Hispanic friend named A. B. Cito.

In a sense, Robinson was empowering himself to be a children's auteur, creating his own Afrocentric universe within the broader *Sesame Street* universe. Though he stayed in New York on weekdays to tape the show, he and his wife, Dolores, who had two children, kept their home base in Matt's native Philadelphia, where, said Dolores, they were part of a circle of "black revolutionary types" that included the educator and civil-rights leader Walter D. Palmer, the playwright and critic Larry Neal, and the poet and essayist Amiri Baraka, who lived in New Jersey but was close with the others.

Neal and Baraka were both key figures in the Black Arts Movement, a loose collective formed in the aftermath of Malcolm X's 1965 assassination to further the creation of distinctly African American literature, art, theater, and music as a means of awakening black consciousness and pride. Other well-known members of the movement were the poets Nikki Giovanni, Audre Lorde, and Gil Scott-Heron. *The Year of Roosevelt Franklin* was Robinson's early-childhood extension of the Black Arts Movement, its intent most explicit in the song "The Skin I'm In," sung by Robinson in character as Baby Ray:

> *I'm not just speakin' for myself now*
> *I speak for all of my kin*

When I tell you just-a once more again
That I love the skin I'm in

The print campaign for *The Year of Roosevelt Franklin* was filled with big-name testimonials. Representative Shirley Chisholm, a year away from becoming the first woman to seek out the Democratic Party's presidential nomination, praised the album for bringing together "children black and white, fat and thin, shy and bold. They are natural children untouched by the polluted minds of adults. It is beautiful." John Lindsay, New York's mayor at the time, said, "This album is a delightful, constructive contribution to the struggle for understanding and equality." Ed Sullivan, nearing the end of his run as CBS's king of Sunday night, wrote, "As a grandfather of five, I recommend it! Not only to the nation's youngsters, but to their parents as well. It offers something to people of all races and creeds." And B. B. King, blues guitarist extraordinaire, gave this endorsement: "I wish albums like this would have been available when I was a kid in Mississippi."

None of the album's new characters made the jump to the TV show. But Roosevelt became so popular that, nearly thirty years before the Elmo-mania of the 1990s begat *Elmo's World*, he was given his own dedicated segment on *Sesame Street*, "Roosevelt Franklin Elementary School." In these sketches, Roosevelt presided over an inner-city classroom, teaching a mouthy, unruly bunch of Muppet pupils who, like Roosevelt, were voiced not by Henson's puppeteers but the show's cast: Manzano as Smart Tina, Long as Suzetta Something, Calloway as Baby Breeze, and Roscoe Orman, Robinson's eventual successor as Gordon, as the shades-wearing Hardhead Henry Harris.

The cast was clearly having a ball, especially Calloway, who imbued the fluffily Afroed, magenta-turtlenecked Baby Breeze with a Muhammad Ali–like bravura and penchant for rhyme. Invited by Roosevelt to guest-lecture the class about the importance of looking both ways at crosswalks, he demonstrated with toy cars and people, saying, "Check this out: If this cat walks across and only digs the *light*, a car's gonna come along and knock him outta *sight*." And, furthermore: "Watchin' the light is very cool, but take a tip from Baby Breeze . . . Not watchin' the car is bein' a *fool*. So watch 'em both, if you please."

— — —

To young audiences, a Roosevelt Franklin segment was the mark of an especially good *Sesame Street* episode, akin to a *Tonight Show* spot where Don Rickles or, later, Robin Williams ambushed Johnny Carson with firecracker shtick: more alive, electric, fun. But unbeknownst to the kids at home who were relishing Roosevelt's every appearance, he was a figure of controversy from the get-go, caught up in the fraught racial politics of his day.

The black members of CTW's senior staff, among them Evelyn Davis, the utilization coordinator, Lutrelle Horne, a producer, and Jane O'Connor, a schoolteacher turned CTW curricular adviser who also edited the monthly *Sesame Street Magazine*, registered misgivings about Roosevelt even before his maiden segment, "Roosevelt Franklin Counts," had been broadcast. Somehow, Robinson had circumvented the Workshop's usual painstaking vetting process and gotten Roosevelt's first segments into the production pipeline without eliciting feedback from his black peers.

O'Connor, who screened "Roosevelt Franklin Counts" only days before it went on the air, made her displeasure known to

Dave Connell, expressing concern that Roosevelt was "simplisti-cally black" and potentially a perpetuator of denigrative stereo-types of black people among white viewers. "I like the idea of black muppets," O'Connor wrote to Connell, but she did not approve of "this one-dimensional use of black muppets."

Cooney, looking to quell O'Connor's discontent, wrote to her explaining that Roosevelt was a risk worth taking, at least in the short term. "We ought to try this kind of thing in an experimental way," she told O'Connor, "since we have been criticized by some Blacks as being 'more Westchester than Watts.'"

Robinson was among the critics to whom Cooney was re-ferring. Speaking to the author Phylis Feinstein, whose book *All About Sesame Street*, published in 1971, was one of the first about the program, Robinson made the case for using vernacular black English, which, indeed, he did not only as Roosevelt but also as Gordon, using such phrases as "Hey, man," "Right on," and "Be cool."

"Why insist on standard English, six-o'clock-news English? It's drab and lifeless," he told Feinstein. "I'd prefer the southern way, where everything's done in analogy: 'as slow as a mule,' or 'walking up a hill is like molasses in January.' Kids flip. The safe but dull norm isn't natural. A standard is imposed, a definite kind of propaganda for certain values. Black English involves all sorts of things. Tone, inflection, pacing. I think we should communicate with children in whatever way they understand."

"Somewhere around four or five," Robinson continued, "a black kid is going to learn he's black. He's going to learn that's positive or negative. What I want to project is a positive image."

But this reasoning did little to assuage the uneasiness of O'Connor and her like-minded black colleagues. In October of

1970, when the Workshop held a training conference in New York for its far-flung team of regional utilization coordinators, Roosevelt was a hot topic. Both Sandra Lindsey, the coordinator for Los Angeles, and Gene Hazzard, from Oakland, wondered if Roosevelt had a father. O'Connor, also at the meeting, tersely responded, "I don't know. Matt Robinson created him." (It should be noted that in "Roosevelt Franklin Counts," after Roosevelt's mother sings, "Whatcha gonna do when you get to three?," he responds, "I'm gonna look my daddy right in his knee." But that is the first and last that we hear of Mr. Franklin Sr.)

Pressed further by the coordinators about Roosevelt, O'Connor said, "There are mixed feelings on the staff," and admitted, "Sometimes I get uptight when I think about how long we've been trying to get away from that language."

Only Aston Young, at the time the utilization coordinator for the New York–Newark metro area, piped up in Roosevelt's defense, saying, "Many people aren't aware of a Roosevelt Franklin type and should be made aware. We can show one side of life or the whole spectrum." To which O'Connor responded, "My objective, now that we're introducing black puppets, [is] that we should introduce at the same time other types of black puppets."

— — —

Robinson was upset by the internal resistance to his creation, believing his critics to have their priorities backward when it came to modeling positive behavior for black children. Robinson was himself an educated black man, a writer with a degree in English from Penn State University whose parents had been a newspaperman and a teacher. He saw no conflict in presenting to the world a character who was simultaneously erudite—sufficiently so that he somehow ran a classroom with no adult supervision—and palpably "black" in his mannerisms.

"It was a sign of the times that there were a lot of black people who were trying to put race under the mat," said Dolores Robinson, who, though she split with Matt in the early 1970s, remains a defender of Roosevelt. "They were so damn bougie that they were *embarrassed* by Roosevelt," she said. "They were busy thinking that the whiter you acted, the better off you would be. Those people were embarrassed by their own culture. It's the same people who were embarrassed by rap when it first started."

For Matt Robinson, the anti-Roosevelt faction was a contributing factor to his decision to leave *Sesame Street* after its third season. He was succeeded in the Gordon role by the actor Hal Miller for Seasons Four and Five, and by Orman thereafter. Upon Robinson's departure, the white puppeteer Jerry Nelson took over the job of performing the Roosevelt character in the classroom sketches—a potentially controversial move that passed muster with Robinson because he and Nelson were good friends.

But by the midseventies, the voices of complaint against Roosevelt had still not abated. As Sonia Manzano noted, Joan Ganz Cooney was always someone who took pains to listen to criticism of *Sesame Street*, and, in the case of Roosevelt, the strongest voices in the debate belonged, in Cooney's words, to "the Evelyn Davises, from the upper middle class of the black community." Though he would make a few scattered cameos on *Sesame Street* in the decades to come, Roosevelt Franklin was dropped as a series regular in 1977.

In the years since, though, Roosevelt has emerged as a totem for members of Generation X, with such figures as Questlove (né Ahmir Thompson in 1971), the drummer and coleader of the

Philadelphia hip-hop band the Roots, and the diversity advocate and #OscarsSoWhite activist April Reign (born in 1970) citing the character as a formative influence. "Within the black community, we ask each other, and others ask us, 'When was the first time that you felt seen on TV? When was the first time you could identify with a character who looked like you or acted like you?'" said Reign. "And for me, Roosevelt Franklin was one of them. He was purple, but he was very clearly a black Muppet. And at that time, he and his mom were the only characters on TV who were clearly representing me, so I gravitated towards them."

The warm regard in which Roosevelt is held speaks to one of *Sesame Street*'s larger accomplishments: that, for all the heat it took in the trip-wire political climate of the early seventies, it introduced children to multiculturalism as no television program or other article of children's culture had before it. "I remember Buffy Sainte-Marie introducing us to Native American culture on TV, singing indigenous songs and teaching Big Bird that she was breastfeeding her son, Cody," said Reign. "I'm sure *Sesame Street* introduced Native Americans into many homes, including my own, because, even as a person of color, I didn't have any exposure to that culture. I learned my first Spanish words from *Sesame Street*. It was the street that we all could walk down and see not only ourselves but folks who didn't look like us, and become comfortable with them."

These lessons in multiculturalism were not a primary objective of *Sesame Street*'s creators, but they have proven to be one of the program's greatest legacies. Though the show was intended first and foremost for underprivileged kids—and underprivileged black kids in particular over its first couple of seasons—*Sesame Street*, by dint of its nationwide popularity across all demographic groups, helped create a new normal in which black culture was not a marginalized subculture but a fundamental part of mainstream American life. It's no coincidence that the first wave of *Sesame Street* viewers was the very same generation that, in its adolescence and young adulthood, embraced and promulgated hip-hop, ensuring its endurance as a wide-scale phenomenon, rather than its passing as a fad.

PART

TWO

Zooming, Rocking,
and Turning It On—
Sesame Street's Heirs

Peggy Charren, the linchpin of ACT, the children's-TV watchdog group.

CHAPTER

THIRTEEN

— — — — — —

"Brownie-Points Shows": Network Appeasement Gestures and *Sesame Street* Knockoffs

The controversy that *Sesame Street* generated was, in part, a consequence of its audacity. It represented so many firsts: the first truly multicultural cast on TV; the first show to integrate educational content with full-on entertainment; the first children's program that adults watched in large numbers. It was a lightning rod, absorbing jolts that its successors didn't have to.

And *Sesame Street*'s success did engender imitation. The commercial networks, which had been resistant to Joan Ganz Cooney's late-sixties inquiries about hosting the show, endeavored in the early seventies to bottle some of *Sesame Street*'s magic, trotting out their own takes on groovy educational children's programming. First up was NBC, which, for the 1970–71 season, introduced a Saturday-morning show called *Hot Dog*.

Aimed at grade-schoolers, *Hot Dog* was made up of segments devoted to answering a single question, such as "Where does honey come from?" or "How do they make baseballs?" Much of its content was simply documentary-style footage of workers going about their business on farms or in factories, with narration provided by the show's creator, Frank Buxton. To liven things up, these segments were interspersed with quick cutaways—inspired, as *Sesame Street*'s pacing was, by *Rowan & Martin's Laugh-In*—to the show's nominal stars: the comedian Jonathan Winters, the actual *Laugh-In* alum Jo Anne Worley, and a stand-up comic turned rising writer-director named Woody Allen.

Hot Dog managed to win a Peabody Award for children's programming, but it was a flimsy excuse for a show, palpably low-budget and made with none of the rigorous forethought and research that went into *Sesame Street*. Allen's comedic interjections, seemingly shot in a single session, found him sitting in a wing chair, extemporizing one-liners of dubious appeal to children. In a segment about the different historical figures who appeared on U.S. paper currency, for example, he said, "There's a picture of, uh, President Nixon on the thousand-dollar bill, and, uh, also little insets of Bob Hope, and, um, Lassie."

Paying more explicit homage to *Sesame Street* were two Sunday-morning programs that premiered in 1971 on ABC, *Curiosity Shop* and *Make a Wish*. The former, conceived by the animator Chuck Jones, who had attended the Children's Television Workshop's 1968 seminars, featured two girls and two boys as its de facto hosts. The children interacted with a gallery of animal puppets who poked their heads through a wall, one of whom was voiced by Jones's longtime collaborator Mel Blanc, of Bugs Bunny and Porky Pig fame. Like a knockoff handbag, *Curiosity Shop* bore

a superficial resemblance to the product that it was imitating—borrowing *Sesame Street*'s mix of live action, cartoons, puppetry, and music—but it was made with less care and with inferior materials.

Make a Wish, produced by ABC's news division, was better, channeling *Sesame Street*'s more freewheeling side. While it lacked a research department, the program hired a seasoned elementary-school educator, Dr. Maureen Miletta, as a consultant. *Make a Wish*'s host was the shaggy-haired folk-rocker Tom Chapin, the younger brother of the more famous Harry, and its psychedelic animated sequences, each of them a free-associative riff on the multiple meanings of a specific word, were supervised by Al Brodax, the man behind the visuals of the Beatles' film *Yellow Submarine*. Of the commercially produced *Sesame* wannabes, *Make a Wish* lasted the longest, running five seasons to *Curiosity Shop*'s two and *Hot Dog*'s one.

But the networks had neither the will nor the expertise to truly match what the Children's Television Workshop was doing; most of their efforts seemed gestural rather than heartfelt.

And, as it happened, there was another reason for the networks' dalliance with educational TV besides the usual industry impulse to copy a successful formula. A year before *Sesame Street*'s debut, an advocacy group called Action for Children's Television—ACT for short—was formed in the Boston area by four women, all mothers of young children. ACT proved formidable in its ability to apply pressure to the networks.

In 1969, ACT filed a petition with the FCC proposing nothing less than the complete decommercialization of children's television. In the group's ideal scenario, the renewal of FCC station licenses would be contingent upon a station's meeting three

requirements: (a) that kids' shows would carry no ads whatsoever, apart, perhaps, from sponsor acknowledgments of the sort that preceded public-TV programs, (b) that no hosts or characters could pitch products in the course of a show, as Buffalo Bob Smith had routinely done on *Howdy Doody*, and (c) that every station would broadcast at least fourteen hours of children's programming a week, with blocs devoted to the specific developmental needs of three different age groups.

These sweeping demands might have been dismissed as the pie-in-the-sky folly of a band of delusional nobodies were it not for two factors. The first was that the climate was right for such an anti-commercial crusade. As the sixties progressed, there was growing parental distress over both the poor quality of children's television, particularly on Saturday mornings, and the volume of noisy, pushy ads with which young viewers were being bombarded. "Commercialism" was increasingly a bugaboo among the educated and enlightened, as evidenced in 1965's *A Charlie Brown Christmas*, in which the spiritually questing Charlie Brown, upon learning that Snoopy had entered a Christmas-lights competition in pursuit of a cash prize, lamented, "My own dog—gone commercial! I can't stand it!"

The second factor was that the founders of ACT, Lillian Ambrosino, Evelyn Sarson, Peggy Charren, and Judith Chalfen, were no pushovers. They were educated, sharp, and politically savvy. Two of the group, Ambrosino and Sarson, were married to programming executives at WGBH, Boston's flagship public television station, and Ambrosino had herself worked in public television and radio.

"I had been a reporter in England and France," said Evelyn Kaye, whose married name at the time was Evelyn Sarson. "Judy

had been very active in politics. Lillian was the brains of the group because she had a lot of professional experience, as a radio producer who knew how government works. And Peggy just talked well. We weren't ignorant about things, and we did feel passionately that our kids were being exposed to rubbish."

All four women were at a point in their lives where their careers were in a state of suspension because they were caring for their children. "We were stay-at-home mothers because there wasn't much alternative," said Kaye. "I went for an interview with the *Boston Globe*, for which I was very well qualified and had written freelance articles, and they told me they never hired women with children. But there was a huge sixties revolution going on around us, with everyone protesting. We couldn't go marching in the streets because we had our kids. So this was our protest, our part of the sixties."

Like Cooney, with whom they forged an alliance, the women of ACT were not anti-television, and, indeed, they believed that TV held enormous educational potential for children. Charren, who emerged as the group's driving force and de facto spokesperson, ran a company that mounted bookfairs for children, and she imagined that kids' TV could be "as diverse and delightful as a good children's library," she said.

But, *Captain Kangaroo* aside, Charren found commercial programming for kids to be egregiously terrible, concocted primarily to reap profits through ads. After ACT was founded, in her Newton, Massachusetts, living room, she and her colleagues undertook a close study of what was on TV for children, and discovered that even *Romper Room*, the long-running, aggressively wholesome syndicated program that featured characters named Mr. Do Bee and Mr. Don't Bee, was ethically compromised: its "teachers," as its female hosts were known, shilled for products during the show and sometimes invited children on set to join them in the shilling.

This was, in essence, a violation of the covenant that ACT believed should exist between broadcasters and the young. In a statement released in early 1970, ACT declared that children should be "considered as a special audience, and not as potential consumers."

Around this time, ACT's founders sought out meetings with the programming chiefs of the Big Three television networks: CBS, NBC, and ABC. Only Michael Dann of CBS, who had informally advised Joan Cooney in CTW's early days, agreed to see the four women. "They were very clever at CBS. They tried to get us on their board, because then we would allegedly be giving our input," said Kaye. "But we would have been outnumbered and outvoted, so we said, 'No, that's ridiculous.' But Mike Dann was very nice."

Still, as a result of ACT's pressure and public-relations campaigns, all three networks felt compelled to create an executive position for a director of children's programming. ABC promoted from within, tapping a twenty-nine-year-old rising star within its ranks named Michael Eisner. Mike Dann, for his part, made a more radical move: after some soul-searching, he reached out to Cooney to see if she might have a position for him. That June, at the age of forty-eight, he forsook his lucrative job at CBS to join the nonprofit Workshop as a vice president.

More consequentially, the FCC published ACT's petition in early 1970, for the purpose of inviting public comment while the commission deliberated over it. The FCC did not formally respond to the petition until the autumn of 1974, when it issued a bland policy statement declaring that "broadcasters have a special obligation to serve children." Though this statement was merely a nudge rather than a new regulation, essentially leaving it to the broadcasters to regulate themselves, the four-year period in which the FCC deliberated was in and of itself effective, in that it made the broadcasters very, very nervous. With *Sesame Street* flourishing as Exhibit A of the glories of noncommercial children's television, the networks felt pressure to do *something*.

"Our mandate," recalled Eisner years later, by which time he had become the chairman of the Walt Disney Company, "was to somehow find a balance between creating popular shows and producing the sort of higher-minded programs that would satisfy our critics."

In 1973, the National Association of Broadcasters agreed upon a series of new, voluntary guidelines to which its members were expected to adhere. One, as prescribed by ACT, was to prohibit in-show pitches for products by children's-program hosts. (*Romper Room* adjusted its hosts' practices accordingly.) Another was to forbid the placement of ads for vitamins and medications during children's shows. The NAB's toughest new measure, albeit still voluntary, was to reduce the number of commercials per hour during children's shows from sixteen to twelve minutes on weekdays, and to nine minutes on weekends.

— — —

Few of these public declarations of good intent yielded quality TV, though—and the networks knew it. In 1972, *Broadcasting* magazine derisively referred to an epidemic of "brownie-points shows," and an anonymous network executive more or less owned up to this assessment, describing his and his competitors' new programs as "appeasement gestures, and expensive ones at that, to placate those who don't think we're living up to our responsibilities in the area of children's programming."

Still, the brownie-points era produced *some* decent results. In 1972, ABC launched *ABC Afterschool Specials*, an anthology series of short films irregularly broadcast on weekday afternoons. Most of them, though not all, traded in themes similar to those covered by Judy Blume in her contemporaneous young-adult novels: feelings of not fitting in, or of being bullied, or of navigating the divorce of one's parents.

To more cynical tweens, the *Afterschool Specials* were maudlin shlock, the stuff of mockery and parody. But the specials played well to the sensitivities of kids going through their own moments of emotional tenderness, and they reached a wide audience— sufficiently enough that the series ran, on and off, for fifteen years. In its launch phase, *ABC Afterschool Specials* also made stars of the young actors Jodie Foster, whose debut special was the Emmy-winning *Rookie of the Year*, in which she played an eleven-year-old who integrated her brother's all-male baseball team, and Kristy McNichol, who sulked through the self-explanatory *Me and Dad's New Wife*.

In 1971, CBS kicked into gear an interstitial mini-program, broadcast between cartoon shows on Saturday mornings, called *In the News*, memorable for its intro and outro bumpers, in which a vector-graphics animation of a spinning globe was accompanied by a blippity-bloop audio loop of what sounded like digital percolation. Narrated in a deadpan baritone by the veteran CBS newsman Christopher Glenn, *In the News* presented two-minute feature reports for viewers of elementary-school age, on subjects ranging from the Watergate scandal to the origins of ketchup. Like the *Afterschool Specials*, it proved to have a long shelf life, remaining a part of CBS's children's programming through 1986.

The most tangibly educational and entertaining of the networks' full-length children's series was *Fat Albert and the Cosby Kids*, which premiered on CBS in 1972. The show owed its placement on the network's Saturday-morning schedule to the convergence of CBS's FCC-placating agenda and Bill Cosby's desire to position himself as an educator and role model. In the early 1970s, Cosby was a prominent face of African American progress: a college-educated stand-up comic who had in the sixties graduated to leading-man TV stardom in the NBC espionage series *I Spy*, for which he won three Emmy Awards. Cosby was also—publicly, at least—the very picture of a family man. In 1972, the year he turned thirty-five, he and his wife, Camille, were the parents of three children, with two more to come, and he exuded a hipster-dad affability that anticipated his 1980s national-treasure status as Dr. Cliff Huxtable on *The Cosby Show*.

In other words, he was a long way from his twenty-first-century outing as a sexual predator and his subsequent conviction and imprisonment on sexual-assault charges. In the world of children's TV, Cosby was a welcome presence. The Children's Television Workshop recruited him to appear in early episodes of *Sesame Street* and was thrilled when he lent his star power to *The Electric Company*, appearing as a regular for its first two seasons.

Cosby, likewise, was drawn to the educational community. In the spring of 1972, he received a master's degree in education from the University of Massachusetts at Amherst. Three years earlier, he had made a pilot for an animated kids' show, based on his stand-up routines, that recalled his and his friends' misadventures during their hardscrabble childhoods in North Philadelphia. Entitled *Hey, Hey, Hey, It's Fat Albert*, the pilot aired on NBC as a one-off special and went no further.

But in '72, with Cosby looking to make a kids' program and CBS looking for educational content—"They felt that they needed to do something that was worthwhile in this area," Cosby later remarked—*Fat Albert and the Cosby Kids* got the green light. Cosby and his team took the task seriously, enlisting a CTW-style advisory panel of experts in child psychology and education, most of them plucked from UCLA, since the show was produced in Los Angeles. Foremost among them was Dr. Gordon L. Berry, an African American professor of educational and counseling psychology.

In the opening credits of each episode, Cosby addressed viewers with the introductory comment, "Here's Bill Cosby, coming at you with music and fun. And if you're not careful, you may *learn something* before it's done." *Fat Albert* was not nearly as ambitious as *Sesame Street*, with neither a research department nor explicit curricular aims. "Its goals differ from *Sesame Street* and *The Electric Company*," Cosby later wrote in his doctoral dissertation, "in that its emphasis is the affective development of young viewers." Each episode imparted a lesson in morality and decency, on such subjects as being supportive of a friend who needs eyeglasses and the perils of playing hooky from school.

Fat Albert was also notable for being, like *Sesame Street*, a TV show where African American children could recognize a version of themselves on-screen. All eight of its core group of kid characters—Fat Albert, Bill, Russell, Donald, Mushmouth, Rudy, Bucky, and Weird Harold—were black, as were nearly all of the adults (teachers, doctors, cops) with whom they interacted. "The program," Cosby said, "attempts to develop positive belief systems and positive self concepts for inner-city youngsters."

Cosby worked out an agreement with the University of Massachusetts to continue his advanced studies from afar as a part-time student—the dean of its college of education, Dr. Dwight Allen, was a consultant on *Fat Albert*—and, in 1977, he received his doctorate, later grandiosely referenced in the credits of *The Cosby Show*, in which he was referred to as "Dr. William H. Cosby, Jr. Ed.D."

Cosby was basically his own case study; creating and writing *Fat Albert* constituted the bulk of his graduate work. His dissertation was entitled "An Integration of the Visual Media via *Fat Albert and the Cosby Kids* into the Elementary School Curriculum as a Teaching Aid and Vehicle to Achieve Increased Learning."

Like Jon Stone's romanticized ghetto-scape, the world of *Fat Albert* was determinedly gritty. The Cosby Kids passed their time sitting on literal scrap heaps, or in trash-strewn vacant lots hard by rail yards, and at the end of each episode they performed a catchy moral-of-the-story song (e.g., "There's no fool like a fool playin' hooky . . .") on instruments constructed out of salvaged objects: an accordion made from a radiator, a harp made from a bedspring, a trombone made from metal piping and an old phonograph's horn.

Filmation Associates, the production company behind the show, was, like Cosby himself, notoriously frugal, and conspicuously reused the same backgrounds and animated sequences over and over again. But as cheapo animations went, *Fat Albert*'s were effectively vivid, particularly where the boys' wardrobes were concerned. Fat Albert was always resplendent in a crimson sweater, Rudy was always stylishly attired in a red flat cap and lavender flares, and, most memorably and inexplicably, Donald always wore a pink knit cap that was pulled over the top half of his face, compelling him to peer through eye-hole cutouts.

The program's goofiness belied the fact that it was about poor black kids whose real-life analogs weren't so carefree—not exactly the stuff of your typical Warner Bros. or Hanna-Barbera cartoon show. Yet *Fat Albert and the Cosby Kids*, which ran into the early 1980s, reached eight million children per episode at its peak, and, along with *Sesame Street*, helped normalize black culture and blackness itself for a national audience: an educational benefit in and of itself.

For Cosby, this benefit was not merely ancillary. His show and CTW's shows, he wrote in his dissertation, helped "establish in the minds of millions of television viewers and educators that black children are not by nature stupid or lazy; they are not hoodlums, they are not junkies. They are you. They are me. The fact that the 'Kids' are black is neither minimized nor exploited. They are people. Their problems are universal."

"Conjunction Junction," somewhere in the Schoolhouse Rock! *rail yard.*

CHAPTER

FOURTEEN

The Sunshiny Poptimism of *Schoolhouse Rock!*

The most appealing of the Big Three networks' early seventies educational offerings for kids was the one with the most unorthodox genesis. *Schoolhouse Rock!*, which aired on ABC, owed its birth neither to reform-minded activists nor the commercial broadcasters' desire to replicate the success of *Sesame Street*. It came about organically, the idiosyncratic vision of its creators rather than of some network suit. And the people who brought it to life were, of all things, advertising men.

David McCall had all the qualifications to be an arrogant, unfeeling shark, the bogeyman of ACT's nightmares. He was born in New York and educated at the Hotchkiss School and Yale University. In the 1950s, he shot up through the ranks of the blue-chip agency Ogilvy & Mather and was tapped by the great David Ogilvy himself to follow in the former's footsteps as the firm's chief copywriter. By 1962, McCall had set up his own shop in New York with a fellow Ogilvy alum named Jim McCaffrey. McCaffrey & McCall, the agency, went on to acquire a roster of prestige clients, including Mercedes-Benz, Rolls-Royce, Tiffany & Co., the ABC television network, and Pepperidge Farm. By the early 1970s, McCall was a prosperous, highly respected adman.

But none of this precluded him from having a conscience. McCall was a passionate advocate for humanitarian causes and an unabashed opponent of the Vietnam War. So when, in 1971, a twenty-year-old undergraduate at Yale named Ira Nerken issued a public proposal for the advertising industry to take an active role in the anti-war effort, McCall, a fellow Yalie, was the first person to take Nerken up on his challenge. McCall rallied other ad agencies to join his own in a coordinated effort to "unsell" the war, via advertisements in print, radio, TV, and on billboards.

The campaign pulled no punches. One print ad depicted a bedraggled and bandaged Uncle Sam, his hand desperately outstretched, above the tagline "I WANT OUT." An intense television PSA featured a matronly woman in a rocking chair, with a framed photo of a uniformed navy sailor, presumably her son, on the table beside her. "Our air force has developed a new kind of bomb," she told viewers. "It's called the mother bomb. Each mother bomb contains 640 baby bombs." These bombs, she explained, had the capacity to rip apart the flesh of "a North Vietnamese soldier, or a water buffalo, or a baby." Her voice quavering, she concluded, "Let's hear it for motherhood. And the flag."

Nearly fifty agencies participated in the "Unsell the War" effort, pro bono, and, more extraordinarily, dozens of media outlets proved willing to run the ads for free. (Hugh Hefner, for one, donated a full page in *Playboy*.) McCall's actions were not without their consequences. He incurred the wrath of a few admen who found his conduct un-American, and McCaffrey & McCall nearly lost the Standard Oil account, one of its biggest, when the energy company reported that it had received letters protesting its employment of a "Communist" agency.

McCall's irrepressible man-of-action qualities surfaced in a different way when, in this same period, he and his family went on vacation to a dude ranch in Wyoming. While there, he observed that his namesake son, Davey, was singing Rolling Stones songs in their entirety as he rode his horse. To the elder McCall, this was noteworthy because Davey was struggling with math at school, experiencing difficulty learning the times tables. Much as Joan Ganz Cooney was spurred to action after noticing how naturally young children learned advertising jingles, McCall hit upon an idea: what if the rudiments of multiplication were turned into lyrics and set to catchy pop melodies?

Curiously, given McCall's professional background and all the press that *Sesame Street* had received for adopting TV-commercial techniques—in CTW's 1969 pitch reel for the show, executive producer Dave Connell flat-out declared, "We're trying to sell the alphabet to preschool children"—McCall's mind did not first turn to television. Instead, once he was back at his New York office, he approached two trusted deputies, George Newall and Tom Yohe, the cocreative directors at McCaffrey & McCall, to discuss the possibility of producing a record album of kid-friendly songs about multiplication.

Newall was the musical one of the three men. He played piano and had majored in music at Florida State University, and spent many an evening at the Hickory House, a restaurant and club on 52nd Street where his favorite pianist, Billy Taylor—the same Billy Taylor who composed songs for *Sesame Street*—regularly performed. Newall had befriended the bassist in Taylor's trio, Ben Tucker, so he hit up Tucker for suggestions for songwriters for the multiplication record.

Tucker recommended his friend Bob Dorough, a well-known bebop pianist with whom Tucker had a side business collaborating on advertising jingles. Dorough, Tucker told Newall, could set anything to music. He had written several novelty songs, including "I'm Hip," a cowrite with fellow jazz pianist Dave Frishberg that became a cabaret staple, and "Do Not Remove This Tag," whose lyrics were lifted from the admonitory little tags that came attached to mattresses.

Dorough, nearly fifty, was a beatific, agreeable beatnik who wore his sideburns long and his hair in a ponytail. As fortune would have it, he was also "kind of a math junkie," as Newall recalled, and he agreed to give the idea of writing a multiplication song a shot. Three weeks later, Dorough returned to McCaffrey & McCall with a demo of his first effort, "Three Is a Magic Number." "We pulled out our Wollensak tape player and played the song," Newall said. "And the minute we heard 'A man and a woman had a little baby,' that was it."

"Three Is a Magic Number" was gentle, infectious, and a little spacey—and as enchantingly, mysteriously attuned to the seventies-kid Zeitgeist as *Sesame Street* was. In a dulcet, blissed-out voice bearing a trace of his roots in Depression-era Texas, Dorough sang an introductory passage that bordered on the inscrutable—"Somewhere in the ancient mystic trinity, you get three . . . as a magic number"—and followed with examples of things that came in threes, such as the corners of a triangle and the wheels of a tricycle. Then came Dorough's most Zeitgeisty, love-power example of them all, sung in multitrack harmony: "A man and a woman had a little baby / Yes, they did / They had threeeee in the family / And that's a magic number."

Dorough proceeded to sing the multiple-of-three times tables, not once but twice, before bringing in the song for a soft landing on a repeat of the "A man and a woman had a little baby" refrain—all of this contained in, appositely, three minutes.

The McCaffrey & McCall men were blown away. Yohe, who was also the head of the firm's art department, was an inveterate doodler, and he started doodling images that the song evoked: a freckle-faced girl with an ice-cream cone bearing three scoops; football players entering a field in groups of three; and the man and the woman and their "little baby," glimpsed first as a swaddled infant and then as a little girl, frolicking with her parents through an Arcadian landscape of flowers, grass, and trees. Soon thereafter, the idea of an LP was dropped in favor of a series of educational films.

The firm's biggest account was with ABC, and the executive in charge of that account, Radford Stone, was aware, through his dealings with his client, that the network was looking for educational programming—and, specifically, a short-form interstitial program that would serve as ABC's answer to CBS's *In the News*.

Stone set up an appointment with Michael Eisner, and he, McCall, and Yohe hustled over to ABC's headquarters on Manhattan's Upper West Side with Dorough's demo and Yohe's storyboard to pitch their concept, *Multiplication Rock*. Eisner invited the animation auteur Chuck Jones, whose *Sesame Street* knockoff

Curiosity Shop was then on ABC, to sit in. Eisner was skeptical, but he deferred to Jones, who loved the presentation and insisted that Yohe draw the animations.

"Three Is a Magic Number" made its debut in 1973, during one of the final broadcasts of *Curiosity Shop*, and thereafter ran, along with ten further *Multiplication Rock* shorts, in between conventional-length ABC programs on Saturday mornings. Improbably, the slick advertising firm of McCaffrey & McCall was now in the educational-TV business.

— — —

George Newall was, in some respects, an unlikely candidate to serve as the creative point man of what would come to be known as *Schoolhouse Rock!* In 1973, he was thirty-nine years old and married, but also childless and not particularly invested in the welfare of children. His biggest claim to fame in the advertising world was a notoriously cheeky campaign for Hai Karate, a budget aftershave that competed with Aqua Velva, whose own ads unironically made the case that the product in question turned its wearers into chick magnets—because "there's something about an Aqua Velva man."

Newall's idea was to *ironically* make the case that Hai Karate turned its wearers into chick magnets. In each ad of the campaign—which was either the apogee of high camp or of retrograde sexual attitudes, depending upon how you looked at it—a poindexterish man in glasses slapped on some Hai Karate and was immediately set upon by hordes of ravishingly beautiful women. The voice-over announcer noted that the aftershave came with "instructions on self-defense in every package," and the commercials concluded with the tagline "Hai Karate—be careful how you use it."

Yet Newall was a devoted David McCall disciple, more than the sum of his nightclubbing, martini-drinking, model-auditioning proclivities: a son of FDR-idolizing parents and a dedicated liberal who was, he said, "completely on Dave's side of everything." Regarding the educational-film project, Newall recalled, "The context was that we were working in an advertising agency and selling shit. And here's a chance to do something that really matters. And as it rolled on, we got more and more fanatical about it. Tom was drawing on the train coming in, in the morning, and at night at his kitchen table."

Multiplication Rock was by no means a pro bono undertaking, but it was something that its creators worked on in their own time, since they still had full-time day jobs at McCaffrey & McCall. The success of the math series in 1973, which caught on immediately with such Dorough-written, Yohe-animated earworms as "My Hero, Zero" and "I Got Six," prompted ABC to request new batches of three-minute films devoted to grammar, American history (timed to the run-up to the United States Bicentennial celebrations of 1976), and science, all produced under the banner *Schoolhouse Rock!* (Actually, McCaffrey & McCall's first choice was *Scholastic Rock*, but Scholastic, Inc., the children's-book publisher, issued a cease-and-desist.)

Yohe's cheerful aesthetic—lots of deeply dimpled faces, freckles, striped shirts, and Robert Indiana–style shadowed lettering and numbering—gave *Schoolhouse Rock!* its visual identity, even when he wasn't handling the animation. His workload dictated that he hire other animators and artists, among them his old mentor at Young & Rubicam, Jack Sidebotham, who drew up the three-generation family of weirdos who ran an adverb store in the episode entitled "Lolly, Lolly, Lolly, Get Your Adverbs Here." Newall persuaded Dorough to stay on as *Schoolhouse Rock!*'s musical director. Together, the two men shaped the project's distinctive musical identity—which, strangely, given the series' title, didn't have a whole lot to do with rock music.

Once again, as with *Sesame Street* and *Mister Rogers' Neighborhood*, jazz players and composers seemed to most intuitively grasp the musical lingua franca of educational children's television: a bright, Tin Pan Alley–influenced pop that borrowed freely from many idioms and was, above all, *communicative.* "It's kind of trite, but jazz is a creative art full of creative people, and as they get involved with something, you're going to find them contributing ideas," said Newall.

He and Dorough called upon an impressive roster of middle-aged hepcat jazzers who had broken through in the fifties and sixties: Grady Tate, the drummer in Billy Taylor's trio, who sang "I Got Six" and "Naughty Number Nine"; the singer Blossom Dearie, who performed "Unpack Your Adjectives" (an original composition by Newall) and "Figure Eight"; and Dorough's pal Dave Frishberg, who wrote a legislative procedural on how a bill gets passed into law entitled "I'm Just a Bill."

"I'm Just a Bill," which first aired in 1975, is a master class in turning dry information into child-friendly narrative. A boy espies a "sad little scrap of paper" sitting on the steps of the Capitol. Yohe, at his most ingenious, depicted Bill, the anthropomorphic main character, as a rolled-up document slumped forlornly like a skid-row drunk, a dog-eared corner of his face acting as the equivalent of a fallen man's tumbling forelock. Bill spills his guts to the boy:

I'm just a bill
Yes, I'm only a bill

And I'm sitting here on Capitol Hill
Well, it's a long, long journey
To the capital city . . .

In the course of the short, Bill explains to the boy how he originated as an idea in his congressman's home state. The two of them then bide their time as Bill is debated over in committee, sent for separate votes in the House and Senate, and then dispatched to the White House, where, after a moment of neurosis over the prospect of a veto, Bill is indeed signed into law, prompting a triumphant "Oh, yesss!"

As he wrote the song, Frishberg decided that it was perfect for Jack Sheldon, a Los Angeles jazz trumpeter who served for many years as the musical director of *The Merv Griffin Show* and had a unique, melancholic vocal delivery: a little sleepy and hungover-sounding, yet friendly enough to connect with kids rather than terrify them. Sheldon sold the hell out of the song, and his own son, John, voiced the boy.

Sheldon also sang lead on what turned out to be *Schoolhouse Rock!*'s most popular short of all, "Conjunction Junction." Newall had come up with the concept of a rail yard where words and phrases get hooked together, boxcar-style, by conjunctions such as "and," "but," and "or." Dorough took the idea and ran with it. He came up with an easy-swinging call-and-response song in which two female singers, Terry Morel and Mary Sue Berry, harmonized like the Andrews Sisters on a question ("Conjunction Junction, what's your function?") and Sheldon drawled his answers ("Hookin' up words and phrases and clauses").

Like *Fat Albert and the Cosby Kids, Schoolhouse Rock!* had neither the budget nor the resources to execute a program on the scale that the Children's Television Workshop could. But the producers did assiduously run every single script past an academic adviser. The *Multiplication Rock* shorts were developed in consultation with the Bank Street College of Education, in New York, on whose board McCall sat, while the history and civics shorts received input from John A. Garraty, a historian at Columbia University.

In some instances, the shorts proved to be not merely educational but also inspirational. Lynn Ahrens was a secretary at McCaffrey & McCall in the midseventies, fresh out of college, when the *America Rock* bundle of Bicentennial-themed episodes was ramping up. It was her custom in those days to bring her guitar to the office, so that she could play songs during her lunch break. Newall happened by Ahrens's desk one day as she was playing and asked her if she wanted to take a crack at writing a *Schoolhouse Rock!* song based on the preamble to the U.S. Constitution.

Ahrens came up with some folk verses that led up to a stirring chorus whose lyrics, sung in country-gospel harmony, were simply the words of the preamble, minus the phrase "of the United States":

We the people
In order to form a more perfect union
Establish justice, insure domestic tranquility
Provide for the common defense
Promote the general welfare, and
Secure the blessings of liberty
To ourselves and our posterity

Do ordain and establish this Constitution
For the United States of America.

"The Preamble," which Ahrens both composed and sang, connected profoundly with a grade-school audience whose members
carried none of their parents' post-Watergate cynicism about America. It was joyously patriotic without being jingoistic, and its chorus became a mnemonic device for a generation of schoolchildren;
Newall and Yohe received reports from teachers that their students
were humming the song during tests.

Ahrens, who would go on to become a Tony-winning Broadway writer and lyricist, was particularly good at uplift. Another
of her songs, "Interjections!," borrowed part of its melody from the
"Hallelujah" chorus from Handel's *Messiah*, and provided Yohe
with the opportunity to draw an arching, rainbow-colored "WOW!"
The song's culmination—a euphoric "Hallelujah, hallelujah, hallelujah, YEA!," set against a field of exclamation points in which a
little girl is jumping—is, quite simply, the distilled essence of 1970s
thirteen-and-under poptimism.

— — —

Schoolhouse Rock!, whose original run carried it into the early
1980s, was as acclaimed by adults as it was loved by kids. For
three out of the last four years of the seventies, the program bested
Sesame Street at the Daytime Emmys, winning for Outstanding
Children's Series in the "Instructional Programming" category.
McCaffrey & McCall became the first advertising agency ever to
win an Emmy Award.

"It was something that we didn't have to do, but we liked it better than what we did have to do," Newall said. "So we pretty much threw ourselves into it. The only guy who took it as just a job was Jack Sheldon."

Sheldon reprised his role, after a fashion, in a 1996 episode of *The Simpsons* in which he provided the voice for an "amendment-to-be" who wanted to be ratified, thereby clearing the path for yahoo extremists to pass laws that previously would have been ruled unconstitutional. ("I'll crush all opposition to me / and I'll make Ted Kennedy pay / If he fights back, I'll say that he's *gayyy*.")

Like Fred Rogers and Ernie and Bert, *Schoolhouse Rock!* made such an indelible impression upon its audience that it became, decades later, the stuff of loving parody (on *Saturday Night Live* and *American Dad*, to provide two more examples) and loving embrace. On its landmark 1989 album, *3 Feet High and Rising*, the hip-hop trio De La Soul included its own spin on "Three Is a Magic Number," entitled "Magic Number." ("Somewhere in this hip-hop soul community / Was born three: Mase, Dove, and me / And that's a magic number.") Dorough, who died at the age of ninety-four in 2018, continued to play *Schoolhouse Rock!* songs into his final year, and in 2013, on the occasion of the series' fortieth anniversary, performed to a capacity crowd at the Kennedy Center for the Arts, in Washington, D.C.

For David McCall, *Schoolhouse Rock!* was a prelude to spending more of his time as an activist. He became deeply involved in organizations devoted to human rights, refugee aid, and the removal of land mines from war zones. He died with his wife, Joan, in a car crash in 1999, while on a Refugees International mission in Albania.

Yohe died a year later, of cancer. But Newall and Dorough lived long enough to see their cocreation receive the ultimate tribute. In

2013, with the government facing a potential shutdown because of a budget impasse in Congress, President Barack Obama commented on the situation to CNN's Chris Cuomo. "Maybe you're not old enough to remember *Schoolhouse Rock!*," he said. "You remember how the bill gets passed? You know, the House and the Senate try to work out their differences. They pass something. They send it to me, and, potentially, I sign it."

Doug and Emmy Jo preside over the
New Zoo Revue, circa 1972 . . .

. . . while Carole Demas and Paula Janis welcome you
to The Magic Garden.

CHAPTER

FIFTEEN

Carole, Paula, and
Other Local Heroes

I t wasn't only the Big Three networks that were feeling the pressure to improve the quality of their children's programming. In 1971, the FCC dropped a heavy hint to the nation's local TV stations by issuing what it called an Ascertainment Primer, a document designed to "aid broadcasters in being more responsive to the problems of their communities" and to "add more certainty to their efforts in meeting Commission standards."

This document was more pointed and specific than the FCC's later statement, in response to ACT's 1969 petition, that broadcasters had a "special obligation" to serve children. Though the primer was, again, a statement rather than a law, it carried the air of a mandate. "Ascertainment" was an FCC term for the process by which stations determined the needs of their local audience, especially where the public interest was concerned. WPIX, a venerable independent station in New York City, quickly ascertained that it needed to up its children's-programming game if it didn't want the FCC breathing down its neck.

Carole Demas was oblivious to these developments, having long moved on from teaching kindergarten with her friend Paula Janis at the decrepit P.S. 7 in Brooklyn. By 1971, she had achieved her dream of becoming a jobbing actress. She had appeared on TV in soap operas, commercials, and the CBS drama *Route 66*, and had just landed her big break: to play Sandy, the female lead, in the first New York production of a new, 1950s-themed musical imported from Chicago called *Grease*. (Barry Bostwick was cast as Danny, and Adrienne Barbeau as Rizzo.)

But when her agent called and let Demas know that WPIX was looking for a young woman with experience both in working with children and performing on television, for a new program aimed at preschoolers, Demas agreed to take a meeting with the station's executives. Their pitch disappointed her: they were merely looking to run cartoons that they already owned, and to hire a cheerful hostess to do wraparound patter. But Demas's idealism prevented her from simply walking away. Instead, she suggested what she believed to be a better idea: that WPIX hire both her and her friend Paula, and allow them to create their own live-action children's program.

WPIX was initially wary of her suggestion, noting that Janis had zero television experience. Janis had spent the better part of the 1960s teaching pre-kindergarten in the New York City school system, and had recently given birth to her first child, a daughter named Victoria. But the station was desperate enough for content that it let Demas and Janis shoot a pilot, most of which consisted of the two young women singing children's songs in harmony, with Janis accompanying on guitar. Their original title for the show was *The Magical Magic Tree.*

The pilot was raw, but it was enough to sell WPIX on Demas's idea, and *The Magic Garden*, as the half-hour show was renamed, went into production in 1972. The program was bare-bones, low-budget, and, out of necessity, hastily assembled. Janis had a new baby to attend to. Demas was busy doing eight performances of *Grease* a week at the Eden Theatre in the East Village. (Though it opened geographically Off Broadway, *Grease* was considered a Broadway production, and, after five months, moved to a major Broadway house, the Broadhurst.)

Wednesdays, Demas recalled, were the days when she had time to kill between the matinee and evening shows, "so Paula would come to the theater with the baby on her back and a sandwich for me." The two women would hash out their ideas for each episode, which generally consisted of a few songs, a story-time segment, and some sort of run-in with Sherlock, a giant pink squirrel performed by the puppeteer and Jim Henson alumnus Cary Antebi. The actual shoots always took place on Mondays, the one day of the week when *Grease* was dark.

Carole and Paula, as Demas and Janis billed themselves professionally, succeeded by guilelessly being themselves. On camera, they wore their long, straight hair just as they did off duty, in pigtails tied with ribbon or colored yarn. Since WPIX had afforded them all of $100 for a wardrobe budget, they generally appeared in their own clothes: jeans and primary-colored blouses with contrast vests for Demas, and slacks and tops in turquoise, brown, purple, and other microfiber-friendly seventies colors for Janis.

They began each episode singing their introductory song, beckoning viewers to "come and see our garden grow," while sitting on tree swings suspended by ropes from the giant tree in which Sherlock lived. (The tree's name was the Magic Tree, and it occasionally lowered a clawlike branch to the women in order to deliver props for the show.) Carole and Paula's single, unchanging set was a bright, idyllic backyard garden of green turf under blue sky, with a stone footpath, sunflowers with smiley faces, and a small bed of quivering, giggling cornflowers known as the Chuckle Patch, whose leaves grew with jokes inscribed upon them. Carole and Paula sometimes sat on a pair of giant, speckled toadstools that resembled *Amanita muscaria*, a common mushroom valued in many cultures for its psychoactive properties.

Demas and Janis avow to this day that they were not consciously counterculturists and definitely not advocates of psychedelics. "There are those who insisted that we were eating the mushrooms," said Janis, "which is so hysterical, because there was nobody who was straighter than we were. *Nobody*."

But *The Magic Garden*'s visual presentation, like *Sesame Street*'s jumbled urban Utopia and Tom Yohe's WOW!-ified *Schoolhouse Rock!* aesthetic, chimed with the times and marked a pivot from such long-running franchised local kids' programs as *Romper Room* and the various iterations of *Bozo the Clown*, which, no matter how hard they tried to adapt, felt square and backward, the starch of the 1950s still in their collars. Carole and Paula simply *looked* like new-vanguard elementary-school teachers of the 1970s, and *The Magic Garden*, which aired Mondays through Thursdays on WPIX, became the most highly rated regional program in the history of children's television—and, by virtue of being in the nation's largest market, attracted a viewership of national-audience proportions, in the millions.

— — —

What made *The Magic Garden* connect was that it was, for all the visual stimulus it provided, a simple program, closer in spirit to *Mister Rogers' Neighborhood* than to the commercial-network extravaganzas of the brothers Sid and Marty Krofft, who at the time were cutting a swath through Saturday-morning television with such fantastical live-action programs as *H.R. Pufnstuf, Lidsville,* and *Sigmund and the Sea Monsters.* The Krofft shows, too, were visually eye-popping, but exponentially more antic and jittery— McDonaldland minus the anthropomorphic burger-people. (In fairness to the Kroffts, their shows were intended as pure entertainment, not as educational material.)

Like Fred Rogers and Bob Keeshan, Demas and Janis had an easy, naturalistic talent for directly addressing the camera and never patronizing their viewers. Furthermore, they didn't have the luxury of postproduction editing, so it was incumbent upon them to sustain their banter in a manner that would hold children's interest. "We worked with big, long units of time," said Janis. "Sometimes we would have to do something that would go on for ten minutes, because there was no other way." In this respect, *The Magic Garden* functioned as a form of counterprogramming, or perhaps a chill-out complement, to the more fast-paced *Sesame Street.*

There was also something to be said for the refreshing fact that *The Magic Garden* was hosted by two young women rather than an older, avuncular man. Carole and Paula nearly always wore pants instead of skirts or dresses—an unthinkable proposition just a few years earlier on television—and came across to young viewers as big sisters or hip kindergarten teachers. Indeed, the budgetary restrictions placed upon the show compelled them to summon the same resourcefulness they had demonstrated in their P.S. 7 days. "We knew this formula worked, because we had made it happen live in a classroom full of kids who had nothing," Demas said.

She and Janis purposefully used everyday household objects for their segments devoted to imaginative play: kitchen implements like eggbeaters and wooden spoons, old clothes from their closets, and lots and lots of cardboard boxes. "They were simple things that even a poor child could relate to and find at home," said Demas. "It wasn't like kids would sit there longing for what we used because it came from Toys "R" Us."

Another echo of their public-school experience came in their performance of "The Hello Song," which was always followed by spoken salutations to their viewers, using names the two women chose for their likelihood to connect with kids watching at home: John, Jessica, Kathy, and Nancy, but also, pointedly, Javier, Luis, José, and Maria.

Janis would sometimes adapt the song in order to teach young viewers how to say "Hello" in other languages. She had studied Swahili at Skidmore College—"I can still remember how to say, 'The cows are grazing on the other side of the riverbank,'" she said—so she taught the kids how to say "*Jambo.*" Her usual methodology, however, consisted of consulting with the proprietors of New York City's multitude of ethnic restaurants: "Just walking into a Chinese restaurant and saying, 'Hey, how do you say "Hello" in Chinese?'" she said.

WPIX, eager to tout its compliance with the FCC's guidelines, took out ads in the trades that namechecked not Carole and Paula but Dr. Rose Mukerji, the chairman of Brooklyn College's Early Childhood Education Division, with whom *The Magic Garden* was "produced in consultation." In reality, Demas and Janis, though they were fond of Dr. Mukerji, had little interaction with her; she was there to lend an imprimatur of educational legitimacy. As Demas recalls it, Mukerji never gave them notes or prescriptive recommendations. They simply recorded their episodes, Demas said, "and then she highly approved of everything she saw that we were doing."

— — —

On Fridays, the one weekday when *The Magic Garden* did not air, its time slot was taken by *Joya's Fun School*, a preexisting children's variety show that had been retrofitted by WPIX, also in response to the FCC's Ascertainment Primer, to appear more explicitly educational. In its original incarnation, as *Time for Joya*, the program had aired on Sunday mornings in 1970 and 1971.

Joya was Joya Sherrill, an effervescent singer in her forties who had been performing on and off with Duke Ellington's orchestra since she was a teenager. Sherrill had quietly made history by becoming the first African American woman to host her own children's TV show. (*Sesame Street*'s Loretta Long preceded her on the air by a few months, but as part of an ensemble.) In the summer of 1970, Sherrill welcomed Ellington onto her program as a guest, in what would turn out to be one of his final TV appearances before his 1974 death. When Sherrill thanked Ellington for agreeing to show up at the unforgiving hour of 8 a.m., he replied with characteristic suavity, "Eight o'clock in the morning—one never gets up. One only *stays* up."

In 1972, the program was reformatted so that Sherrill's set more closely resembled a classroom, and there was no longer a studio audience of children. In look and spirit, *Joya's Fun School* was much more old-fashioned than *The Magic Garden*, though notable for its impressive roster of African American talent. Just as Fred Rogers had the jazz pianist Johnny Costa providing expressive accompaniment on keys, Sherrill had the Juilliard-trained Luther Henderson, a longtime Ellington associate and renowned Broadway orchestrator, operating in the same capacity. On the show, Joya called him "the Professor." The *Fun School*'s resident art instructor, a graying, goateed gent known as Mr. B.B., was Brumsic Brandon Jr., whose then new comic strip, *Luther*, was one of the first to feature a black character in its lead role.

The programming combo of *The Magic Garden* and *Joya's Fun School* aired on WPIX through the remainder of the 1970s and into the early 1980s. Remarkably, only fifty-two episodes of *The Magic Garden* were ever made, and none later than 1973. *Joya's Fun School* had even fewer episodes to its name and ceased production in 1972. But as CTW's leaders had already figured out, preschoolers were a renewable resource, which guaranteed a long shelf life for nearly any decent children's TV show.

— — —

Another juggernaut of inadvertent children's psychedelia was *New Zoo Revue*, a syndicated half-hour program that premiered early in 1972. Like *The Magic Garden*, its look was lysergic-pastoral, its main set rich with greenery, flowers, a bright-blue pond, and cheery yellow gazebos. The *Revue*, too, had two young hosts, in its case a real-life married couple named Douglas Momary and Emily Peden, who, on the show, called themselves Doug and Emmy Jo.

Doug and Emmy Jo's costars were three biped animals, actors in oversize costumes: the childlike Freddie the Frog, who, despite his species, wore a turtleneck; the wise but ornery Charlie the Owl, who wore a scholar's mortarboard; and the Blanche DuBois–esque southern belle Henrietta Hippo, who wore polka-dot dresses with petticoats. Produced out of Los Angeles, with a somewhat larger budget than *The Magic Garden*'s, *New Zoo Revue* splurged on animal costumes designed by none other than Sid and Marty Krofft.

But *New Zoo Revue* shared with *The Magic Garden* an effective naiveté, its obliviousness to TV-production norms lending it an un-network-like innocence. And it, too, had a corporate benefactor keen to burnish its reputation by underwriting a quasi-educational children's program. In the *Revue*'s case, this benefactor was Mattel, Inc., the toy-making giant—precisely the sort of plastic-peddling behemoth whose ads so grated on the members of ACT.

The marriage of Mattel and *New Zoo Revue* came to be in a roundabout way. In 1970, Doug Momary was still an undergraduate at California State University, Fullerton, a theater major with aspirations to become a Broadway composer, when he was approached by a woman named Barbara Atlas, who owned a toy store in the nearby town of Whittier. Atlas had created a beanbag frog toy that she named Freddie, and she was keen to develop a children's TV show around her new product. She asked Momary's mother, who worked in the shop, if she had any ideas of who could aid her in this project. "Of course, my mom being a good mom, she said, 'You ought to read some of my son's plays,'" said Momary.

Atlas and Momary met and agreed to give a partnership a go. Soon thereafter, the whole vision poured out of Momary: a campfire-worthy sing-along song that began, "It's the *New Zoo Revue*, comin' right at you / Where three delightful animals have fun at what they do!" Charlie and Henrietta, inventions of Momary's, were the two animals who would star alongside Freddie. Originally, Momary had planned to preside over the show's action as a character named Zenophenes Zoo. But he decided to simply play himself, an ordinary-looking young man named Doug who had horn-rimmed glasses, a mustache, matted dark hair of medium length, and a modish suede jacket. He enlisted his girlfriend, Peden, a beautiful young woman who was working toward her master's degree in speech therapy at the University of Southern California, to play Doug's "helper," Emmy Jo.

Momary and Peden's first audition together, for a financial TV station that was looking for family-oriented programming in order to retain its broadcasting license, didn't elicit an offer. But Atlas, working her connections in the toy industry, secured an audition for the couple at Mattel, which was based in Hawthorne, California. Mattel and the ad agency it used, the L.A.-based Carson/Roberts, were seeking a sort of public penance for a perceived misdeed: namely, producing an animated Saturday-morning cartoon for ABC, *Hot Wheels*, that critics deemed little more than a half-hour advertisement for Mattel's line of toy cars of that name.

It was actually a rival toy manufacturer, rather than an advocacy group such as ACT, that first kicked up a fuss about *Hot Wheels* to the FCC. The commission investigated the situation and took action, compelling ABC to log a percentage of the show's broadcast time as advertising rather than as original programming. Soon thereafter, in 1971, ABC canceled *Hot Wheels*, less than two years into its run.

But ACT, too, was unhappy with Mattel. Along with other organizations, it charged that the company's regular spots for Hot Wheels cars on Saturday-morning TV were deceiving, tricking gullible kids, via sophisticated camerawork, into believing that the little cars were capable of greater playtime performance than they could deliver. The Federal Trade Commission agreed. In 1970, it drafted a formal complaint against Mattel for producing commercials for Hot Wheels that "convey a sense of involvement or participation that falsely represents their actual use." Mattel called the complaint unjustified, but by this point it needed a public-relations win.

In Mattel's sumptuous in-house theater, Momary and Peden, now newlyweds, performed a few songs and sketches in front of the company's board of directors, including its president, Ruth Handler, the creator of the Barbie doll, and her husband, Elliot (the "el" in Mattel, which he cofounded with his friend Matt Matson).

The company agreed to pay for a pilot of *New Zoo Revue*, and to come on board as a sponsor. Hershey Foods, the chocolate-maker, was the program's other major sponsor. That a toy manufacturer and a candy peddler would get behind a lo-fi program of vaguely hippieish vibe speaks to the pressure that big companies were under to do the right thing. "On commercial television, a lot of the Saturday-morning shows were getting questions about 'Are they really just trying to sell sugar cereals?' It was a big issue with mothers," said Stephen Jahn, who, at the time, was a young actor transitioning into producing, with *New Zoo Revue* becoming his first production.

"And in the marketplace, people saw the success of what *Sesame Street* was doing," Jahn said. "So, if you connect the dots, *Sesame Street* was doing its thing, and commercial TV was really problematic, and here's a show that's something like *Sesame Street*, contributing positive moral messages to children. And all of a sudden, it made sense."

— — —

Jahn lined up financing for *New Zoo Revue* from an unlikely source: W. Clement Stone, a self-made insurance tycoon from Chicago who was an early self-help guru—like his friend Norman Vincent Peale, he published several books about the power of positive thinking—and a major political donor to President Nixon. ("Stone had a real heart for children," said Jahn.) The program got another major boost from Eddie Smardan, an adman who handled Mattel's media programming at Carson/Roberts. Smardan had been one of the producers of the *Hot Wheels* TV show and was therefore personally invested in doing some reputational repair work for Mattel. Acting as a consultant for *New Zoo Revue*, he hustled 150 local stations into carrying it, covering about 70 percent of the national marketplace.

What this meant was that *New Zoo Revue*, which finally went into production in 1971, didn't have to struggle to grow a viewership. It helped, too, that the program was so eye-catchingly strange, with three anthropomorphic animals galumphing around and the visual mismatch of Doug and Emmy Jo: he, an affable if nerdy fellow of grad-studentish mien, strumming a guitar (think Eugene Levy in nebbish mode); and she, a vivacious, brown-haired knockout who grooved and sang in miniskirts and go-go boots (think Ann-Margret crossed with Lady Miss Kier of the 1990s pop group Deee-Lite).

"I got a lot of 'How did a guy like you get *her*?,'" Momary said. "It was not calculated to be sexy, though it did turn out that way.

We got a lot of fan mail from guys." (Momary and Peden remain married to this day.)

Momary was prolific, churning out 196 episodes and more than six hundred songs over the course of the *Revue*'s 1971–75 production run. His songs and plotlines, wholesome and earnest, were the antithesis of the lucre-seeking cacophony of *Hot Wheels.* Unlike his showrunner counterparts on the East Coast, Momary had no consultants or academic advisers at his disposal, or even a specific mandate from his benefactors. But his instincts were sufficiently on target that the program was endorsed by the National Education Association. Given creative carte blanche, Momary, a young, liberal man animated by the spirit of the times, turned *New Zoo Revue* into what he called "a 'how kids behave' kind of show," and what Jahn called "morals through music."

"I was concerned about the next generation and what we were teaching our kids," Momary said. "So I came up with a show about behavior and treating all people with respect and dignity no matter who they are, and no matter what color they are." In one episode, Freddie the Frog got bad grades on his report card and declared that he was going to quit school and run away with the circus. Emmy Jo led the gang in a hypnotic, *Astral Weeks*–like jazz-folk song entitled "Stay in School" that convinced Freddie of his self-worth, and of the virtues of "expanding your mind."

Momary acknowledges that the *Revue* had a "kind of trippy" quality, but this, he said, was more attributable to the show's look and his musical influences—his favorites were the Beatles and Crosby, Stills & Nash—than to any illicit substances. Indeed, one episode was explicitly anti-drug. Charlie the Owl, the show's brainiac, had invented something he called a "happiness pill," and things went awry with predictable consequences: he oversampled his own product, went on a manic bender, took flight, and smashed into a hickory tree. The gang (including, bizarrely, the future game-show host and conservative firebrand Chuck Woolery, who had a recurring role as an elderly postman named Mr. Dingle) sang a cautionary song that warned, "Drugs are not cool, and they're not fun / Why play around with your life? / It's your only one."

As hokey as *New Zoo Revue* could be, Momary brought some authentic moral courage to it. "It's amazing to me that some of those shows were accepted," he said, "especially given that our first advertiser was Mattel. Their mission is to sell toys. Here, we had a very altruistic show that *they* were sponsoring." Momary ran into some opposition when he wrote an episode about money and greed. But in the end, his was the opinion that prevailed, and Charlie led the cast in an up-tempo screed against materialism that, quite literally, was music to ACT's ears:

Buying things may make you happy for a while
But they can't give you a lasting smile
That's got to come from within yourself
No amount of buying will ever really help

— — —

By 1973, *New Zoo Revue*, which in the New York market aired five days a week on the same station as *The Magic Garden*, WPIX, was the region's highest-rated commercially produced TV program for kids, Saturday-morning shows included.

WPIX's FCC- and activist-appeasing strategy, no matter how grudgingly it had been hatched, had proven mightily effective, with no less an eminence than Joan Ganz Cooney praising *The Magic Garden* as "a lovely little show."

By the same token, ACT was proving its own effectiveness. Lloyd Morrisett, Cooney's more retiring CTW partner, played a significant role in ensuring ACT's long-term viability. The year of *Sesame Street*'s launch, 1969, he left the Carnegie Corporation to become the president of the smaller John and Mary R. Markle Foundation, which, under his direction, focused on how the public good could be better served by the mass media and the entertainment industry.

ACT, for all the press it was generating and dues-paying members it was attracting, was hanging on by a thread financially. ACT's Peggy Charren sought out Morrisett and Markle for funds to pay for her organization's ongoing research and reform-promoting efforts. Morrisett delivered: in 1971, Markle granted a sum of $164,500 to ACT, the first of nine grants the group would receive from the foundation.

The organization's growing clout also resulted in its successful enlistment of some major names to its advisory board, which, by 1974, included, in addition to Cooney, Fred Rogers; Margaret Mead, the celebrated cultural anthropologist; Albert J. Solnit, an eminent Yale child psychiatrist; and H. A. and Margret Rey, the creators of the *Curious George* books.

In 1973, ACT started giving out its own awards for Achievements in Children's Television, effectively bestowing a *Good Housekeeping*–style seal of approval upon the stations, networks, and programs that fulfilled its criteria. Though most of ACT's love was directed toward public television, WPIX, too, came in for honors: specifically for putting *The Magic Garden* and *Joya's Fun School* on the air.

*Rita Moreno and Morgan Freeman bring the
ham (and milk) on* The Electric Company.

CHAPTER
SIXTEEN

"Hey, You *Guyyys!*":
Powering Up
The Electric Company

L
loyd Morrisett was also the prime mover in initiating the development of one of ACT's favorite shows of the 1970s, *The Electric Company*. Mere weeks after *Sesame Street*'s launch, he made the case to Cooney that CTW should keep its foot on the gas pedal, using the goodwill generated by its first program to create a second: this time for kids in the next age group up. Cooney was reluctant.

"I remember saying, 'Oh my God, we just got *Sesame Street* on the air. We have to turn around and do *another* show?,'" she recalled. "But he said, 'You don't want to become a one-show house—you want to keep going.'"

The well-connected Morrisett was alert to the fact that the Nixon administration's newly announced Right to Read campaign against illiteracy was the pet project of the First Lady, Pat Nixon, who, notwithstanding the *Sesame Street* cast's unpleasant visit to the White House under her auspices, remained a figure the Workshop was keen to court. A new CTW program devoted specifically to reading would be right up Mrs. Nixon's alley. There was a catch, though: in order to receive government funding, this show would need to be framed as a *remedial* reading program, not as a straight-up fun educational program for kids.

So, while the popular perception is that *The Electric Company* was simply the logical next step for *Sesame Street* "graduates," the newer program was, at least in its early days, presented by CTW to the public as a show whose target audience was, as one press release stated, "the child in the lower half of the second grade in reading achievement." Not that this wasn't an area of genuine concern in American education circles; the Workshop's own internal report concluded, earnestly if inelegantly, that "some 20 million or 40% of elementary and secondary school students are reading cripples, and this despite their intelligence, emotional stability, and being in a good school program."

This public emphasis on remedial instruction also allowed *The Electric Company* to pick and choose how it taught reading skills in any given sketch. "If you said it's beginning reading, you would walk into a buzz saw of ideology about how reading should be taught in the very beginning," Cooney said. "But if you said it's a *remedial* program, that it's for seven-to-nine-year-olds who are having problems with reading, you walked into no problems at all. And then you could teach both whole words and phonics. You could mix up the ideologies. And these were *ideologies* in that world."

What this meant in practical terms was that *The Electric Company* could feature both a sing-along song (written by Clark Gesner, the composer of the stage musical *You're a Good Man, Charlie Brown*, and another member of the *Captain Kangaroo* diaspora) whose lyrics consisted almost entirely of whole words that kids could recognize from street signs—"Jane Street! Jones Street! Park Avenue / No Right Turn, No Left Turn / What can ya do?"—*and* sketches and songs that broke down words into their phonetic components.

The most memorable segments in this latter category featured what the Workshop labeled "silhouette blending": rhythmically recited sequences, set to music, in which a man and a woman, seen in intimate, silhouetted profile, effectively practiced procreative word copulation, each providing his or her own half-word in order to conceive a whole:

HIM: Ch-
HER: -at
TOGETHER: Chat
HIM: Ch-
HER: -in
TOGETHER: Chin

The silhouette-blending bits were emblematic of CTW's flair for cool: phonics as Pop Art. For all the laudable efforts being made on commercial TV with the likes of *Schoolhouse Rock!* and *The Magic Garden*, no one would ever out-hip the Workshop. Nor would any commercial-TV producer ever come close to CTW's level of preparatory rigor.

— — —

As swingy and simple as the silhouette-blending segments were, they didn't come about casually. Initially, the *Electric Company* team believed that the best placement for words on a television screen was at the bottom, simply because that's how subtitles had always worked in film and television. But Ed Palmer's research team determined, with the help of an eye-movement study conducted by the University of Toronto, that the eye is initially drawn to the middle of the screen—which is where the show's "blended" words ended up—and that even nonreaders are intuitively inclined to scan a screen from the top to the bottom. Hence, in most sketches, words appeared above *The Electric Company*'s actors rather than below them.

The Electric Company's development was more or less a recapitulation of *Sesame Street*'s, only on a tighter, more streamlined schedule: a feasibility study was quickly followed by two Gerry Lesser–led seminars (as opposed to *Sesame Street*'s five), which were followed by testing by Palmer's team, which was followed by an order of 130 episodes for an "experimental" first season. Each *Electric Company* episode would run for half an hour rather than an hour, though the program was nearly as expensive to produce as *Sesame Street*, with its maiden season, 1971–72, costing $7 million. The same lineup of funders—the U.S. Office of Education, the Ford and Carnegie Foundations, and the Corporation for Public Broadcasting—were the show's primary benefactors.

CTW's Sam Gibbon was put in charge of bringing the program to fruition, with Dave Connell overseeing the process from his executive-producer perch. Gibbon's deputy was the twenty-four-year-old Naomi Foner, who was given a big promotion from the ranks of *Sesame Street*'s production assistants.

It was easy to see why. Like Cooney before her, Foner had an uncommon résumé that combined social activism with television literacy. A Brooklyn native, she had graduated from Barnard College at the age of twenty, worked for the Head Start program in its very first summer, served as the director of media for the short-lived 1968 presidential campaign of the liberal Minnesota senator Eugene McCarthy, spent a short stint in the election unit of NBC News, and received a master's degree in developmental psychology from Columbia University—all before joining the Workshop.

Gibbon and Foner spent nearly a year on the road in 1970, as Cooney had a few years earlier, to put together their feasibility study. They observed inner-city schools in Oakland where children struggled to reconcile written English with the vernacular "black English" spoken in their homes. They visited a U.S. Army base where functionally illiterate enlistees, unable to navigate their own gun manuals, were being taught to read and write via a genre that held their interest: pornographic literature.

This approach was more instructive to CTW than it sounds. "Kids who are seven to ten aren't as containable or directable as they'd been when they were younger, so you need to get their attention," Foner said. "So, what would appeal to them? We were trying to make the show hip, so it didn't seem to talk down to them, as if they were little babies."

— — —

The Electric Company's creators opted to lean heavily on sketch humor as their attention-getting device, with *Rowan & Martin's Laugh-In* once again frequently invoked as a model. The Workshop brought in the comic actor and improv veteran Paul Dooley, later better known as a repertory player in the films of Robert Altman and Christopher Guest, to serve as a consultant.

"Paul had the idea of doing a show that was based on burlesque and vaudeville," said Skip Hinnant, a member of *The Electric Company*'s cast, "because the golden rule in those two media is say everything three times: 'My dog had fleas!' 'Your dog had fleas?' 'My dog had *fleas!*' Which made it an ideal format to map the words. For a reading show, it just seemed like the way to go."

Though nominally the program's head writer, Dooley acted more as a comedy whisperer, coming up with sketch ideas and inventing such recurring characters as Morgan Freeman's Easy Reader, who dressed like Jimi Hendrix and spoke like Sly Stone ("Top to bottom, left to right . . . Readin' stuff is outta sight!"), and Hinnant's mustachioed, trench-coat-wearing Fargo North, De-coder, who "decoded" jumbles of words by arranging them into co-herent sentences.

Foner, who took charge of the show's animated segments, showed no hesitancy in reaching out to big-name talent. She had loved *The Critic*, an Oscar-winning short in which Mel Brooks, voic-ing an irritable old Jewish man, supplied baffled commentary while a series of abstract animations played before him on a screen. Foner managed to convince Brooks to provide his voice-acting services for a short entitled "I Am Cute Very," in which his charac-ter, yet another cranky old man, ordered the animators to place the "very" in its correct place. For a running animated bit called "The Adventures of Letterman," about a superhero who habitually saved the day by ripping a letter off his varsity sweater—for the purpose of, say, transforming a jar back into a car—Foner enlisted Joan Rivers to be the narrator, and Gene Wilder and Zero Mostel to play, respectively, Letterman and his nemesis, the Spellbinder (which, in Rivers's Brooklyn accent, came out as "Spellbindah").

"A lot of it was simply a matter of 'Who has a kid and is inter-ested in having their kids see them as a hero?,'" Foner said. "That was also how we got a lot of people on *Sesame Street*." Both Riv-ers and Rita Moreno, a charter member of *The Electric Company's* live-action cast, had daughters of *Sesame Street*–watching age, and were excited to do work that their children could actually watch.

"The interesting thing was that I talked to actor friends, and every last one of them said, 'Don't do it,'" said Moreno. "The idea being that this might very well put me in a category where I might not get to play dramas anymore or be cast in anything but other children's shows. I thought about it very carefully, and I looked into my beautiful little girl's face, and I thought, 'Yeah, but *this* is what it really means—this is what's important.' And I said yes."

Whereas Jon Stone had cast *Sesame Street* instinctively, by feel, *The Electric Company* went for tenured performers. The marquee "gets" were Bill Cosby, already an Emmy winner for his work opposite Robert Culp in the TV series *I Spy*, and Moreno, an Academy Award winner for her portrayal of Anita in the 1961 film version of *West Side Story*.

Cosby stayed for only a season and a half, but the show's lesser-known cast members were every bit as gifted. The blond, boyish Hinnant had originated the role of Schroeder in the first New York production of *You're a Good Man, Charlie Brown*. Judy Graubart, whose flaky, off-kilter presence enlivened such characters as Jennifer of the Jungle and Julia Grownup, had been a member of Chicago's Second City comedy troupe. And Freeman, though a long way from his future film stardom, was getting noticed in the theater; at the time that he was cast, he was understudying Cleavon Little in the lead role of a Broadway musical called *Purlie*.

"Dave Connell was frantic, because we had to keep rescheduling around Cosby, who was never there. But it was great for Morgan, because he got to play a lot more than he would have otherwise," said Tom Whedon, who joined *The Electric Company*'s writing staff at the eleventh hour, when CTW realized it wasn't generating scripts fast enough, and who quickly took over as the show's actual head writer.

"Morgan could do anything," Whedon said. "I kept thinking of new things I wanted him to do, because whatever it was, he succeeded. I figured, *I'll give him a real challenge*, which was an effete George Washington who just didn't quite get it, and it became one of my favorite characters. He couldn't remember Yankee Doodle's name. I think it's probably the only time that 'Yank my noodle' was ever said on a children's television show."

— — —

Like *Sesame Street*, *The Electric Company* had a racially diverse cast. Moreno and Luis Ávalos, an actor who joined the show in its second season, were born in Puerto Rico and Cuba, respectively. Lee Chamberlin, best known for playing Vi, the proprietor of the show's diner, was of Afro-Brazilian heritage. When she left after two seasons, she was succeeded by Hattie Winston, one of *The Me Nobody Knows*'s African American stars. Cosby and Freeman were black, and Hinnant, Graubart, and Jim Boyd, best known for his grouchy character, J. Arthur Crank, were white.

The program also featured an all-kid rock band named the Short Circus (another Paul Dooley coinage), whose original lineup included June Angela, of Japanese and Italian descent, and three of *The Me*'s youngest alums: Irene Cara, a Latina, and the black actors Douglas Grant and Melanie Henderson, the latter of whom was the daughter of Luther Henderson, aka the Professor on *Joya's Fun School.*

Whereas *Sesame Street* had been pointedly multicultural, *The Electric Company*, coming along just two years later, was almost casually so; the Workshop's first program blazed a path for its second. In one sketch, Hinnant and Winston played a couple whose interracial marriage had nothing to do with anything. The premise was simply that Hinnant's character was eagerly awaiting the arrival of a new loudspeaker that, alas, turned out to be a "loud speaker": a man played by Boyd, who, once unboxed, spoke in a voice so earsplitting that it caused Hinnant and Winston to pass out. In another sketch, built around a Tom Lehrer song about contractions called "N Apostrophe T," Boyd, dressed as a little boy, sweet-talked Chamberlin, dressed as a little girl, into coming out to play: "Isn't, couldn't, didn't, wouldn't / Is that all you can say?"

"I thought that was one of the great things that the Children's Television Workshop did, that color and gender never, ever entered into any of these things," said Moreno. "Luis Ávalos and I weren't playing Hispanic characters. We were just playing *people.*"

Indeed, Moreno, who was nearing forty when *The Electric Company* began, had struggled since *West Side Story* to find parts that were worthy of her talent. Much as Emilio Delgado's acting options were mostly limited, prior to his joining *Sesame Street*, to playing street criminals, Moreno kept getting offers from Hollywood to play stereotypically, demeaningly "Puerto Rican" roles (e.g., the hot-tempered spitfire and the chatterbox maid).

But right before joining *The Electric Company*, Moreno secured one of the better roles of her recent career, in a prestigious film directed by Mike Nichols and written by Jules Feiffer. There was, however, a catch: the movie was called *Carnal Knowledge*, and Moreno was playing a prostitute. Moreno had accepted the part because she liked Feiffer's script and her character was not specifically denoted as being Latina, or any ethnicity, for that matter. But *Carnal Knowledge* wasn't exactly the ideal lead-in to this new phase of her career as a children's performer.

It occurred to Moreno that she owed Dave Connell a heads-up about her participation in the movie, which would be released a few months ahead of *The Electric Company*'s premiere. "I took him aside and said, 'I did a movie with Mike Nichols and Jack Nicholson,' and he said 'Wow,'" Moreno recalled. "And I said, 'Yeah, but I need to tell you the context of the scene.' I proceeded to tell him about this hooker person and the character that Jack played, and said, 'It comes to this point near the end of the movie where he is unable to function sexually unless he is talked into it. I play that hooker who talks him into an erection, and then I disappear from the camera, and ostensibly I'm doing fellatio.'"

Connell blanched. "The look on his face was priceless," Moreno said. "It's as though the blood drained from his entire body, starting with his head, and landed in a pool around his ankles. He just stared at me for several minutes. Then he finally said, 'Oh, my God.'"

In a more prudish or outrage-prone era, that would have been the end of Moreno's time on *The Electric Company*. But Joan Cooney, as ever putting her faith in the creative team, was not as bothered as Connell was, and Moreno remained in the cast.

— — —

Still, within CTW, there were occasional moments of contention between Whedon's writing team and the research and production staffs about racial and gender stereotypes. The Workshop's African American staffers were wary, as they had been in the case of *Sesame Street*'s Roosevelt Franklin, of presenting black characters in a potentially unflattering light. Whedon had written a song called "Fear" specifically for Freeman, in which the actor would play a hunter who was afraid of animals (and knew how to emphasize the vowel sound that "ea" makes). "But the black caucus said, 'You absolutely cannot have a black man being afraid, because it's denigrating to black men,'" Whedon recalled. The song was given to Boyd instead.

Whedon encountered similar resistance to his suggestion that all of the actors should play both male and female roles. As he remembered it, "The thinking was, if you have a man playing a woman, you're making fun of women. And if you have a woman playing a man, it indicates that she has to be a man in order to do what men do." One of Moreno's signature characters, Millie the Milkman's Helper, was nearly a casualty of this debate, given that she was originally conceived as a trainee milk*man*. But Millie survived, wearing a long skirt rather than trousers, and her clueless greeting to her still-sleeping customers—a full-throated cry of "Hey, you *guyyys!*"—became the program's catchphrase, eventually tacked onto the very top of the show, before its opening credits.

The Electric Company, which premiered on October 25, 1971, roared onto the screen—aurally and aesthetically more of a chrome-coated dragster than *Sesame Street*'s wholesome hippie hayride. Joe Raposo nailed his assignment for the theme song, composing a driving, soul-inflected tune whose jubilant group vocals, delivered in the pop-revival style then current in such Broadway shows as *Godspell, Jesus Christ Superstar,* and *Hair,* began with the words "We're gonna turn it on, we're gonna bring in the power!"

Just four years earlier, the BBC had banned the Beatles' song "A Day in the Life" from the radio because of what it had deemed the "sinister" implications of the lyric "I'd love to turn you on." But by the early seventies, the trappings of psychedelia had infiltrated the mainstream, and *The Electric Company* "turned it on" in a manner considered entirely family-friendly: with Peter Max–inspired sets;

amoeboid graphics in such colors as avocado, rust, and brown; and a glinting logo in the ITC Neon font. Unlike *The Magic Garden*, *The Electric Company* was consciously, wittingly of its time.

Even the use of the word "gonna" in the theme song was a sign of more relaxed mores. *Sesame Street*, in its first years, came in for a lot of criticism for using casual, conversational speech, and—Roosevelt Franklin excepted—tended to tread carefully where spoken language was concerned. But *The Electric Company* simply went for it. Mel Mounds, the shades-wearing DJ who introduced the Short Circus's songs (played by Freeman in an Afro wig and a gold earring), spoke exclusively in jive: "Say hey there, melody mavens, it's your old disco tech . . . *nician.*"

To manipulate words and diphthongs so that they appeared to float above and zip around the actors, the show used such state-of-the-art technologies as Scanimate, the same computer-animation system that allowed words to shimmer and undulate during the Oompa-Loompas' songs in the contemporaneous hit children's film *Willy Wonka and the Chocolate Factory*. ("Who do you blame when your kid is a BRAT? / Pampered and spoiled like a Siamese CAT?") Indeed, it was this emphasis on technology that inspired the program's name, CTW's Dave Connell explained. "Our job was to get print on the screen in a lot of different ways so people would want to watch it," he said, "and that meant electronic gadgetry, and the show became *Electric Company.*"

— — —

By design, given its slightly older demographic, *The Electric Company* was goofier and more rambunctious than *Sesame Street* was. "I looked at an early pilot of the show, and they asked me what my suggestions would be," Whedon said. "I said, 'I think it needs a gorilla.' It was too teachy. You need a character who wants to break things and just rush around, and there's no teaching involved in him at all. I got the gorilla."

The gorilla was named Paul, after Dooley, and played by Boyd, who muttered gibberish from inside an oversize, furry suit, usually while being the straight man to Graubart's Jennifer of the Jungle. Freeman regularly appeared in skits as a vampire, performing utterly barmy songs to which he fully committed. In one, he fondled squashes and cucumbers lasciviously while identifying himself as "Vincent, the vegetable vampire." In another, he lathered himself with bubble soap, shirtless, while sitting in a coffin and singing, "I love to take a bath in a casket." Helpfully, the word "casket" appeared above him.

"It was really a burlesque show for children," said Moreno. She and Freeman had a running sketch in which Moreno played Otto, a short-tempered movie director, and Freeman played her terrified cue-card holder, whose cards Otto whacked viciously with a pointer every time one of her flighty actors (usually Graubart) flubbed a line. Moreno assigned Freeman's mute, trembling character the name Marcello, and it took all of their actorly powers not to break in these sketches. "I was always so close to peeing when we did those things," Moreno said.

As of *The Electric Company*'s fourth season, the show also included a series of vignettes called "Spidey Super Stories," produced in collaboration with Marvel Comics and Spider-Man's creator, Stan Lee. The Spidey character, played by the dancer and Jim Henson puppeteer Danny Seagren, did not speak, communicating only through speech and thought balloons ("Danger!"), thereby providing the sketches with their reading-comprehension content.

The theme song for these sketches was written and performed

by Gary William Friedman, who, thanks to his track record as the composer of *The Me Nobody Knows*, was tapped to be *The Electric Company*'s musical director when Raposo temporarily left the Workshop.

"I sat at my piano and I thought, 'Spider-Man, he doesn't speak. He's a weird guy—like, nobody knows who he is,'" Friedman said. "So I came up with *Spider-Man, where are you coming from? / Spider-Man, nobody knows who you are!*"

Friedman's kitschy, Paul Shaffer–ish "rock" delivery suited the absurdity of the Spidey series, which had none of the solemnity and grandeur of Marvel's twenty-first-century Spider-Man films. In one characteristic episode, the superhero contended with a lumbering yeti (Boyd, again in a giant, furry suit) who was wreaking terror on the town of Paramus, New Jersey, by sitting on civilians' ice-cream cones and soft drinks.

"I found the show at times sort of tasteless," said Cooney, who, in *The Electric Company*'s early days, recoiled at its vaudevillian brashness and shouty, pun-laden sketches. But the show grew on her as she came to recognize that its madness was working toward a miraculous end: it was actually teaching kids how to read. "I now think that *Electric Company* is more brilliant than *Sesame Street* in its way," she said. "But at the time, I was so used to sweet little *Sesame Street* that I was not used to the sensibility of seven-to-nine-year-olds. Sam Gibbon and Dave Connell and Naomi Foner were."

— — —

As Cooney soon learned, children were more ready for *The Electric Company* than she was. And teachers were more amenable than they had been in the pre-*Sesame* days to buying into TV—especially CTW-produced TV—as a pedagogic tool. *The Electric*

Company was quickly embraced by American educators. Within two months of its introduction, the show was being used in nearly a quarter of all primary schools in the United States as a teaching aid. It was also reaching an audience of roughly two million children, who were watching at home after school.

Both of these numbers would continue to trend upward. A year after the show's premiere, Sid Marland, the U.S. commissioner of education, described *The Electric Company*'s incorporation into school curricula as "one of the remarkable events in the history of instructional television." These words, coming from a Nixon appointee, spoke to how far Cooney and Morrisett's grand experiment in using television as an educational medium had come in just half a decade, and how enthusiastically Americans of all stripes had taken to CTW as a trusted brand. To this day, no TV program has been more widely used in U.S. classrooms than *The Electric Company* was in its seventies heyday.

If there was a downside to the program's public reception, from CTW's point of view, it was that it wasn't generally perceived as remedial. While the Workshop was quick to tout surveys of teachers who attested to *The Electric Company*'s efficacy in helping problem readers, the reality was that the show was an across-the-board hit, enjoyed by primary-school-age viewers who, unlike *Sesame Street*'s, were completely aware that they were watching educational television.

But this was a good problem to have: the more viewers the show found, the better. CTW also discovered, to its surprise, that *The Electric Company* was being watched by immigrants who were using it as a de facto ESL course, and by *Sesame Street*–age children already prepared to take the next step: as Jim Boyd put it, "Really bright three- and four- and five-year-olds."

Moreno recalled that her husband's elderly aunt, an illiterate old-world Ashkenazic Jewish woman known within the family as Tante Shoshi, became a daily watcher of the program, mainly because she enjoyed seeing her nephew's wife perform. "But to her amazement and surprise and delight—and mine, too—she began to learn to read," Moreno said. "I remember one day she called me up and said, 'Rita, dahlink, I'm in the supermarket—and I'm reading a can of peas!'"

— — —

For the second time in three years, the Workshop, through a combination of rigorous research and the leeway that Cooney allowed her TV professionals, had uncannily attuned itself to the wavelength of kid viewers, creating a program that had no precedent or equal in its category. In its way, CTW had become as formidable a force in 1970s television as such West Coast production shops as MTM Enterprises, the creators of *The Mary Tyler Moore Show* and *The Bob Newhart Show*, and Norman Lear's Tandem Productions, the company behind *All in the Family, Sanford and Son, Maude*, and *Good Times*. Posterity has proven this era to be a golden age of U.S. television, and CTW was as much a part of it as the networks were.

By the early 1970s, the Workshop had built up a considerable stable of in-house creative talent: to name just a few, Whedon, Foner, Friedman, Raposo, Elaine Laron (who, as a lyricist, collaborated with Raposo on such *Electric Company* standards as "Punctuation," "Old Double 'E'," and Easy Reader's theme), Jeff Moss, Christopher Cerf, Jon Stone, and Bob Cunniff, a Whedon pal and fellow former *Dick Cavett Show* writer who came aboard *Sesame Street* in 1972, when Stone was promoted to the position of executive producer.

Many of these individuals were good friends, members of a smallish, bourgeois, bohemian circle that just so happened to be exerting a considerable influence on children throughout the United States. Many of them produced children who also became creatives. Three of Whedon's sons, Joss, Jed, and Zack, are successful screenwriters. Cunniff's daughter, Jill, cofounded the band Luscious Jackson. Foner's children are the actors Maggie and Jake Gyllenhaal.

But what truly distinguished this circle from a typical close-knit group of show-business machers was that its members were creating entertainment in pursuit of a higher calling than entertaining—and with the federal government's backing, no less.

"I've always felt that what we were doing was a form of community service," said Moreno. "It had all the aspects of that, because it certainly didn't pay very well. But I thought it was a noble, noble undertaking."

"I saw myself as a political person," said Foner, "and to me, this was a smart, savvy way to reach many people with information power that they wouldn't otherwise have had."

And while none of the CTW writers took a vow of poverty—Whedon would go on to write for *The Golden Girls*, and Stone, a *Sesame Street* lifer, would lament in his later years that he had lacked the financial acumen that made Jim Henson a rich man—they passed up on more lucrative opportunities because they were committed to the Workshop's mission.

"It's the thing that I've done that I'm proudest of, because it changed the world, and all for good," said Foner, who herself later became a screenwriter and director. "When I went to Hollywood, I found it crass—very hierarchical, and very much about money. It was welcoming enough, but it didn't give me the same feeling."

The second cast of Zoom's third season, including Mike Dean (with cap), whose tonsillectomy was chronicled in 1974.

CHAPTER

SEVENTEEN

We're Gonna Teach You to Fly High: *Zoom* Invents User-Generated Content

In Boston, a similar circle of educated, creatively inclined sophisticates formed around WGBH, that city's public television affiliate. While New York had Big Bird, it was WGBH that created more programs central to PBS's identity in the 1960s and 1970s than any other public station in the country.

Among them were the cooking shows *The French Chef* (1963), with Julia Child, and *Joyce Chen Cooks* (1966); *Masterpiece Theater* (1971), the Anglophile anthology series hosted by Alistair Cooke; *Nova* (1974), the science-for-laymen show; *Crockett's Victory Garden* (1975), a gardening-for-food how-to; and *This Old House* (1979), the home-improvement program that made Bob Vila's name. Like the Asylum Records logo and the Levi's orange pocket tab, WGBH's station-identification

sting—an insectoid gibble-gabble overtaken by a sunrise cre-
scendo of synthesized strings, composed and played on a Moog
by the electronic-music pioneer Gershon Kingsley—was a mark
of 1970s quality.

"It was just this incredible buzz of activity. We didn't know
what we were doing, that we were creating public television for
the next twenty, thirty years," said Christopher Sarson, a WGBH
producer and the driving force behind *Masterpiece Theater*. Sarson attributes the fecundity of WGBH in this era to Hartford Gunn,
a founding employee of the station and its general manager from
1957 to 1970, and Michael Rice, who took over as general manager
not long after Gunn left to become PBS's first president. Both were
well-educated men with wide-ranging interests: Gunn, a Harvard
MBA and navy veteran who was also a gearhead, fluent in the
technology of television, and Rice, a former Rhodes scholar who
was only twenty-eight years old when he ascended to the helm of
WGBH.

From its inception, WGBH was a bastion of tolerance and progressivism. Its very first broadcast, on May 2, 1955, was a simple
program for preschoolers entitled *Come and See*. The first figure
seen on the program, performing its theme song accompanied
only by his acoustic guitar, was Tony Saletan, a wiry, bespecta-
cled folk singer whose credentials were beyond question: It was
he who, during the folk-revival movement of the 1950s and 1960s,
fostered the popularization of two African American spirituals
that at the time were relatively obscure, "Michael, Row the Boat
Ashore" and "Kumbaya." Saletan taught the former to Pete Seeger,
of the Weavers, and the latter to Joe Hickerson, of the Folksmiths.
The Weavers' and Folksmiths' recorded versions caught on, and

both songs entered the American canon, becoming staples of music classes in nursery and primary schools.

As the heads of WGBH, Gunn and Rice fostered an atmosphere of open-mindedness and intellectual freedom. Within WGBH's tight, familial community, they commanded respect and adoration for their willingness to indulge their producers' ideas. One such producer, Michael Ambrosino, the husband of Lillian Ambrosino of ACT, came up with the idea for *Nova* after seeing a similar program in Britain called *Horizon*. Rice gave him the go-ahead to bring the show to fruition.

Christopher Sarson, too, was an ACT husband, married to the organization's founding president, Evelyn Sarson. The Sarsons were English and impressively credentialed. Back home, she had been one of the *Guardian* newspaper's first female reporters, and he had been a young producer for Granada Television. They were introduced to each other by a mutual friend, the actress Eleanor Bron, to whom the Beatles sang "You've Got to Hide Your Love Away" in *Help!* "We decided to go to America for our honeymoon, and we came by ship," Christopher said. "The sea sickness turned out to be morning sickness, so we had a baby, bought a house, and never went back to England."

Under Hartford Gunn's guidance, Christopher Sarson carved out a niche for himself at WGBH, creating a slate of educational programming intended for in-school use called *The 21-Inch Classroom*, its title a reference to the diagonal distance across a standard TV screen in the 1960s. For its time, *The 21-Inch Classroom* was innovative, but Sarson acknowledges that it didn't measure up to the futuristic CTW shows that came in its wake. "We had math programs and science programs and all the good things that you were supposed to do, but I don't think there was much imagination in those days," he said. "Quite honestly, I don't think people expected a lot of imagination."

Masterpiece Theater, however, was a big step forward for Sarson. Recognizing that his native Britain excelled in a television format in which the United States was lacking—the limited-edition serialized drama—Sarson suggested to Stan Calderwood, who was briefly the chief of WGBH between the tenures of Gunn and Rice, that the station should secure the rights to such series. Calderwood embraced the idea, cut a deal with the BBC, wangled a grant out of the Mobil Oil Corporation, and *Masterpiece Theater*, which is now the longest-running prime-time drama series on television (its title truncated in 2008 to *Masterpiece*), was born.

But at the dawn of the seventies, Sarson felt himself being pulled back into children's television. The impetus was not so much his wife's involvement in ACT, he said, as the fact that their two kids, a girl born in 1963 and a boy born in 1965, "were getting into their preteen ages, and I was interested in the way that they would go into a situation where there were lots of other kids. They were cautious. It was 'We would like to be your friend, but we don't want you to laugh at us.'"

Sarson came up with a general outline for a program in which a cast of children of preteen age would perform songs and sketches and create craft projects based on scripts and premises sent in by home viewers in the same age group. On-screen and off, kids would learn from one another rather than from an adult authority figure. "If the emphasis is on learning rather than teaching, you achieve a lot," Sarson said. "If the kids are learning rather than *being taught*, they'll be more sure of themselves and enjoy life more. So, it was this feeling of getting kids in a position where they could be thinking for themselves."

The more thought Sarson gave to his idea, the more its specifics came into focus: there would be a cast of seven children, local Boston-area kids, ethnically mixed, and none of them trained performers. There would be no adults. Sarson decided to call the program *Zoom In, Zoom Out*, he said, "because it was 'We're gonna zoom in on the kids' lives, and we're going to zoom out on how that affects you in the world.'"

—   —   —

But surprisingly, given his impressive track record at WGBH, the powers that be at the station gave Sarson's pitch a hard pass. "They didn't like it very much. They said, 'No. Not for us,'" he said. So, Sarson trucked his idea over to Boston's CBS affiliate, WBZ, to see if its brass were interested. They were, but on a condition that ran counter to Sarson's vision: he had to incorporate Rex Trailer, a star of Boston children's television since the 1950s, into the program.

Trailer was a television oddity: a singing cowboy and an authentic son of Texas who had become an institution in Yankee New England, hosting a weekend show for kids entitled *Boomtown*. Beloved as it was, by the early 1970s, *Boomtown* was passé and nearing the end of its run, even though Trailer was only in his forties and still commanded tremendous goodwill in Boston.

Sarson suggested a compromise to WBZ. They would allow him to film two pilots: one constructed around a cast of kids, and the other a vehicle for Trailer. WBZ agreed to the plan. As things turned out, the station preferred the Trailer pilot, and, without Sarson, developed it into a science program with the very 1970s title *Earth Lab*.

But Sarson, for his troubles, was at least left with a tape of a completed pilot for his adult-free kids' show. He decided to take it back to WGBH, figuring that, this time, he stood a better chance with some concrete evidence of how his concept would play out. His instinct proved correct. "Michael Rice, he wasn't particularly fond of children, and he didn't particularly like the idea, but he let it happen," Sarson said. "He kept prodding me with ideas that were quite wrong, but they made me think of ideas that were quite right, which I put into the show."

The program, renamed *Zoom*, was made on the cheap, starting with a $30,000 surplus left over from another program's budget. Sarson's cast of seven kids, ranging in age from nine to thirteen, needed a unisex uniform: blue jeans and some sort of top. The thriftiest option was found at Sears, where children's rugby-striped jerseys were selling in multiple sizes for $5 apiece.

The stripes would become *Zoom*'s visual motif, adorning not only the children but also the big Z-O-O-M letters that stood, Stonehenge-like, at the rear of the set. "The idea of the stripes came from the shirts," Sarson said. "The only way we could afford to make a set was to cut out big pieces of cardboard in the shape of the letters and stick the stripes on them."

For music, Sarson reached out to a classically trained musician named Newton Wayland, who at the time was a pianist and harpsichordist for the Boston Symphony Orchestra. A burly, thickly bearded man who was evangelical about getting kids interested in music, he served as *Zoom*'s music director and composer. His theme song began with an unrefusable invitation: "We're gonna zoom-a, zoom-a, zoom-a, zoom / Come on and zoom, zoom, zoom-a zoom," and ended with a sweetly encouraging plea:

> *Come on, give it a try*
> *We're gonna show you just why*
> *We're a-gonna teach you to fly high!*
> *Come on and zoo-oom! Come on and zoom-zoom!*

The children performed this song to boisterous choreography by Billy Wilson, an African American director and choreographer who was the head of the dance department at Brandeis University. Their execution was more raggedy than pinpoint, and all the more exciting for it: hanging off the giant letters, arraying themselves into a shimmying group, and then splitting off from one another, running barefoot (with the blessing of an on-set physician) into the far reaches of WGBH's cavernous Studio A, where, in a corner out of view of the camera, Julia Child's *French Chef* kitchen set stood dormant.

The optics of this opening sequence alone—preteens leaping and gallivanting freely, alike but different, white boys with great, thick mops of unregulated hair, black boys with tight Afros, girls of various ethnicities with center partings—were beguiling to young viewers. *Zoom* presented a picture of children's liberation that, while rife with youthful energy, was orderly and cooperative rather than a *Lord of the Flies*–like Hobbesian state of nature.

The program was also, way before the term became fashionable, a showcase for user-generated content. Its stars encouraged kids at home to send in their ideas, with Wayland ingeniously turning the show's mailing address into a patter song, part rapped and part sung—"Box Three-Five-Oh, Boston, Mass., *Oh-Two-One-Three-Four*! Send it to *Zoom*!"—that seventies children committed to memory as if it were the Pledge of Allegiance.

The resulting content was resolutely low-tech bordering on Luddite. The Zoomers, as the child performers were known, demonstrated viewers' recommendations for, say, tie-dying T-shirts or for playing a homemade game called "cotton race," in which two players, using flexible plastic straws, blew a cotton ball back and forth. On the more sophisticated end of the spectrum, the Zoomers obliged a girl's request to perform "some of the old-time oldies," executing a medley of the Tin Pan Alley songs "Flat Foot Floogie" and "Mairzy Doats," with musical and choreographic assistance from Wayland and Wilson, respectively.

Joan Ganz Cooney was enchanted by *Zoom*'s pilot episode and quickly got behind the program, playing a significant role in ensuring that it was, from the off, widely distributed via the PBS network. The half-hour show launched in 1972, airing once a week in most markets, usually in the early evening. The early 1970s were still an era of limited viewing options for children, particularly in the tween demographic, and *Zoom* zoomed to national prominence: a euphoric watch for preteens and an aspirational one for their little siblings. *Life* magazine, during *Zoom*'s first year on the air, described the program as "graduate school after *Mister Rogers' Neighborhood*."

The striped shirts, born of budgetary necessity, became iconic, as did Ubbi-Dubbi, the *Zoom*-popularized pig-Latin variant in which "ub" was inserted before the vowel sound in each syllable of a word, so that "Hello" came out as "Hub-ell-ub-o." At its mid-1970s peak, the program was receiving twenty thousand letters a week from children at home, some suggesting ideas, others requesting a coveted *Zoom* Card, a postcard that, on one side, featured a color photograph of a cast member, and, on the other, step-by-step instructions for a crafts project or a game featured on the show.

— — —

The cast members themselves became short-term celebrities. Each Zoomer was asked to come up with a signature move or gesture to accompany his or her introduction in the opening song, and these alone could make a mark. "I'm Mike," said a Season Three boy whose bushy blond hair protruded from beneath a flat cap, left-handedly tossing a baseball as a few notes of "Take Me Out to the Ball Game" played. "I'm Berna-*dette*," said a Season Two Chinese American girl who performed an interlocking-elbow maneuver that tricked the eye into believing that her forearms wrapped around each other as if bonelessly, her hands rapidly fluttering like hummingbird wings. Bernadette's "arm thing" became the subject of national preteen fascination.

Sarson ensured that no *Zoom* cast stayed together for more than thirteen episodes—partly because some kids aged out of its demographic, and partly because he expressly wanted to avoid the performative kiddie professionalism that had caused Fred Rogers despair when he worked at NBC in the 1950s. As such, Zoomers generally pulled no more than two thirteen-week shifts before being phased out via the "Goodbye Song," in which the kids who were remaining bade farewell to those who were departing.

Zoom was arguably the most stylistically radical of all the children's shows of its period, in its empowerment of its cast and viewers, and in its general lack of artifice. Flubbed lines and missed cues were left in. The same Mike who tossed the baseball was also diagnosed with tonsillitis while he was in the cast, which set off a light bulb in Sarson's head. "I called the hospital and, believe it or not, asked them to hold up the operation for a couple of hours, while we got our crew together," he said.

The show ran a taped *vérité* segment in which Mike's doctor, at the hospital, announced to him that he was going to administer an anesthetic into Mike's rear end. "Michael said in his squeaky tonsillitis voice, 'Why are you going to give me a jab in the rear end? Why don't you do it nearer the tonsils?,'" Sarson recalled. "No adult would have ever come up with a question like that. But it's just the kind of thing that interested kids, and that kids wanted to know."

More audacious still was a regular segment entitled "*Zoom Rap*," in which the Zoomers, given prompts from home viewers, sat in a circle and, unscripted, discussed big philosophical ideas: the meaning of friendship, where they imagined themselves in ten years, what it felt like to be on TV. Here was Fred Rogers's assertion that "feelings are mentionable" taken to its logical conclusion: allowing children to discuss their feelings among themselves as the cameras rolled.

The results could be both funny and achingly poignant. In the "ten years from now" discussion, a petite African American girl named Andrae said, "I'll probably be a storywriter or I'll be an actor, because I can imagine things. Like, I have this imaginary friend George, but he's gone now. I think that he helped me through auditions and everything. My mom said it's good to have imaginary things and stuff. Some people say, 'Are you stupid?,' but it's not. In ten years from now, I wish I could be something like that."

In the same discussion, Tracey, a white girl with a pronounced Boston accent, said, "I'm not gonna get married, no way! 'Cause I just don't like the idea of me being a 'Mrs.' Bleah! I'm gonna just go to New York, have an apaht-ment."

Zoom was deliberate in assembling its casts, which were composed of black, white, Hispanic, and East Asian children. To Sarson, this wasn't a powerful statement of intent but simply an articulation of how things should be for children: a preemptive strike against prejudice. The first season of *Zoom* predated by two years the apex of the Boston busing crisis, in which some white Bostonians, reacting to a court-ordered plan to desegregate public schools by busing black kids to predominantly white schools and vice versa, demonstrated angrily, pelted buses full of black students with eggs, and withdrew their own children from school in protest.

The busing crisis prompted a departure from *Zoom*'s generally Utopian outlook in the form of a *Zoom* Rap addressing what was going on. An Irish American girl from South Boston, Tishy, stated that "the whites should stay with the whites, the blacks should stay with the blacks, [and] the Puerto Ricans should stay with the Puerto Ricans." The other Zoomers strenuously voiced their objections, albeit with remarkable comity, and without ostracizing Tishy.

— — —

Zoom went a step beyond *Sesame Street*, whose small children said little, and *The Electric Company*, whose Short Circus kids were supporting players (and showbiz professionals to boot), in providing a clear picture of youth integration in its idealized state. The national breakout stars of Seasons One and Two, based on viewer mail, were, respectively, Nancy, a black girl, and Berna-dette, the Asian girl who did the arm trick.

And the Zoomers were themselves enlightened and trans-formed by the process of participating in Sarson's experiment. A case in point is Bernadette, whose full name is Bernadette Yao. By her own account, she was a shy child with no aspirations to be-come a performer. She was a twelve-year-old middle schooler in Weston, Massachusetts, to the west of Boston, who on Saturdays attended a Mandarin-language class organized by the parents of local Chinese American kids.

"I don't know how WGBH found the school, but somebody rep-resenting *Zoom* called and asked if the children wanted to audi-tion. Because my friends were going to the audition, I went along with them," Yao said.

She and her fellow students in the Mandarin class, about thirty kids, were seated cross-legged on the floor in a circle alongside members of *Zoom*'s production team, Sarson included. Right away, Yao said, she felt herself experiencing a new dynamic. "There was a democracy here," she said. "With the adults sitting *with* us, and not in front of us, and not above us."

The audition, such as it was, involved passing an imaginary ball around and improvising an interaction with it. To her surprise, Yao and one other girl were advanced as "the finalists from the Chinese group," she recalled, to participate in a more traditional audition that involved singing and acting. Yao was chosen for the second and third of *Zoom*'s three thirteen-week shifts in its second season, which ran from 1972 to 1973.

Given the busing protests that loomed on the horizon, Yao's after-school commute to WGBH on Wednesdays, the day that

Zoom held its rehearsals, represented a rosy alternative reality to what was to come, closer to what Boston's architects of desegregation had in mind. The station sent a cab to pick up Yao, but first the cab stopped in nearby Dover, where a black castmate, Leon Mobley, was attending school as part of METCO, a voluntary Massachusetts program in which gifted and talented children from poor urban neighborhoods were bused to schools in the prosperous suburbs in order to receive better educations.

Mobley was a true child of the Great Society: a former Head Start kid who, with his three siblings, was being raised by his single mother in Boston's Cathedral Housing projects. Early on, he flashed his abilities as a musician and actor, and was placed at the Elma Lewis School of Fine Arts, whose namesake founder, an African American woman, had created the school to provide arts education to Boston's "deprived children," as she put it. The black kids in *Zoom*'s first season, Nancy Tates and Kenny Pires, had been recruited from Elma Lewis, and Mobley was tapped for Season Two. By the time that season began taping, Mobley was living part-time with a white host family in Dover and going to the public elementary school in their district—where, he recalled, "I was in a classroom with just twenty children, with telephones and TV and everyone getting their own desk. I was used to forty kids in a classroom."

Yao, who had barely interacted with black people up to that point in her life, became fast friends with Mobley, and with the other kid on their route, a white girl named Lori Boskin. "It was such a joyful thing," Yao said. "It was just like 'This is my other family.'"

"I was the first one to get picked up in the taxi, and we had a black driver, so he and I would listen to music and sing," Mobley said. "Bernadette was so quiet, but I was friendly as hell. I would involve her in the songs and games that we played, and she came out of her shell. And Lori was funny and cool. We had some interesting cab rides, interesting conversations. Even about the different dynamics in our families, because my father wasn't around and Bernadette was really close to her father."

This cab-ride routine repeated itself on Fridays, the days of *Zoom* tapings, which began at 6 p.m. and sometimes went all the way to midnight. (The taping day was carefully chosen so that the Zoomers could sleep in the next morning.) Yao, Mobley, and Boskin would rev each other up for the taping, and arrive psyched, Yao said, "to get on our striped shirts, take off our shoes, and go into Studio A."

Beyond the exhilaration of performing, Yao was energized by working and playing in an environment where her opinion was sought out and respected. The daughter of parents who fled China shortly after the Communist Revolution of 1949, she came, she said, "from a background where we showed respect for the elders by calling them Auntie This or Auntie That. It was more like 'Be seen but not heard so much.' But when we got to the studio, Christopher Sarson would always say, 'Call me Chris.' It was great that they wanted us to give our input."

By the same token, *Zoom* instilled in Yao the confidence to embrace and publicly discuss her Chinese background. At school in Weston, where most of her classmates were Caucasian, she was shy about bringing in her lunch, "because people would make fun of me for the smell and the odd-looking greens," she said. But when the prompt for a *Zoom* Rap was "What's your favorite food?," Yao had grown comfortable enough among her peers to reveal, to their shock, that she had never been to a McDonald's or eaten pizza.

When the other Zoomers asked her what she did eat, Yao described how her mother cooked. "Eventually, we started inviting each other over to each other's homes, and people got to try Chinese food in my house from Boston, Roxbury, Newton, Lexington, all the different areas of MetroWest," she said. "Everybody loved the food, and I felt more confident about sharing my culture."

"Oh, man, I got to know about Chinese culture, Jewish culture, Italian culture," said Mobley, who is now the percussionist in the band of the blues-rock guitarist Ben Harper, and who, during Barack Obama's presidency, traveled overseas as an arts envoy for the U.S. State Department. Even when young, Mobley had a diplomatic disposition, having had more experience moving among white and Asian children than his fellow Zoomers had had among black kids. "We always got a bathroom break, and I'm not going to name any names, but one boy, he asked me if my sperm was black!," Mobley said. "I started laughing like crazy. I wasn't offended. I just found it hilarious. He was like, 'Why are you laughing?' I was like, 'You don't *know*? What makes you think I'm different from you?'"

— — —

As for Yao's celebrated "arm thing" (which is what she actually calls it), it, too, was a product of her Chinese background. As the Season Two cast members were figuring out what their signature moves should be, Yao despaired of not having one, and envied Boskin, a gifted gymnast who performed a back walkover.

She spoke of her dilemma with her father, who suggested the arm trick. "It was from the Chinese opera. His father used to take him to performances when he was young," she said. "It was a move that the warlords did with swords, like blades on a helicopter, going around and around, three or four times."

Yao's father, a research scientist and mechanical engineer, taught Bernadette how to perform the maneuver, albeit without a sword. "I was like, 'Oh my gosh, I'm trying to be so American-ized and here they see I'm coming from China. People are going to make fun of me.' But I had nothing else," she said.

The next day, Sarson asked Yao what she had prepared, and she did the arm thing. "He says, 'Great! Let's do it!,' and I do it, no big deal," she said. But a few weeks after *Zoom*'s second season began airing, Sarson invited her to his office, where he emptied an enormous container of letters onto a desk. "We weren't allowed to read the mail—we knew that there was mail, but we never saw it," Yao said. "So this was unusual. And all the letters were 'How do you do that arm thing?'"

Zoom subsequently devoted a segment to Bernadette, in which, working slowly, she demonstrated to the viewing audience, step-by-step, how to do her thing.

— — —

As spartan as its set was, and as simple as its concept was, *Zoom* was very much the product of careful forethought—much like its public-TV peers *Sesame Street*, *The Electric Company*, and *Mister Rogers' Neighborhood*. Its quality and popularity ratified an idea that ACT had inferred if not stated outright: that public television was better at churning out watchable, effective educational children's programming than commercial TV was.

The educational kids' shows that found success on commercial TV, like *The Magic Garden* and *New Zoo Revue*, were generally the products of happy accidents and serpentine roads to realization. Even *Schoolhouse Rock!*, with its roots at an ad agency, was unconventional, with no backing from a major network in its formative stages. But there was one quality commercial program that, because its star and chief conceptualizer had a network pedigree, proved an exception to this phenomenon.

Marlo Thomas and Harry Belafonte prepare to shoot
"Parents Are People" on the steps of the Metropolitan Museum of Art.

CHAPTER

EIGHTEEN

"Propaganda at Its Height": Marlo Thomas Gets Political with *Free to Be ... You and Me*

In 1971, Marlo Thomas signed off from *That Girl*, the sitcom that had made her a star. The show, which had run on ABC for five years, was a daffy, spun-sugar confection with an aesthetic debt to such pastel-tinted big-city "women's pictures" of the 1950s as *Woman's World* and *The Best of Everything*. Still, *That Girl* was considered groundbreaking, if not radical, in that its protagonist, Ann Marie, played by Thomas, was not a wife or a homemaker but a single working woman—a struggling young actress in New York City who bounced from job to job.

Thomas was closely involved in *That Girl*'s production, pushing back against scripts that hewed to the conventional notion that a young woman could only be fulfilled by marriage to a man. Nevertheless, the sitcom's final episode gave in a little—it ended with Ann Marie getting engaged to her longtime boyfriend, Donald, played by Ted Bessell, and tossing her luxuriant hair in slo-mo ecstasy.

Prime time was not as progressive as the Children's Television Workshop was in 1971. The original premise of *The Mary Tyler Moore Show*, whose first season coincided with *That Girl*'s last, was that Moore's character, Mary Richards, had moved to Minneapolis in the wake of a divorce. But CBS, wary of accusations of immorality, rejiggered the setup so that what Mary had experienced was merely a broken engagement.

These strictures annoyed Thomas. In *That Girl*'s later years, she had developed a friendship with Gloria Steinem, at the time the most prominent voice of second-wave feminism. Steinem encouraged Thomas to affirm her feminism publicly, shrewdly recognizing that the actress, by dint of her *That Girl* popularity, had the power to pitch the Women's Liberation Movement to mainstream America without facing the usual charges leveled against feminists, that they were man-haters and anti-family radicals.

Not that Thomas needed any nudging in this regard. In 1969, her sister, Terre Gordon, had given birth to a daughter, Dionne. Thomas, in her capacity as Dionne's doting aunt, was taken aback by the paucity of early-childhood literature that portrayed girls as boys' equals. "I was reading books to Dionne, and I was shocked that the children's stories were the exact same stories that Terre and I had read as girls," Thomas said. "I mean, with all that was changing: women running for office, the marches that were happening, the laws changing."

Searching for fresh children's titles, Thomas came across a picture book called *I'm Glad I'm a Boy! I'm Glad I'm a Girl!*, by Whitney Darrow Jr., a longtime cartoonist for the *New Yorker*.

Portraying children as adorable little mini-adults, in a spare style not unlike that of early Charles Schulz, Darrow captioned his drawings with glaringly sexist captions, such as "Boys are doctors. Girls are nurses," "Boys are pilots. Girls are stewardesses," and "Boys build houses; girls keep houses."

Given Darrow's pedigree as a liberal, New England–based satirist, and the timing of his book's publication—1970, the same year that Steinem testified before the U.S. Senate in support of the Equal Rights Amendment and wrote a landmark essay for *Time* magazine entitled "What It Would Be Like If Women Win"— it's likely that Darrow intended his book as a dark sendup of outmoded gender stereotypes. (He never publicly commented on his intentions.) Nonetheless, the book was stocked in the children's section of bookshops and libraries, and its humor was likely lost on most of its readers. It certainly was lost on Thomas, who recalls "almost having a heart attack" when she first encountered it, late in 1971.

Thomas, thirty-four years old and free of her *That Girl* obligations, resolved to create some sort of mass-media, family-friendly manifesto against gender stereotyping. Like David McCall, the godfather of *Schoolhouse Rock!*, she initially decided that the best medium for her message would be a record album, featuring a collection of songs and stories. She found a willing creative partner in Carole Hart, a young TV writer who, along with her husband, Bruce, had worked on Jon Stone's staff in *Sesame Street*'s first season. Bruce Hart had been Joe Raposo's collaborator on the title song for that program, contributing its famous "Sunny day, sweepin' the clouds away" lyrics.

But Thomas wanted a woman to serve as her coproducer, and that woman turned out to be Carole Hart. In its earliest stages, their record was not even necessarily going to be targeted at children. "We talked about doing something for adults," Thomas said. "And then we said, 'No, teens.' And then we said, 'No, you really have to start with the youth.' It's like the Catholics or the Nazis. They start on kids when they're young. You can't wait 'til they're fifteen—by then, it's too late."

Thomas had no indoctrinatory malevolence in her heart, but she made no bones about her intent. *Free to Be…You and Me*, as the record would end up being called, was "propaganda at its height," she said. "You know how people often say, 'I had no idea the impact this was going to have'? I actually had a planned impact."

— — —

Before she had even partnered with Hart, Thomas, upon the recommendation of her friend Shel Silverstein, met up with the sixty-two-year-old Ursula Nordstrom, then nearing the end of what would be a thirty-three-year tenure as the head of Harper & Row's children's division. Nordstrom, in a letter to one of her authors, Mary Rodgers, seemed both intrigued and amused by the go-getting Thomas.

"She is very caught up with Women's Lib (which I know you are not particularly) and she has been upset by some of the 'sexist literature' being fed to children," Nordstrom told Rodgers. "She hoped I could find her some writers who would contribute brief stories and/or poems which in some way will counteract the sexist stuff. . . . I told Marlo that we just didn't have a lot of authors who write therapeutic material for the sake of therapy, but that I would try to think of a few who might be interested at least in talking to her. Would you be?"

Though Nordstrom remained a creative force in children's

literature, with Rodgers's body-switching novel *Freaky Friday* and Silverstein's poetry collection *Where the Sidewalk Ends* in the pipeline at Harper & Row, Thomas found the once revolutionary publishing doyenne too behind the times for her purposes.

"Without mentioning names, most of the writers that Ursula recommended were just too pedantic," Thomas said. "They belonged to another time."

Thomas found a more simpatico collaborator in the pages of *Ms.* magazine, whose first issue had recently been published as an insert in the December 20, 1971, issue of *New York* magazine. *Ms.*, soon to be a stand-alone feminist monthly, was the creation of Steinem and the African American activist Dorothy Pitman Hughes, with some logistical and financial help from Clay Felker, *New York*'s editor. Within its debut issue was a lengthy article by Letty Cottin Pogrebin, a friend of Steinem's and one of *Ms.*'s editors, that was right up Thomas's alley. Entitled "Down with Sexist Upbringing!," it was both a protest against American society's heavy-handed conditioning of girls and boys to fulfill prescribed gender roles (Pogrebin lamented the familiar sight of "little girls' rooms that are so organdied, pink, and pippy-poo one would never dream of besmirching them with Play-Doh") and a call to create new paradigms. "Let your boy know the challenge of tackling a recipe," Pogrebin wrote. "Let your girl know the challenge of tackling another kid."

Pogrebin's path to activism was not unlike Thomas's. In the 1960s, she had established herself as a bright young publishing executive, albeit one unfamiliar with the precepts of women's liberation. Her first book as an author, *How to Make It in a Man's World*, which came out in 1970, was an accommodationist primer on succeeding in the workplace on men's terms; the illustration on the book's cover depicted her as a blond bombshell in sunglasses and a green tank, perched at her desk while three hunky men hovered over her. But on July 10, 1971, Pogrebin attended the founding conference of the National Women's Political Caucus, a grassroots organization devoted to cultivating female candidates for public office. It was at this conference that she met and befriended Steinem and experienced an awakening.

"I had not been paying attention," Pogrebin said. "I was horrified by myself. So I drilled down into all the alternative literature: Ti-Grace Atkinson, Robin Morgan, Vivian Gornick, Anne Koedt's *The Myth of the Vaginal Orgasm*." She also accepted Steinem's invitation to join the staff of *Ms.*

Pogrebin differed from her peers at the magazine in that she was the mother of young children: six-year-old twin girls named Abigail and Robin and a four-year-old boy named David. In her season of awakening, over the summer and autumn of 1971, she rethought her entire approach to being a parent. One day, she purchased a Nerf basketball set and, upon bringing it home, hung the plastic hoop on her son's bedroom door. It was her husband, Bert—who, Pogrebin said, was "living my feminist transformation day by day"—who called her out on this action. "He said, 'How come you put the hoop on David's door? He can hardly walk.' And Robin and Abby were already good athletes." The Nerf hoop was duly moved to the girls' room, and Pogrebin, still not done, relocated some of the cups from the girls' toy tea sets to David's room.

This, she came to realize, proved an effective means of raising feminist children, unbound by older notions of gender roles. In 1973, young Abby Pogrebin wrote a letter of protest to General Mills, taking issue with its TV campaign for Wheaties breakfast cereal in which a little boy was seen participating in sports while a man sang in a rich baritone, "He knows he's a man—he's ready for Wheaties."

"This is a 8 year old girl speaking," Abby's letter began, the word *girl* underlined three times. "When ever I see your Wheaties commercial I sing the opposite of a boy knowing he's a man. I sing the girl knows she's a woman. . . . I'm just warning you that I'm not even touching one tasty bit of those Wheaties till theres a girl on that t.v. commercial."

Pogrebin's "Down with Sexist Upbringing!" article in the inaugural issue of *Ms.* concluded with a reading list, headlined "For the Liberated Child's Library," that she had drawn up from her own experiences in seeking out relatively enlightened story-time material for her kids. Pogrebin granted that her list was imperfect. "Despite some flaws," she wrote, "each book was chosen because of a redeeming theme or constructive moral." Among the titles she recommended were L. Frank Baum's venerable *The Wizard of Oz*, which Pogrebin labeled "a fantasy for feminists and humanists of all ages," and a new book by Cecily Brownstone, better known as the food editor of the Associated Press, called *All Kinds of Mothers*, which demonstrated, Pogrebin wrote, that "black and white mothers, working and stay-home mothers all have an important quality in common—their love for their children."

This list became the template for a regular section in *Ms.*, curated by Pogrebin, called Stories for Free Children. "We were the only women's magazine, ironically, that had anything for children," she said. "Even though the slur in the media was that feminists hate children."

Steinem recognized that Pogrebin was already doing a version of the work that Thomas hoped to do, and brokered an introduction between the two women, who met for lunch on the first of March in 1972. "It was instantly obvious that we were soul mates," Thomas later recalled. "We both wanted to save the world and agreed the place to start was with its children." Pogrebin joined Thomas and Hart's project in an advisory role, serving, in her words, as "the sensitivity reader, the sexism strainer. Nothing got through that had the vaguest kind of stereotype: racism, sexism, ableism. I remember wanting to create principles of respect and collaboration, so it wasn't 'boy ghetto' and 'girl ghetto.'"

Thomas and Hart, meanwhile, called upon their own friends and loved ones for help. Throughout the spring of '72, Thomas hosted get-togethers at her apartment on East Seventy-First Street in which, over pizza and wine, she, Hart, and Pogrebin brainstormed with such writers as Silverstein; Hart's husband, Bruce; Thomas's then boyfriend, Herb Gardner, the playwright; Mary Rodgers, who agreed to join the project; and the screenwriters Peter Stone and Paddy Chayefsky. "We examined gender stereotypes and identified other elements in our culture that prevented children from being and expressing their true selves," Carole Hart said.

Gardner, thinking back to his own boyhood, told the group that he wished that some adult had told him that it was all right to cry, and that doing so publicly didn't make him weak, or a sissy. Thomas admitted that she longed for a fairy tale in which the princess heroine wasn't blond and didn't get married to a handsome prince at the end.

Here, six years on from the dinner party at Joan and Tim Cooney's place in which the seeds of *Sesame Street* were planted, was another gathering of the cultural elite in a New York City apartment, with the future of America's children the topic of discussion. But a lot had changed. The idea of using songs and TV programs for educational purposes was no longer met with skepticism, as it had when Joan Cooney and Lloyd Morrisett were developing *Sesame Street*; rather, the *Sesame Street* model was now the paradigm, and the media literacy of small children was a given. Indeed, Thomas flatly stated that she couldn't count on old-timey methodologies in the new environment of the 1970s, in which, she said, "kids had rock concerts coming into their living rooms."

And whereas the founders of CTW had aimed to quantitatively improve children's learning skills, Thomas and her *Free to Be* crowd were hoping to do nothing less than shape the very ethos of a generation, thereby creating a more just, enlightened future. As Steinem later wrote of the project, "Civil rights, feminism, and other social justice movements were at last beginning to sift down into children's worlds. With *Free to Be . . . You and Me*, this went wide and deep." Thomas, Steinem, and their colleagues were setting their sights on a goal more lofty and ambitious than even Cooney and Morrisett's, and their success or failure would not be measurable until their test subjects reached adulthood.

— — —

Nonetheless, Thomas and her partners were women in a hurry, eager to get their record out in time for the 1972 holiday season. Thomas leveraged her connections—she had grown up in show business, the daughter of Danny Thomas, the star of the 1950s sitcom *Make Room for Daddy*—to rope in such A-list participants as Diana Ross, Mel Brooks, Harry Belafonte, and Alan Alda. Hart turned to her husband, Bruce, for title ideas. He suggested "Free to Be You and Me Jamboree." Carole liked it but thought it worked better truncated and assigned Bruce the task of writing the record's theme song. What he came up with, in tandem with the composer Stephen Lawrence, his frequent collaborator, was a recruitment ballad that used simple words to invite children into the new Utopia:

> *There's a land that I see*
> *Where the children are free.*
> *And I say it ain't far*
> *To this land from where we are.*

Lawrence conjured up the melody with a specific group in mind: the New Seekers, a UK-based soft-rock combo whose lead singer, Eve Graham, "had the perfect voice for the song, a gentle mid-range sound with an occasional touch of brass," he recalled. The New Seekers were at that point best known for their 1971 hit, "I'd Like to Teach the World to Sing (In Perfect Harmony)," a reworking of a jingle for Coca-Cola, "I'd Like to Buy the World a Coke," that proved so popular that it was expanded into a full-length song.

Like the Coke ad, whose TV version featured young men and women from all over the world assembled upon a bucolic Italian hilltop, "Free to Be . . . You and Me," the song, promised a better world than the one that old white men in power had gunked up with pollution and war. Lawrence, later to become a prolific composer for *Sesame Street* in the 1980s (writing the music for, among other songs, "If Moon Was Cookie" and "Fuzzy and Blue"), painted a vivid sound picture to match Hart's lyrics. He came up with a figure on his piano—TWANG-twanga-langa, TWANG-twanga-langa—that he reassigned to the banjo, which he thought had a more "invitational" quality. Eric Weissberg, best known for the "Dueling Banjos" song from the movie *Deliverance*, was brought in to do the honors.

After the banjo-led opening verses, the song pedaled furiously into its sugar-rush chorus ("In a *land* where the river runs free / In a *land* through the green country"), before settling gently on the tagline, "And you and me are free to be . . . you and me," with the final words awash in Beatles-style descending harmonies by the New Seekers. In a pointed bit of vocal arranging in the last verse, Eve Graham was assigned the line "Every boy in this land grows to be his own man," while Peter Doyle, the group's tenor, sang "In this land, every girl grows to be her own woman"—a demonstration that boys could take cues from women, and girls from men.

The Hart-Lawrence composition provided an inspirational framework for the rest of the album. Carole Hart reached out to Carol Hall, a singer-songwriter who later wrote the hit Broadway musical *The Best Little Whorehouse in Texas*, to bring some of the *Free to Be* brain trust's song ideas to fruition. Pursuant to Herb Gardner's expressed wish that someone had told him as a boy that it was acceptable for boys to cry, Hart decided to include a new story by the children's author Phil Ressner about a boy, Dudley Pippin, whose kindly male principal encouraged young Dudley to let out his tears. (On the album, the story was performed as a sketch, with the actor Robert Morse voicing Dudley.)

Hart asked Hall if she could write a companion song to the Dudley Pippin story. Hall, a single mother of two, went to her children's school and interviewed a classroom full of five-year-olds about the act of crying. One told her that "crying gets the sad out of you." Another said, "It's like raindrops from your eyes."

"I stole those lines and never looked back," Hall later remarked. She wrote a simple, sweet acoustic song called "It's Alright to Cry," which was enthusiastically accepted at the *Free to Be* headquarters. Bruce Hart, a die-hard fan of the New York Giants football team, suggested that the retired defensive tackle Rosey Grier, who had spent half of his pro career with the Giants and the other half as part of the Los Angeles Rams' famed Fearsome Foursome defensive line, might be just the guy to do justice to Hall's composition.

Grier was a Zelig-like figure in the late 1960s and early 1970s. In his capacity as an unofficial member of Robert F. Kennedy's security detail, he helped disarm Sirhan Sirhan after the latter fatally shot RFK in the kitchen of Los Angeles's Ambassador Hotel in 1968. While still playing football, Grier had begun to branch out into acting and singing, and in 1970 he became a series regular on *Make Room for Granddaddy*, Danny Thomas's short-lived sequel to his old TV program. Most memorably and significantly, Grier, in the early seventies, had taken to presenting himself as a new-paradigm manly man, appearing on talk shows to espouse the joys of his favorite hobby, needlepointing. On the dust jacket of his 1973 book, *Rosey Grier's Needlepoint for Men*, he wrote of his male detractors, "'Smile all you want,' I tell them, 'but if you try it once, you'll keep on coming back for more,' and that's the truth, brother."

In light of all this, Grier was happy to oblige the *Free to Be* team, asking only if they could put a beat under Hall's song. Lawrence recast the song as an R&B slow jam, with Grier talk-singing in his deep baritone and improvising a spoken kicker that was too good not to use: "It's alright to cry, little boy. I know some big boys that cry, too."

Hall's other major contribution to *Free to Be . . . You and Me* was an engagingly poppy duet between Thomas and Belafonte entitled "Parents Are People." Its central premise was that mommies and daddies, no matter their gender, could do "a lot of things." Mommies could be ranchers, taxi drivers, or doctors. Daddies could be cellists, painters, or, in a sly nod to Marlo Thomas's father, "funny joke tellers."

Thomas got her wish for a princess story that did not end in marriage. Betty Miles, one of the children's-book authors who had attended Gerry Lesser's 1968 seminars to help develop *Sesame Street*, adapted a story from Greek mythology about a fierce, fleet female hunter named Atalanta. In Miles's telling, narrated on the record by Thomas and Alda, the newly ascendant star of the hit CBS sitcom *M*A*S*H*, Atalanta was a hyperintelligent princess whose sexist-pig father, a king, determined that his daughter would marry the winner of a footrace that he was organizing. Atalanta insisted that she, too, be allowed to participate in the footrace, a condition that the king granted. Meanwhile, a principled villager named Young John took note of these local developments and thought to himself, "For surely, it is not right for Atalanta's father to give her away to the winner of the race. Atalanta herself must choose the person she wants to marry, or whether she wishes to marry at all."

Atalanta and Young John ended up outrunning their male competitors and crossing the finish line together. The king declared that Young John had proved himself worthy of "the prize," his daughter. But the principled Young John demurred, saying he had run the race simply "for the chance to talk with Atalanta." Atalanta and Young John proceeded to picnic together in a field, and they became fast friends. The following day, they set off on separate trips. At the story's end, Miles switched from the past to the present tense: "By this time, each of them has had wonderful adventures, and seen marvelous sights. Perhaps someday they will be married, and perhaps they will not. In any case, they are friends."

— — —

These songs and stories were a radical proposition for a children's anthology in 1972, a year before the Supreme Court ruled on *Roe v. Wade* (Miles's words "Atalanta herself must choose" carried an extra resonance) and also a year before the American Psychiatric Association's members voted to remove homosexuality from the APA's *Diagnostic and Statistical Manual of Mental Disorders*. For all the clout that Marlo Thomas carried in the entertainment industry, she and her colleagues had a hard time finding a major record label willing to take on *Free to Be ... You and Me*. Hart remembered one prominent music executive saying, "What would I want with a record produced by a bunch of dykes?"

Ironically, the most controversial of all the record's stories and bits was one of the few that came about as a result of Thomas's meeting with Ursula Nordstrom, the woman who purportedly belonged to another time. Just as the *Free to Be* project was getting underway, Nordstrom's longtime deputy at Harper & Row, the fifty-seven-year-old Charlotte Zolotow, herself a children's author, was about to come out with a new book, entitled *William's Doll*. Illustrated by William Pène du Bois, Zolotow's book told the story of a little boy, also named William, who, though he enjoyed such reassuringly heteronormative activities as shooting baskets and playing with his electric-train set, wished for a doll—and not just any doll but a doll with "blue eyes and curly eyelashes and a long white dress and a bonnet."

William's brother derided his wish as "creepy." The boy next door called him a sissy. William's father, deeply concerned, cried out, "Why does he need a doll?" William ultimately got his wish thanks to his beneficent grandmother, who bestowed the doll upon the boy and explained to his father that, through his doll play, William would benefit. "When he's a father like you," she said, "he'll know how to take care of his baby and feed him and love him and bring him the things he wants."

The *Free to Be* team liked the substance of Zolotow's book but found its tone "a bit too earnest for our purposes," as Hart put it. They turned to Sheldon Harnick, the lyricist for *Fiddler on the Roof*, and Mary Rodgers, who was not only a children's-book author but also, like her father, the Broadway legend Richard Rodgers, a talented composer.

Together, Harnick and Rodgers fashioned a three-minute, fifteen-second operetta of childhood trauma whose nyah-nyah chorus—of children cruelly chanting "A doll! A doll! William wants a doll!"—was destined to lodge itself in the brain of every boy and girl within listening distance. Alan Alda sang the narrator's part, Thomas sang William's, and, together, they sang the taunting chorus. The song concluded, as the book did, with William's grandma saving the day. She reassured William's father, "When he has a baby someday, he'll know how to dress it, put diapers on double, and gently caress it to bring up a bubble."

"William's Doll," the song, was a powerful statement on behalf of gender-neutral parenting. But its references to sissydom, even though they were framed unflatteringly, were bound to make some listeners uncomfortable. Any intimation of effeminacy in a boy was still widely regarded as troubling in the early seventies, and having a gay child was still often considered to be an outright family tragedy. One of the focal points of the serialized fly-on-the-wall documentary *An American Family*, filmed in 1971 and broadcast on PBS in 1973—attracting 10 million viewers and making the cover of *Newsweek*—was when Lance Loud, the eldest of five children in the affluent California family featured on the show, came out as gay, much to the consternation and befuddlement of his guy's-guy father, Bill Loud.

Even Pogrebin, while decrying in her "Down with Sexist Upbringing!" article the flawed notion that "superficial masculine and feminine identities and activities will prevent sexual confusion," quoted an expert, Dr. Robert E. Gould, the director of adolescent psychiatry at Bellevue Hospital in New York, who offered a retrograde explanation of homosexuality. While Gould tried to allay parental concerns that participating in "feminine" activities turned boys gay, he still stigmatized queerness (and undermined his own scientific authority) by telling Pogrebin, "Boys become homosexual because of disturbed family relationships, not because their parents allowed them to do so-called feminine things."

Thomas would later come to believe that "William's Doll" was, if anything, too timid, in that William's love for his doll didn't need to be rationalized as preparation for his presumably heterosexual adult life as a father. "Not everybody wants to be a daddy," she said. "That didn't need to be the reason why William wants a doll. It still had a little tip of a stereotype on it. But I didn't realize that until twenty years later."

In any event, *Free to Be . . . You and Me*, finding no takers among the major labels, was released in November of 1972 by Bell Records, a small subsidiary of Columbia Pictures Industries, with a modest first pressing of fifteen thousand copies. Attributed to Marlo Thomas and Friends, the album had a pink cover and the *Ms.* logo stamped on its front. Thomas did her best to hustle the LP, granting as many interviews as could be arranged.

Ms., in its November '72 issue, ran a house ad whose headline proclaimed, "LIBERATE LITTLE EARS!" "The sounds of sexism are all around us—and children are the first to hear them," read the copy. "Outmoded values and rigid sex roles have long been part of the singsong repertoire of childhood." The new album, by contrast, was "the very first record that is designed for use by children of all ages, colors, and sex, without being preachy or moralistic—a record that teaches human values by celebrating laughter, love, and freedom of choice."

— — —

To the surprise of nearly everyone involved, the album swiftly went gold, selling five hundred thousand copies in the United States, and then platinum within two years. The populace was more ready for *Free to Be* than the recording industry was, and the record received overwhelmingly positive reviews. As with *Sesame Street*, the loudest critical voices came not from the right but from the left, most of them targeting a sketch called "Housework," written by Sheldon Harnick and performed by the Broadway star Carol Channing.

A rhyming monologue intended to alert kids that TV ads for cleaning products were a sexist con—because, as Channing stated in a breathless rush, they featured actresses who were *paid* to smile as they extolled a certain "soap or detergent or cleanser or cleaner or powder or paste or wax or bleach"—"Housework" went off the rails as it neared its conclusion. "Remember," said Channing, "nobody smiles doing housework but those ladies you see on TV. Your mommy hates housework, your daddy hates housework, *I* hate housework, too. And when you grow up, so will you!"

Several women wrote in to *Ms.* complaining about the "Housework" sketch, noting that, as one reader put it, "it seemed too demeaning and insensitive" to those who actually derived satisfaction from doing housework, including cleaning women for whom housework was their livelihood. And though Channing's monologue was meant to de-gender the act of performing house-hold chores—at the very end, she told listeners that "when you're big husbands and wives ... make sure, when there's housework to do, that you do it together"—many parents protested that *Free to Be* was sending a message that housework was inherently hateful, something to be grudgingly endured.

This controversy proved to be a minor one, though. *Free to Be ... You and Me* sold so well that it was an unexpected financial boon to the newly formed Ms. Foundation for Women—established by Thomas, Steinem, Pogrebin, and Patricia Carbine to provide grants to women-led organizations and businesses—and to *Ms.* magazine itself, which, because of its unabashedly political, feminist content, had difficulty attracting big-ticket advertisers.

The next step was to extend *Free to Be* into other media, as a book and a TV special. While the self-assured Thomas saw these developments as the logical and inevitable progression from what was a brilliant and righteous idea to begin with, some of her peers couldn't get over the impact and reach of the now multimedia project. Francine Klagsbrun, who edited the book version of *Free to Be* for the Ms. Foundation in coordination with the McGraw-Hill Book Company, had shortly beforehand overseen the publication of *The First Ms. Reader*, an anthology of articles from the magazine's first year in business. Of the process of assembling the *Free to Be* book, Klagsbrun later wrote, "It was as though the serious and provocative essays I had gathered for *The First Ms. Reader* had danced off the pages of that book, rearranged themselves in color and song, and come back to teach children painlessly the achingly difficult lessons many of their mothers had struggled to learn. This children's book, I decided, was downright subversive, in the best sense of the word."

For the TV special, Thomas made a deal with her old network, ABC, and its then head of entertainment, Martin Starger, to produce a one-hour *Free to Be* special that would air in March of 1974. Most of the gang from the record album happily reconvened to perform their sketches and songs on camera.

This included Mel Brooks, who, with Thomas, voiced a pair of newborn babies—now fully realized as puppets with hairless, football-shaped heads, designed and operated by the puppeteer Wayland Flowers—who debated which baby was which gender. (Brooks: "I'm a little noivous, I don't know if I'm a girl or a boy yet.") Brooks's baby, in his Gold's Horseradish rasp, declared that he must be a girl, because he had dainty feet and wanted to be a cocktail waitress when he grew up. Thomas's baby, he said, must be a boy because she wanted to be a fireman. Only when a nurse came to change their diapers, and they got a good look at their genitals, did they come to recognize their genders. (Thomas took particular pleasure in exulting in this reveal, gasping with delight and saying, "Look at that! You see there? I *am* a girl!")

Thomas and Harry Belafonte, looking more beautiful than any two human beings had the right to be, reprised "Parents Are People" in locations throughout a gorgeously autumnal New York City, with Thomas appearing as a cabdriver, a hard-hatted construction worker, and a doctor, while Belafonte appeared as an ice-cream man, a baker, and a painter. "Atalanta" and "William's Doll" received full animations. The impact of "It's Alright to Cry" was enhanced by the very sight of Grier, massive in the widest of wing-collar shirts and a maroon leisure blazer, a guitar in his lap. "It's no accident," Thomas said, "that we got one of the biggest, blackest football players in the world to say, 'This is absolutely all right, for little boys to cry.'"

"Housework" was dropped from the TV version (and modified for the book to remove any mentions of "hate"), and, in an acknowledgment that the original album contained no contributions from black writers, the television special included an animation of "Three Wishes," a short story by the African American poet Lucille Clifton about a girl and boy, named Zenobia and Victorious, who bond over a lucky penny.

As credible as the *Free to Be* brand already was, Thomas encountered some pushback before the special made it to air. "I delivered it to the network, and they asked me, quite specifically, to take out Rosey Grier and 'William's Doll,' which they thought would turn every boy into a homosexual," she said. Thomas was also told that "Parents Are People" wouldn't fly in the South, because it included a scene where she and Belafonte were pushing matching baby carriages down Fifth Avenue—suggesting, possibly, that they were an interracial couple.

But Thomas held her ground. Starger convened a focus group of female secretaries at ABC, "women anywhere from their twenties to forties," Thomas said. "And they just loved it. They didn't have any problem with it."

The special was broadcast on March 11, 1974, without any of the demanded cuts, and with 27 percent of all televisions in the United States tuned in to it—a huge number for a prime-time program aimed at school-age children. Its credit sequence alone packed a wallop. Lawrence had reconfigured the title song to begin with a calliope before the banjo kicked in, and the show opened on a shot of a multiracial group of young kids (including Pogrebin's) atop horses on a carousel in Central Park. During the final chorus, the children transformed into animated kids whose horses came alive and stampeded off the carousel, flying upward and into an Arcadian landscape not dissimilar to the one inhabited by the man and the woman who had a little baby in *Schoolhouse Rock!*'s "Three Is a Magic Number."

— — —

Free to Be . . . You and Me represented the culmination of the children's-liberation movement. Its celebratory, inherently optimistic approach, which owed a considerable debt to *Sesame Street,* was an efficient delivery system for the mass distribution of what was, in effect, a revolutionary children's primer on feminism and gender politics. As Pogrebin described it, *Free to Be* was "not just a junior anthem of the women's movement but a lighthearted symbol of massive social change."

Indeed, the *Free to Be* phenomenon unfolded in a world that would have been unrecognizable from the vantage point of 1966, the year of the fateful Cooney-Morrisett dinner party. This was true both superficially—with Thomas and such stars of the TV special as the singer Kris Kristofferson literally letting their hair down, barely resembling their more straitlaced midsixties selves—and philosophically, with racial integration now a given (other guests on the special included Michael Jackson, Roberta Flack, Cicely Tyson, and Dionne Warwick) and a roster of songs and sketches unabashedly devoted to children's feelings: all this, just a handful of years after Senator John Pastore had received Fred Rogers's testimony as if it were a transmission from some exotic new psychological frontier.

Thomas, Carole Hart, and their program were showered with awards, most notably a Peabody and the 1974 Emmy for Outstanding Children's Special. But more significantly, *Free to Be . . . You and Me* slipped directly into the bloodstream of primary-school-aged children of the 1970s and 1980s. The LP was played repeatedly on home turntables, the book version was a bestseller, the songs became a staple of school assemblies and community theater, and the TV special was adapted for classroom use in 16 mm and filmstrip versions.

The cultural historian Lori Rotskoff has pointed out that even the sales and ratings figures don't tell the full story of the *Free to Be* phenomenon, because, to cite just one medium, "many children who did not own a copy of the record at home heard it replayed in schools and other social settings," making its influence "greater than those numbers alone suggest."

"I would argue that back then, because there were only seven TV channels and a few newspapers that smart people read, real change happened faster," said Pogrebin. "Because it was a shared culture." Indeed, Thomas's multimedia project caught on virtually everywhere in the United States: on the coasts and in interior big cities *and* in the traditionally conservative Deep South. In 1977, Pogrebin, in her capacity as a *Free to Be* adviser, was welcomed as a keynote speaker at a convention held in Shreveport, Louisiana, by the Southern Association on Children Under Six (SACUS), an organization devoted to improving children's education. SACUS's member states were Alabama, Arkansas, Florida, Georgia, Kentucky, Louisiana, Mississippi, North Carolina, South Carolina, Oklahoma, Tennessee, Texas, Virginia, and West Virginia.

Free to Be . . . You and Me, in its various formats, is arguably the most widely and warmly embraced artifact of progressive propaganda in United States history. "There was miraculous buy-in based on the perfectibility of humanity, which at that point was still believed in," said Pogrebin. "The Vietnam War wasn't over until 1975, basically. We were in the streets, taking our kids to Central

Park for demonstrations. I think that when there's that much fervor for change, it becomes a pattern for fixing other issues. The women's movement in the 1970s was replicating the methodology of the civil-rights movement and the anti-war movement. So now you have this third movement that is taking on the notion that you can change the world if everybody buys in: we can raise our children better than we've been doing it."

Such is the power of *Free to Be* that fifty years after it first came about, in an era decidedly more skeptical of "the perfectibility of humanity," its influence is still felt. "To this day, I get mail, or hear through my office, that a teacher has done some sort of program based on *Free to Be*," Thomas said.

What's more, her project has had unintended consequences that she and her collaborators never even anticipated. Despite the fears of its detractors, "William's Doll" didn't turn children into homosexuals. But, as Thomas learned decades later via multiple tearful testimonials from grown men, the song, along with "It's Alright to Cry," helped many a young gay boy achieve self-acceptance. The comedian and actor Billy Eichner, born in 1978, said that his first inkling that he might have a future, both as a performer and as a viable adult, came when he auditioned for a school production of *Free to Be . . . You and Me.* "I was singing 'It's Alright to Cry,'" he said, "and everyone turned around and was like, 'Whoa, this fat Jewish gay kid can really sing!'"

Abby Cadabby, Big Bird, and Elmo, citizens of the latter-day, tidied-up Sesame Street.

CHAPTER

NINETEEN

Sun Shot

There was no emphatic end to the sunny days, no single calamitous event that curbed the further development of artful educational television for children. In 1975, Maurice Sendak finally got into the children's-TV game in earnest with *Really Rosie*, an animated half-hour special that he wrote and directed, based on a collection of his illustrated books from the early 1960s. Carole King, whose 1971 album, *Tapestry*, was one of the best-selling LPs of the seventies, wrote the special's music and voiced its title character. *Really Rosie* received positive notices when it aired on CBS and was expanded into a stage musical that played multiple cities and enjoyed a fruitful second life as a staple of school productions.

As for *Sesame Street*, it moved from strength to strength in the 1970s, and reached the apogee of its capacity for innovation and daring in 1983, when the program was forced to reckon with the death of Will Lee, who played the street's kindly elder, Mr. Hooper.

Lee died unexpectedly of a heart attack on December 7, 1982, at the age of seventy-four. He had already taped several segments for the season in progress, so it was not until the 1983–84 season that CTW was compelled to address his absence, and to consider how it should be handled: by recasting the role, perhaps, or concocting a plotline in which Mr. Hooper had moved away. But the Workshop chose to address the subject head-on: *Sesame Street* viewers would learn that Mr. Hooper, like the actor who played him, was dead.

The broadcast date of the episode, on Thanksgiving Day 1983, was deliberately chosen to ensure that children watching at home had adults around them to answer any questions that they might have. Norman Stiles, the show's then head writer, came up with a complementary story line in which a baby had been born to neighbors down the street, the subject of much excited discussion among the show's grown-ups, Susan, Gordon, Bob, Maria, Luis, David, and Olivia. Happening upon this group, Big Bird presented each adult with a sketch that he had made of them. (The drawings were actually the work of the inhabitant of Big Bird's costume, Caroll Spinney.) Big Bird then held up his drawing of Mr. Hooper, eliciting compliments from everyone.

"I can't wait till he sees it," Big Bird said. An uncharacteristically tense and awkward silence followed.

It was Sonia Manzano's Maria who stood up to explain: "Uh, Big Bird, don't you remember what we told you? Mr. Hooper died. He's dead." The other cast members, speaking through real tears, took turns answering Big Bird's questions as he cycled through confusion, sadness, anger, and acceptance. Three segments later, at the episode's conclusion, Big Bird, having hung his portrait of Mr. Hooper above his nest, was greeted by Luis, who announced that the neighbors had brought by their new baby, a boy named Leandro, for a visit. Cheered by Leandro, Big Bird said, "You know what the nice thing is about new babies? Well, one day, they're not here, and the next day, here they are!"

This unflinching yet gentle handling of the subject of death demonstrated how far *Sesame Street* and attitudes toward it had traveled since 1969, when the *San Francisco Chronicle*'s TV reviewer had dismissed the show's pitch reel as "jabberwocky" and Loretta Long's parents had feared for her sanity when she told them that she would be working alongside a giant yellow bird. Now the yellow bird was a grief counselor, and Long noted that, for years afterward, she was greeted by grateful parents who told her, "Now we can explain what happened to Grandma or Grandpa."

— — —

But as the seventies progressed into the eighties, there was, overall, a gradual diminution in passion and urgency in the realm of smart TV for children. This was, at least in part, a consequence of generational turnover and how efficiently the better kids' programs had built up back catalogues of reusable work. Fred Rogers suspended production of *Mister Rogers' Neighborhood* in 1975. Though he was only forty-seven years old, Rogers had already more or less completed his life's work, having produced 455 half-hour episodes in color that PBS stations could broadcast to a new wave of young children who were none the wiser that they were watching "old" shows. Rogers reactivated the program in 1979, but at a production rate of only fifteen new episodes a year, versus the more taxing workload of sixty-five episodes a year that he had taken on in the late sixties and early seventies. The final season, consisting of just five new episodes, aired in 2001.

The Electric Company stopped making new episodes after the 1976–77 season, its sixth. For Joan Ganz Cooney, this was a difficult but necessary decision: she was facing pressure to cut budgets at CTW, and *The Electric Company*, unlike *Sesame Street*, wasn't approaching self-sustainability through the sales of records, books, and merchandise.

"Product tie-ins, unfortunately, are what killed *The Electric Company*," said Tom Whedon, the show's head writer. "Because the Workshop had the goose that laid golden eggs in *Sesame Street*. But they were at the point where they were afraid that public television couldn't afford two shows this expensive, and so they dropped *The Electric Company*. It's too bad, because we were way, way ahead of where we were in year one. We were getting better at actually teaching reading." *The Electric Company*'s final two seasons were explicitly conceived for repeat broadcasts, and, though the program closed up shop in 1977, it aired on PBS into the mid-eighties.

The success and cultural ubiquity of *Sesame Street* also masked a hard truth about CTW: that it never again approached the level of invention that it had with its first two programs. The Workshop's third original program, *Feelin' Good*, was a health-education show aimed at adults rather than children. Early on, in its developmental phase, it endured a PR crisis when rumors circulated among pro-life groups that the new show would offer information on abortion and, furthermore, that *Sesame Street* and *The Electric Company* would soon be including pro-abortion propaganda in their broadcasts.

These allegations were false. The Workshop, in the course of its usual painstaking show-preparation process, had held some seminars about public-health issues, one of which was devoted to family planning. A Planned Parenthood member who attended the family-planning seminar wrote in his organization's newsletter that some attendees had expressed pro-abortion views. "He led his readers to believe that family planning as a curriculum item on the series was a foregone conclusion," CTW reported in its March 8, 1974, newsletter. This wasn't the case, but the rumor mill went into overdrive, resulting in sensationalistic extrapolations by pro-life advocates and a statement from Cooney, issued under duress, declaring, "No plans have ever been discussed for treating such adult themes on the children's programs."

The bigger problem with *Feelin' Good* was that it never figured itself out tonally. Originally an hour-long sketch show set in a shopping-mall store called Mac's Place, with a cast that included the Broadway veterans Rex Everhart, Priscilla Lopez, and Joe Morton, it was an unwieldy mix of *Sesame Street*–style variety and earnest health-care tutorials. Eleven weeks into its run, *Feelin' Good* was reconceived as a half-hour program hosted by Dick Cavett, and, soon thereafter, it was gone from the airwaves.

CTW had better luck with two programs launched in the 1980s, the science show *3-2-1 Contact*, which lasted for seven seasons, and the mathematics show *Square One Television*, which lasted for five. But neither program captured the public's imagination or nailed the Zeitgeist as *Sesame Street* and *The Electric Company* had. By 2000, with these shows out of the picture, the Children's Television Workshop doubled down on its most successful and durable enterprise, rechristening itself Sesame Workshop.

— — —

In the commercial-TV sphere, the FCC's unenforced but reasonably effective prescriptions for broadcasters to offer programming of educational value to children were undone by the deregulatory philosophies of Ronald Reagan, who was sworn in as president of the United States in 1981. A few months after Reagan was inaugurated, he appointed as chairman of the FCC a communications lawyer and former campaign aide named Mark S. Fowler, a bomb-thrower who rolled his eyes at the very idea of TV's obligation to serve the public interest. He was, effectively, the anti–Newton Minow.

Fowler famously, and controversially, described the television set as nothing more than "a toaster with pictures," a consumer-electronics device with no moral imperative attached to it, no duty to serve the public. His goal, Fowler said, was not merely to deregulate the industry, as even some of his liberal predecessors had made moves to do, "but [to] *unregulate*, and that's the difference. We're going to finish the job."

Too often, Fowler declared, educational programming was an anti-commercial millstone, inhibiting broadcasting companies' ability to make money. "Broadcasters would often bury public-affairs and instructional programming in the so-called graveyard hours because it was a tune-out; nobody listened to it," he said in 1981. "This suggests to me that the public didn't particularly like the kind of programming the government mandated to serve 'the public interest.'"

Which programs did and didn't run on TV, Fowler said, should be determined by "the *public's* interest" rather than the public interest—the distinction being that the former was what the marketplace determined was popular, whereas the latter was what the government deemed necessary. If the marketplace demanded nothing more than a vast wasteland, then so be it; this wasn't an issue for the government to get mixed up in. In 1982, taking a cue from Fowler's FCC, the National Association of Broadcasters eliminated its voluntary code regarding the volume and kinds of advertising that should run during children's programs. In 1984, the FCC repealed its policy statement from a decade earlier that dictated that broadcasters "have a special obligation to serve children."

"That was the death knell of *The Magic Garden*," said Carole Demas. For all of their patchwork-denim, sixties-hangover datedness, the program's episodes, filmed entirely in the early seventies, remained a staple of WPIX's daytime rotation into the early 1980s, as did the similarly limited and dated episodes of *Joya's Fun School*; small children didn't care about the outmoded fashions and hairstyles. "We still had a good audience at that time," said Demas. "But a new programming director came on board and saw the opportunity for a show in our time slot that could run commercials and make money, and there was no more obligation. So goodbye." *The Magic Garden* left the airwaves in 1984, two years after *Joya's Fun School* did.

In the years that followed, children's TV programs based on toys proliferated, a reversal of the *Hot Wheels* controversy that had kick-started the development of *New Zoo Revue*. Among the new shows were *My Little Pony 'n Friends*, *Teenage Mutant Ninja Turtles*, *He-Man and the Masters of the Universe*, *The Transformers*, and the nominally more educational *Rubik, the Amazing Cube*, whose title character was voiced by Ron Palillo, the actor who played Horshack on the 1970s sitcom *Welcome Back, Kotter*.

Letty Cottin Pogrebin, who reviewed toys for *Ms.* in addition to children's books, noted a backslide into "gendered" marketing of these products: "Boys on active toys, girls on tea sets," she said.

Asked to ascribe this change to a specific event or phenomenon, she pantomimed slitting her throat and said, "Reagan. That was it. It couldn't have been clearer."

Though the White House was occupied by a Democrat, Jimmy Carter, in the late 1970s, the period saw a rise in the profile and power of the self-anointed New Right, a collection of political groups dedicated to a "family values" agenda that was anti-feminist, anti–Equal Rights Amendment, and anti-gay. In 1977, James Dobson, an evangelical leader with an atypical background for someone in his line of work—he had a doctorate in psychology from the University of Southern California and was the author of a pro-corporal-punishment parenting guide entitled *Dare to Discipline*—founded a conservative activist organization called Focus on the Family. Two years later, the New Right leaders Paul Weyrich, Richard Viguerie, and Howard Phillips teamed with the evangelical Baptist minister Jerry Falwell to found the Moral Majority, a group of similar intent. These groups mobilized behind Ronald Reagan's campaign, helping to elect a president sympathetic to their stances, which were antithetical to the pluralistic, progressive outlook of the CTW programs and *Free to Be . . . You and Me.*

Pogrebin recalls feeling the chill winds of change in 1977, when the National Women's Conference, an event held in Houston whose speakers included the then First Lady, Rosalynn Carter, as well as her predecessors Lady Bird Johnson and Betty Ford, along with several prominent feminist leaders, was upstaged by a counter-rally organized by the anti-ERA activist Phyllis Schlafly. "That was when we started to feel the pushback, the backlash," Pogrebin said. "Phyllis Schlafly sent busloads of women to Houston who said that we didn't respect the Bible and that women should be submissive to men." Indeed, Schlafly confidently declared to the gathered press, "Houston will finish off the women's movement. It will show them off for the radical, anti-family, pro-lesbian people that they are."

While this was a rabid overstatement, the ascension of Reagan to the presidency effectively spelled the end of the original sunny-days era. In his 1981 annual report for the Markle Foundation, Lloyd Morrisett gravely took note of how the political ground was shifting beneath his feet. "Increasing amounts of federal funds are no longer being directed towards new educational efforts," he wrote. "The flow of money that funded an advance in children's television has stopped. In addition, the current popular philosophy of deregulation has killed any hope that the FCC will mandate programming to serve children. Almost none of the forces that supported growth in quality television for children in 1969 remain strong." It was no longer so easy to sweep the clouds away.

"I was in a rather despairing mood," Morrisett said in 2019 of his mind-set in 1981. "We were worried about the future. I don't think we necessarily thought that we were at the end of the experiment, but we believed we were still very fragile."

— — —

The 1990s offered more hope, though. At the very beginning of the decade, the Children's Television Act, introduced in the House of Representatives in 1989 by Representative John Bryant, Democrat of Texas, became law. The law set caps on the amount of advertising that could run during children's-programming hours, and it required the FCC to police TV stations and cable providers, making sure that they logged and published summaries of the educational content that they were broadcasting.

This second component of the law was not especially effective—the FCC's oversight was lax, and stations got away with denoting their broadcasts of *The Flintstones* and *G.I. Joe* as "educational"—but the Children's Television Act fostered a new awareness of the need for better, smarter, more expressly educational TV programming for kids.

The nineties and early aughts saw a mini-renaissance of quality children's shows, among them Nickelodeon's *Blue's Clues* (1996) and *Dora the Explorer* (2000); the Disney Channel's *Bear in the Big Blue House* (1997), produced by the Jim Henson Company; and WGBH's *Between the Lions* (2000), a creation of the former *Sesame Street* writers Christopher Cerf, Norman Stiles, and Lou Berger. And in 1995, three years after she finally disbanded ACT, believing that it had run its course, Peggy Charren was awarded the Presidential Medal of Freedom by Bill Clinton for her contributions to the welfare of American children. Aptly, Cooney was accorded the same honor that same year.

Concurrently, the maturation of Generation X-ers into parents and unrelenting nostalgists precipitated reboots of many of the programs and stage shows they had held dear in their own childhoods—with varying results. *Zoom*, whose original version had ceased production in 1978, came back for a second run in 1999 that lasted until 2005. Gary William Friedman and Herb Schapiro reconvened to create a de facto sequel to *The Me Nobody Knows*, entitled *Bring In the Morning*, which opened Off Broadway in 1994. The old *Schoolhouse Rock!* gang of George Newall, Tom Yohe, and Bob Dorough got back together in the mid-1990s to create an eight-episode series called *Money Rock*, tutoring kids on financial management and how taxes worked. Later on, in 2009, *The Electric Company* was brought back by Sesame Workshop for a three-season run. The same year, the *Schoolhouse Rock!* team, minus Yohe, who had died in 2000, offered up one last round of educational shorts, an environmentalist series entitled *Earth Rock*.

With the exception of *Zoom*, which captured some of the raw, amateurish energy of its forebear, these reboots were generally underwhelming, unanimated by the zealous, amped-up campaigner's spirit that sparked the originals. Of *Earth Rock*, Newall said, "I don't think the level was quite up to the level of the original. I think we did some shitty songs. I know I did one."

— — —

With Fred Rogers's retirement in 2001 and his death in 2003, the one sunny-days program that has kept on chugging along uninterruptedly since its inception is *Sesame Street*. In recent decades, it has become a rite of passage, and a sign of one's arrival as a significant figure in American life, for famous actors, musicians, athletes, and political figures to appear on the show. A sampling of *Sesame Street* guests from the 1990s to the present includes Michelle Obama, Robert De Niro, Oprah Winfrey, Alicia Keys, Lin-Manuel Miranda, Julia Roberts, Elvis Costello, Venus Williams, David Beckham, Kobe Bryant, Hillary Clinton, Paul Rudd, Ice-T, Tina Fey, Sonia Sotomayor, Rebecca Lobo, Stephen Colbert, Ricky Gervais, Julia Louis-Dreyfus, and Natalie Portman.

But the *Sesame Street* that airs today is markedly different from the one that debuted in 1969. In 1990, Cooney relinquished her role as the chairman and CEO of the Workshop and was succeeded by a longtime CTW executive named David Britt. Jon Stone, who had always sought to promote from within, bristled at the infusion of outsiders that accompanied Britt's ascension, and at the changes that were imposed by the new executive team.

He was adamantly against CTW's decision in 1993 to expand the program's set, allowing for a new array of locations and characters "Around the Corner," to use the Workshop's term for the added real estate. The set extension was too gentrified for Stone's tastes, "looking more like the South Street Seaport than 127th Street," he complained. And, while he admired the actress Ruth Buzzi (a veteran of Cooney's beloved *Laugh-In*), he disliked Ruthie, the whimsical new Around the Corner character that she played, describing her as "the stereotypical kiddie-show character which we had so long eschewed."

Stone's beefs were partly a reflection of the intransigence of an employee who had probably stayed in one workplace for too long. *Sesame Street* was bound to evolve with the times, and it couldn't stay locked forever in the jivey, umber-colored early seventies. But there was indeed a sensibility shift afoot. In 1992, *Barney & Friends*, created by a Texas schoolteacher named Sheryl Leach, became the new darling of PBS. A massive ratings hit, albeit a scourge to intelligent parents everywhere, the program starred a dopey purple dinosaur who sang his cloying goodbye song ("I Love You") to the tune of "This Old Man."

Larry Rifkin, the executive at Connecticut Public Television who developed the show with Leach, said that the character appealed to him precisely because Barney "wasn't as neurotic as Big Bird." Barney was on TV primarily to cheer and entertain, not to teach or to help kids explore the idea, as Fred Rogers had put it decades earlier, that "feelings are mentionable and manageable."

— — —

Sesame Street remained head and shoulders in quality above any TV program for young children, but its production side did feel pressure, in Sonia Manzano's words, to "make the show more cutie-pie." The little red monster Muppet Elmo, a minor character through the first half of the 1980s, began to rocket in popularity after the puppeteer Richard Hunt grew tired of operating him and handed him off to his colleague Kevin Clash. Clash assigned Elmo a falsetto voice, a relentlessly cheery disposition, and a tendency to talk about himself, as toddlers sometimes do, in the third person ("Elmo loves his goldfish!").

In the late 1990s, after the Workshop's research department determined that the average viewing age of *Sesame Street* was getting lower, with more viewers than ever in the two-to-three range, it was decided that each episode would include a fifteen-minute show-within-a-show called *Elmo's World*. With its simple, crayon-drawn set and emotionally constant red blur of a host, *Elmo's World* was the most elemental that *Sesame Street* had ever been.

Elmo's World presaged an overall reconfiguration of the show, in which Muppets received increasingly more airtime than *Sesame Street*'s human cast did, with particular attention paid to newer Muppets such as Elmo, Zoe (a ballet-obsessed orange monster modeled on three-year-old girls, introduced in 1993), and Abby Cadabby (a winged fairy-in-training introduced in 2006). The expansion in the number of female Muppet characters on *Sesame Street* was long overdue, but the new characters lacked the esoteric verve and personality of their predecessors, and were more than a little cutie-pie.

In 2014, Sesame Workshop found itself operating at a loss of $11 million. Between the atomization of the media marketplace, a decline in the revenue brought in by old-fashioned soft toys and action figures, and the streaming revolution's obliteration of the home-video market, the nonprofit Workshop could no longer cover its high production costs. The following year, the Workshop cut a controversial deal: HBO would become the primary funder of *Sesame Street* for the next five years, eradicating the program's operating losses, on the condition that HBO had first dibs on releasing the latest episodes. PBS, covering about 10 percent of the show's budget, would be permitted to broadcast the new episodes nine months after their HBO debut.

The optics of this arrangement weren't great: a program created to benefit the poorest and most resource-deprived of America's children was now hosted by a premium cable and streaming service. But it was preferable to the alternative: a severely diminished *Sesame Street*, or even an extinct *Sesame Street*. Prior to the HBO deal, the Workshop had already cut back its production rate drastically. Relying heavily on its library of old clips, *Sesame Street* produced only twenty-six new episodes in the 2003 season, and in the years since, including those of the HBO era, the show has averaged just thirty-odd new episodes a season. Under the Workshop's latest deal with HBO, agreed upon in 2019, new episodes of *Sesame Street* will air exclusively on HBO Max, a digital-only streaming platform.

"We've been able to keep the budget within the bounds we can finance, but it's nothing like 130 hours," said Morrisett. "That just isn't in the cards. If you ask me, Do you think the federal government would step up to revive something like that? Not this government."

— — —

Sesame Street remains a laudable program. What it isn't, frequently, is particularly watchable—at least to longtime devotees like me. Now cut down to a half-hour format, the show is essentially

an expanded, extravagantly art-directed *Elmo's World*. The DNA
of the original program remains evident, especially in the design
and operation of the Muppets, which are still lovingly created in
New York (specifically in Long Island City, Queens) by employees
of the Jim Henson Company.

But the hipness, depth, and variety that made *Sesame Street*
transcend its intended audience of small children is no longer
there. Ernie, Bert, and Grover, among the program's most evolved
Muppet characters, are still present, but only as bit players.

To some degree, *Sesame Street* has become less a children's
show than, to use Stone's term, a kiddie show. Tellingly, the DVD
anthologies of *Sesame Street*'s first five seasons, from the hairy
years before CTW had put up its sensitivity guardrails, are mar-
keted toward adults rather than to children, as a pure nostalgia
watch. A disclaimer at the beginning of the anthologies states,
"These early *Sesame Street* episodes are intended for grown-ups
and may not suit the needs of today's preschool child." (Anec-
dotal evidence involving latter-day preschoolers' exposure to these
DVDs indicates that this disclaimer is bosh.)

But then, consider HBO's incentive to invest in *Sesame Street*:
that the program is still, after all these years, the gold standard of
what children's television is capable of. Even if the show has lost
some of its relevance, it has not lost its luster. Nor has the Workshop lost its bravery or sense of mission on the humanity front. In
2002, the South African and Nigerian versions of *Sesame Street*
introduced a female Muppet, named Kami, who is HIV-positive
as a result of a tainted blood transfusion. In 2011, the U.S. show
introduced a Muppet named Lily, who struggles with hunger because her family lacks the resources to feed her consistently; Lily's
narrative was expanded in 2018 to reveal that she was now also

homeless, with her family making do by staying with friends. In 2013, in a home video entitled *Little Children, Big Challenges: Incarceration*, a blue-haired little-boy Muppet named Alex hung his head as he told his peers, sheepishly, that his father is in prison. In 2017, the U.S. version of *Sesame Street* added a new Muppet character to its cast of regulars, a flame-haired four-year-old girl with green eyes named Julia, who is autistic. And in 2019, in a new online video series, the Workshop introduced a furry green monster Muppet named Karli whose mother "was away for a while because she had a grown-up problem" (i.e., drug addiction).

Taken together, these developments might read like parody, a methodical ticking of every box on the bleeding-heart liberal's checklist. But the new story lines actually hearken back to *Sesame Street*'s origins as a program for the marginalized and disadvantaged—and to the empathy that motivated Cooney and Morrisett to put themselves through their grueling paces in the first place. The Workshop's unending quest to identify the difficulties that children go through, and to address them through research, cheeriness, humor, and song, is unique in the realm of entertainment. No other effort on children's behalf has come close to matching CTW's work.

I can attest firsthand to the benefits of the Workshop's thoroughgoing efforts to cover all the bases of childhood. When the elder of my two children was three years old, an MRI revealed a tumor in her brain that needed to be removed surgically. The hardest part of the experience, apart from the shock of receiving the news, was figuring out how to explain to a three-year-old why she was going to spend the better part of a week in the hospital, and what being in the hospital would be like. Fortunately, there was a VHS home video (this was the late 1990s) entitled *Sesame Street*

Visits the Hospital. Written by Manzano, the video detailed how Big Bird was admitted to the hospital to have his tonsils removed, how he overcame his fears, how parts of the hospital experience were boring (Christopher Cerf wrote a calypso-style number, sung by Maria and an orderly named Jim, whose lyrical hook was "You gotta be patient to be a patient"), and how everything turned out okay in the end.

We watched the video with our girl repeatedly in the week before the surgery, and it did the work it was supposed to do—it gave my wife and me the vocabulary and reference points to explain to our little child what was going on. It also gave us some songs to sing to her. And everything turned out okay in the end.

— — —

It would be facile to end this book on a note of disillusionment: to point out that *Sesame Street, Free to Be . . . You and Me,* and *Schoolhouse Rock!* did not solve inequities in education and quality of life, and that there is still no Equal Rights Amendment, and that many of the ideologies and messages advanced by these programs are now derided by a segment of the population as emasculating and naive.

But just because a series of insanely ambitious projects fell short of their goals doesn't mean that they failed. Bob McGrath recounted to me how he has frequently been told by adult black men, through tears, that *he* was the father figure of their childhood. "You stop to think about that, for all of the cast," he said. "I'm sure we've all been mothers and fathers to millions of kids who either didn't have one or had very bad ones. That still gets to me."

The creators of and participants in *Sesame Street* and its ilk were not infallible. Jon Stone could be as prickly as he was brilliant, and his marriage to Beverley Stone fell apart. So did Jim Henson's marriage to Jane Henson. So did Matt Robinson's to Dolores Robinson. So did Joan Ganz Cooney's to Tim Cooney. And while Joan Cooney is fond of saying that *Sesame Street*'s journey was stalked by good luck, some of its central figures encountered tragic fates—or, perhaps, the arduous creation and perpetuation of the program took an untold toll on them. Joe Raposo died way before his time, at the age of fifty-one in 1989, of non-Hodgkin's lymphoma. A year later, Henson died at the age of fifty-three of a bacterial infection. And Stone was felled by amyotrophic lateral sclerosis, or Lou Gehrig's disease, at the age of sixty-four in 1997.

But for all their frailties, these were extraordinary people. The world would be a harsher, less tolerant place without their contributions. I prefer to regard the sunny days of late sixties and early seventies children's culture not as a failed epoch but, rather, as an inspirational example of what humanity is capable of when it extends its reach: the potential, latent but still present in us today, to accomplish inconceivably great things. The sunny-days era happens to have coincided with the flight phase of NASA's Apollo program: just four months before *Sesame Street*'s November 1969 premiere, the Apollo 11 mission realized John F. Kennedy's almost recklessly ambitious 1961 pledge to reach the moon before the decade was over.

Cooney, when I met with her, reflected, with some degree of astonishment, upon her own reckless ambition. "I was born to do this job," she said. "That's what I said to Lloyd when he asked, 'Can you be married and do this job, something that will take this kind of time?' I said, 'Lloyd, I was *born to do this job*.' And I knew I was. I knew we would succeed. It was just as clear to me as could be.

It's strange looking back, how arrogant I was. Why didn't someone slap me down?"

The answer is that Cooney, like the stolid Apollo astronauts and engineers, had the strength and vision to persist no matter the obstacles, and no matter how long the odds. Just as returning to the moon is not a question of logistics but of will, so is the idea of creating something new for children that will be as great as *Sesame Street*. Except it won't be a moon shot; it will be a sun shot.

ACKNOWLEDGMENTS

I am grateful to everyone who granted me an interview during the reporting process of this book. Loretta Long, Bob Mc-Grath, Sonia Manzano, Emilio Delgado, and Rita Moreno—you have *no idea* what a life event it was to meet each of you in person. Profuse thanks are also due to Joan Ganz Cooney, Lloyd Morrisett, and Newton Minow for their patience with me and their sharp recall of events that transpired more than fifty years ago.

Let me also thank, for talking, facilitating connections, and/or helping me out in other ways, the following people: Jill Cunniff, Lois Cunniff, Carole Demas, Crescent Dragonwagon, Billy Eichner, Trey Ellis, Naomi Foner, Gary William Friedman, Sam Gibbon, Robert Douglas Grant (R.I.P.), Ben Greenman, Cheryl Henson, Stephen Jahn, Paula Janis, Steve Joseph, Evelyn Kaye, Gregory Kiss, Stephen Lawrence, Naomi Levinson, Sandra Lindsey, Betsy Loredo, Leon Mobley, Doug Momary, George Newall, Frank Oz, Abby Pogrebin, Letty Cottin Pogrebin, Robin Pogrebin, April Reign, Dolores Robinson, Matt Robinson Jr., Alexis Rosenzweig, Christopher Sarson, Mark Schapiro, Fred Silverman, Dulcy

Singer, Beverley Stone, Polly Stone, Don Terry, Marlo Thomas, Pam Webber, Tom Whedon (R.I.P.), Janet Wolf, Norton Wright, Eli Yamin, and Bernadette Yao. A big tip of the hat to Kathryn A. Ostrovsky for sharing with me her inventive and insightful doctoral dissertation, "An Aural History of the 1970s Through the Sounds of *Sesame Street*."

Librarians and archivists are unsung heroes of our society who deserve more public recognition and exaltation (and better pay). So, all due high praise for Emily Uhrin at the Fred Rogers Center at St. Vincent College in Latrobe, Pennsylvania; Mike Henry and his colleagues at the University of Maryland's Special Collections and University Archives in the Hornbake Library in College Park, Maryland; and Karen Falk and Susie Tofte at the Jim Henson Company in Long Island City, New York.

At Simon & Schuster, thanks to Jonathan Karp for believing in the idea for this book, to Emily Graff for gently and wisely guiding it to realization, and to Lashanda Anakwah for pushing it past the finish line. Thanks also to Marie Florio, Elizabeth Gay, Felice Javit, David Litman, Richard Rhorer, Elise Ringo, and Lewelin Polanco.

At the William Morris Endeavor agency, thanks to Suzanne Gluck, Andrea Blatt, and Clio Seraphim.

Thanks to Adam Nadler for copyediting, Abby Field Gerry and Marion Rosenfeld for research assistance, and Mark Jacobson for photo research. Thanks to Andrew Corsello and Don MacKinnon for being supportive early readers. Thanks to Joe McKendry for the stoop illustration. Thanks to Ahmir Thompson for his thoughtful foreword.

Thank you to my sister and brother, Alice and Ted, for being cultural trailblazers, enabling their youngest sibling to pretend to have fluency in events that predated his birth. Thank you to my late father, Seymour Kamp, for cheerfully countenancing the utterly 1970s upbringing of his children despite being an utterly 1940s guy. Thank you to my children, Lily and Henry, for reawakening the child in me—with, arguably, embarrassing consequences for them. Thank you especially to Aimée Bell, my wife, for everything. I don't mean "everything" in some abstract, generic sense—I mean for every single thing she does, in every facet of our lives together.

Finally, I'd like to thank my mother, Lola Kamp, to whom this book is dedicated. She embodies the values of the sunny days written about herein. What's more, she has never wavered from them, remaining as active as ever in her advocacy for human rights, civil rights, women's rights, fairness, kindness, and equality. Like her fellow appreciator of things green, Kermit, she pursues these goals with lightness rather than solemnity—an ideal model for her children and grandchildren.

NOTES ON SOURCES

Most, though not all, of the individuals quoted in this book were interviewed by me. I interviewed Lloyd Morrisett twice, in 2017 and 2019, and his partner in founding the Children's Television Workshop, Joan Ganz Cooney, once, in 2018. That said, I have also drawn upon interviews that my sources gave to other writers and interlocutors. For example, Morrisett and Cooney were interviewed extensively by Michael Davis for his authoritative book *Street Gang: The Complete History of Sesame Street* (New York: Viking, 2008), which will be referred to as "Davis" after first reference. Morrisett and Cooney also downloaded their thoughts and life experiences for the Television Academy Foundation's impressive video series *The Interviews: An Oral History of Television*. These will be referred to as "Television Academy Foundation" after first reference. Morrisett and Cooney did the same for the Carnegie Corporation's oral-history interview series, which is held by Columbia University and will be referred to as "Carnegie Corporation" after first reference.

Gerald S. Lesser's *Children and Television: Lessons from Sesame Street* (New York: Random House, 1974) will be referred to as "Lesser" after first reference.

Jon Stone, who passed away in 1997, left behind a manuscript for a memoir that was never published. He completed the book, entitled *The Road to Sesame Street*, not long before his death. His daughter, Polly, was kind enough to entrust me with a copy. Most of the quotations attributed to Jon Stone in *Sunny Days* come from this manuscript, which was written in a loose, conversational tone that, his daughter says, accurately captures his voice. It will be referred to as "Stone" after first reference.

I also leaned heavily upon the following archives:

Children's Television Workshop Archives, Special Collections in Mass Media and Culture, Hornbake Library, University of Maryland, College Park, Maryland (referred to as "CTW Archives" after first notation).

Fred Rogers Archives, Fred Rogers Center, St. Vincent College, Latrobe, Pennsylvania (referred to as "Fred Rogers Archives" after first notation).

The Jim Henson Company Archives, Long Island City, New York (referred to as "Henson Company Archives" after first notation).

INTRODUCTION

xii   *"I doubt whether I shall live"*: Edward Robb Ellis (1911–98) was "the most prolific diarist in the history of American letters," according to NPR. This entry comes from Box 13 of the Edward Robb Ellis Papers at the Fales Library and Special Collections at New York University.

xiv   *"The place is in the unavoidable present"*: Stefan Kanfer, "Who's Afraid of Big, Bad TV?," *Time*, November 23, 1970.

xiv   *"I said to my mom"*: Author interview with Loretta Long, 2017.

xv   *"None of us was going to get rich"*: Jon Stone, *The Road to Sesame Street*, 122.

xv   *"human wealth"*: Author interview with Lloyd Morrisett, 2017.

xix   *"stalked by good luck"*: Author interview with Joan Ganz Cooney, 2018. (Though Cooney has been using this phrase for years.)

CHAPTER ONE

3   *"My big interest . . . from the beginning"*: Author interview with Newton Minow, 2017.

4   *"When I was a child"*: Author interview with Minow. Robert F. Kennedy used similar rhetoric in his speeches in the early 1960s.

5   John Bartlow Martin's reports on the state of TV were published in the autumn of 1961 in the *Saturday Evening Post* as "Television USA: Wasteland or Wonderland? A Famous Writer's Close-up Report on the Controversial State of TV," October 21, 1961, and "Television USA: The Big Squeeze," November 11, 1961.

6   *"To which I would say"*: Author interview with Minow.

7   *"I became a very looked-down-upon person"*: Author interview with Cooney.

9   *"Yes, I know, but I've seen enough"*: "Interview: Mr. Fred Rogers," *The Wittenburg Door*, June/July 1977.

10   *"hiring handsome but mute men"*: William Gill, "Around the Corner," *The Pittsburgh Press*, December 11, 1960.

10   *"I think it was then"*: Ibid.

11   *"I don't know why"*: "Interview: Mr. Fred Rogers," *The Wittenburg Door*, June/July 1977.

14   Carl Hovland's work for the OSS is chronicled in Timothy Glander's *Origins of Mass Communications Research During the American Cold War* (Mahwah, NJ: Lawrence Erlbaum Associates, 2000), 95; John Gardner's is chronicled in Richard Harris Smith's *OSS: The Secret History of America's First Central Intelligence Agency* (Berkeley: University of California Press, 1972), 26.

15   *"We found that too many children"*: Author interview with Morrisett.

16   The statistics about American nursery schools, and the lack thereof in the 1960s, come from the National Center for Education Statistics' 1970 survey of enrollment of three-, four-, and five-year-olds in preprimary programs, and from CTW's own promotional booklet that it published prior to *Sesame Street*'s premiere, itself simply entitled *Sesame Street*, which I viewed at the Henson Company Archives.

17   *"The reality of what we found"*: Author interview with Carole Demas and Paula Janis, 2016.

21   The Morrisett-Cooney dinner party was described to me by both Lloyd Morrisett and Joan Ganz Cooney, and is also recounted in detail in Michael Davis, *Street Gang: The Complete History of Sesame Street* (New York: Viking, 2008), and in the Television Academy Foundation's *The Interviews: An Oral History of Television*.

CHAPTER TWO

23   *"A number of our staff members felt"*: Author interview with Morrisett.

24   *"And whether it was"*: Cooney, in the Carnegie Corporation's oral-history interview series.

24   *"The real question behind that title was"*: Ibid.

25   *"Friday morning"*: Stone, 61.

26   *"milky turquoise"*: This and other details of Henson's early life and professional ascent come from Brian Jay Jones's *Jim Henson: The Biography* (New York: Ballantine Books, 2013). And much of Henson's early work—on TV programs, in advertisements, and in short films—is available on the Jim Henson Company's YouTube channel.

29   The Cinderella ordeal is described both in Jones's book and Stone's memoir.

CHAPTER THREE

35 *"good books for bad children"*: Leonard S. Marcus, *Dear Genius: The Letters of Ursula Nordstrom* (New York: HarperCollins, 1998), 64. This line comes up in a letter that Nordstrom wrote in 1953 to the children's author Meindert DeJong, after she had turned down an offer from Harper management to be "promoted" to its adult-books division. Nordstrom's letters, as collected by Marcus, provide wonderful insight both into the woman herself and the books she published.

36 *"My great curiosity"*: Maurice Sendak as quoted by Selma Lanes in *The Art of Maurice Sendak* (New York: Harry N. Abrams, 1998).

37 *"Where the signposts clearly pointed out a choice"*: Stone, 16. In his memoir, Stone writes at length about his admiration for Bob Keeshan, as well as his grievances toward his complicated mentor.

CHAPTER FOUR

39 I was able to view some footage of *The Children's Corner* at the Fred Rogers Archive in Latrobe, where a few episodes have been transferred to digital format. The show is a bizarre, enchanting specimen of early local television, remarkable in its spirit and resourcefulness, especially given its nearly nonexistent budget.

42 *"I'm more convinced than ever"*: Rogers in a letter to his parents on Hotel Pierre stationery, July 29, 1955. From the Fred Rogers Archives. Quoted with permission of the McFeely-Rogers Foundation.

43 *"to promote the intellectual and cultural growth"*: Joan Cooney, "Television for Preschool Children: A Proposal" (New York: Children's Television Workshop, 1968).

43 Nordstrom's sexuality is examined thoughtfully in Kelly Blewett's essay "Ursula Nordstrom and the Queer History of the Children's Book," published in the *Los Angeles Review of Books*, August 28, 2016.

44   *"This isn't for us"*: Author interview with Cooney. Again, it's another of her stories oft told, and versions of it exist in several interviews.

44   For anyone looking for a deeper dive into how Morrisett and Cooney raised the initial funds for *Sesame Street* and the Children's Television Workshop—a process I've vastly simplified here—I recommend Davis, 105–29.

46   *"I'm putting together a children's show"*: Stone, 71, and author interview with Beverley Stone, 2016.

CHAPTER FIVE

49   The details of Jon Stone's transformation come from his memoir as well as the recollections of his ex-wife, Beverley, and his daughter, Polly, both of whom I interviewed in 2016.

51   *"was not aimed solely at minority or inner-city children"*: Cooney, Television Academy Foundation.

51   *"I had never heard anyone involved"*: Stone, 74.

51   *"probably the best children's-material writer"*: Cooney recalling Gibbon's words, Television Academy Foundation.

52   *"I said, 'I feel as though I should do something more'"*: Author interview with Sam Gibbon, 2018.

53   *"what was left: the shape of the show to come"*: Stone, 88.

53   *"was in the assumption that a teacher"*: Stone, 73.

54   *"I think he had the same sense of play"*: Author interview with Frank Oz, 2018.

55   *"It was like 'Hmmm, here are a bunch of blocks'"*: Author interview with Cheryl Henson. Cheryl is the president of the Jim Henson Foundation, which advances and celebrates the art of puppetry, and is an especially thoughtful explicator of her parents' art, child-rearing habits, and motivations.

55   Further insight into Jim and Jane Henson's involvement in the Mead School was derived from Karen Falk and Karen Frederick, "Jim and Jane Henson Create the Muppets and More," *Connecticut Explored*, fall 2017.

56 *"Jim knew that deep within kids"*: Author interview with Norton Wright, 2018.

57 *"was filled floor-to-ceiling with"*: Stone, 113.

57 *"I joined Jim when I was nineteen"*: Author interview with Oz.

58 *"It was like this breeze coming through"*: Author interview with Long.

58 *"Schmaltz, 1920s, oompah Bavarian"*: Stone, 138.

59 *"Most geniuses, I have found"*: Cooney, Television Academy Foundation.

59 *"I am positive"*: Stone, 122.

60 *"Dave Connell and I were sitting up front"*: Author interview with Cooney. This tale of Cooney's initial fearfulness of the bearded man—Jim Henson—is another one that she has often told at her own expense.

61 *"any creative product must be conceived intuitively"*: Gerald S. Lesser, *Children and Television: Lessons from Sesame Street* (New York: Random House, 1974), 54.

61 *"Will you guys please speak English?"*: Author interview with Cooney. Also recounted in Lesser, *Children and Television*.

61 *"The drawings were incisive"*: Stone, 82–83.

61 *"maybe, just maybe"*: Author interview with Cooney.

62 The ups and downs of the 1968 seminars, and their ultimately fruitful outcome, are chronicled with candor by Lesser in his book *Children and Television: Lessons from Sesame Street*.

CHAPTER SIX

65 *"with a very special ordination"*: "Interview: Mr. Fred Rogers," *The Wittenburg Door*, June/July 1977, 10.

65 I was able to watch some episodes of *Misterogers*, Rogers's fifteen-minute show for the CBC, at the Fred Rogers Archives. Fred was new to the camera, but a natural from the start.

66 *"I am anxious to make a lasting contribution"*: "MISTEROGERS' NEIGHBORHOOD: Proposal for a Children's Television Project,

Submitted by WQED Pittsburgh," November 1964, from Fred Rogers Archives.

67   Rogers's working relationship with Margaret McFarland has been chronicled in many publications. I relied primarily on Sally Ann Flecker, "When Fred Met Margaret," *Pitt Med*, winter 2014; Rogers's own recollections of McFarland in "Interview: Mr. Fred Rogers," *The Wittenburg Door*, June/July 1977; and the Margaret McFarland page on the official misterrogers.org website.

69   Rogers spoke extensively over the years about the care he put into his episodes about children and their bodily fluids. His striking tale of intuiting a correlation of a girl viewer's fear of the factory fire depicted on his program with her own toilet-training issues comes from his 1977 interview with *The Wittenburg Door*.

70   *"clowns and cartoons and too much noise"*: Johnny Costa as interviewed in 1973 in Volume 1, Edition 8, of *Around the Neighborhood*, a newsletter published for a time by Rogers's production company, Family Communications.

70   *"He wrote kid songs, but"*: Liner notes from the album *It's You I Like*, John Ellis, Criss Cross Jazz, 2012.

71   *"little wimpy thing"*: from the album *National Lampoon: That's Not Funny, That's Sick*, Label 21, 1977.

72   *"a plea not to leave the children isolated"*: from Rogers's speech to the National Symposium on Children and Television in Chicago, 1971. This speech is quoted more fully in Maxwell King, *The Good Neighbor: The Life and Work of Fred Rogers* (New York: Abrams Press, 2018).

73   *"Every night, the TV set brought you bad news"*: Cooney, Carnegie Corporation.

CHAPTER SEVEN

76   *"It is one thing to be liberal and talk"*: Herbert Kohl, *36 Children* (New York: Signet, 1967), 13.

76   *"It was the easiest job in the world"*: Author interview with Steve

Joseph, 2016. I interviewed Joseph a second time in 2018. His recollections of *The Me Nobody Knows* and its genesis come from both of these conversations.

78 *"The good kids never made any mistakes"*: Author interview with Naomi Levinson, 2017.

80 The children's poems and essay fragments come from *The Me Nobody Knows: Children's Voices of the Ghetto* (Lincoln, NE: iUniverse, 2004), edited by Stephen Joseph; the original version was published by Avon in 1969.

80 *"a book for teachers, children, and for all"*: Julius Lester, "A Visible/ Invisible Minority: The Me Nobody Knows," *New York Times*, February 16, 1969.

81 Though other ads survive from the Urban Coalition's "Send Your Kid to a Ghetto for the Summer," I was unable to locate a viewable version of the one that inspired Stone. It is described in detail, however, both in Davis, 154, and in "Commercials: The Spoilers," *Time*, November 15, 1968.

81 *"For a pre-school Harlem child"*: Stone, 126.

82 *"She listened intently"*: Stone, 128.

83 *"I was determined that our neighborhood"*: Ibid.

83 *"you could solve all the problems in the world"*: Author interview with Mark Schapiro, 2018.

84 *"a ghetto Under Milk Wood"*: Miriam Friend, "Show's Saga: Slum School to Hit," *The Princeton Packet*, July 22, 1970.

85 The genesis of *The Me Nobody Knows* as a show was described to me by Herb Schapiro's two sons, Mark Schapiro and Gregory Kiss, as well as by Gary William Friedman and Steve Joseph.

85 *"I loved it. I loved its understanding"*: Clive Barnes, "Stage: Vivid and Honest; 'Me Nobody Knows,' a Musical, Bows," *New York Times*, May 19, 1970.

86 *"The Me Nobody Knows gets it all across"*: John Simon, "Theatre Chronicle," *Hudson Review*, winter 1970–71.

87 *"one of the few people who raised the idea"*: Author interview with Steve Joseph.

CHANGE CHAPTER EIGHT

89 *"the inner-city ghetto"*: Joan Ganz Cooney, "Sesame Street at Five: The Changing Look of a Perpetual Experiment" (New York: Children's Television Workshop, 1974).

90 I drew upon various internal CTW memos and clippings pertaining to the development and implementation of the Workshop's Department of Utilization that were found in Boxes 2, 32, 45, 219, 224, 229, 230, and 238 of the CTW Archives.

91 *"We didn't find many being thrown away"*: Evelyn Davis as quoted in Herman W. Land, "The Children's Television Workshop: How and Why It Works" (Jericho, New York: Nassau Board of Cooperative Educational Services, 1972). Land's study provides great real-time insight into *Sesame Street* as it was in its early "experimental" years, with compelling quotes from Cooney, Davis, and Stone.

92 *"the Czarina of Watts"*: Memo from George Broadfield to Evelyn Davis, August 19, 1970, Box 238, CTW Archives.

92 *"It took quite a bit of convincing"*: Author interview with Sandra Lindsey, 2019.

93 *"Joan Baez types"*: Author interview with Loretta Long.

96 *"I felt immediately that this was where I wanted to be"*: Author interview with Bob McGrath, 2018.

97 *"Big Bird had to be totally re-dyed"*: Author interview with Long.

97 *"When we first tested four-year-old black children"*: Author interview with Naomi Foner, 2019.

98 *"The black children in my class feel very good"*: "First Impact Studies," *Children's Television Workshop Newsletter*, February 9, 1970, Henson Company Archives.

98 Sonia Manzano chronicles the difficulties of her childhood and her time at Carnegie Mellon in her memoir, *Becoming Maria: Love and Chaos in the South Bronx* (New York: Scholastic Press, 2015).

98 *"It was just such a shocking image"*: Author interview with Sonia Manzano, 2018.

CHAPTER NINE

101　The *Sesame Street* pitch reel is viewable on YouTube. Rowlf and Kermit were a good team, broken up too soon.

104　*"The excerpts shown were foolish grotesques"*: Terrance O'Flaherty, "'J' Is for Junk," *San Francisco Chronicle*, May 8, 1969.

105　*"A lot of what the programs create is really art"*: Renata Adler, "Cookie, Oscar, Grover, Herry, Ernie, and Company," *The New Yorker*, May 27, 1972.

106　*"the closest thing we have to a childhood songbook"*: Lin-Manuel Miranda as quoted in Melena Ryzik, "How 'Sesame Street' Started a Musical Revolution," the *New York Times*, August 22, 2019.

108　*"Fuck, they did it"*: Steve Martin, *Born Standing Up: A Comic's Life* (New York: Scribner, 2007), 166.

108　*"the greatest thing that ever happened to television"*: Orson Welles's comment was noted in the *Children's Television Workshop Newsletter*, December 31, 1970, CTW Archives.

108　*"destroyed God knows how much writing"*: George Plimpton as quoted in W. Stewart Pinkerton Jr., "How 'Cookie Monster' Destroys Work Habits of George Plimpton," *Wall Street Journal*, April 22, 1971.

109　*"We watched it at Keeshan's shop"*: Author interview with Norton Wright.

110　*"Adults falling down stairs"*: "Interview: Mr. Fred Rogers," *Wittenburg Door*, June/July 1977. In the same interview, Rogers spoke of the virtues of his being, in contrast to other children's programming, "not fast paced."

110　*"unhip"*: On July 5, 2018, Frank Oz tweeted, via his @TheFrankOz Jam account, "CONFESSION: In my 20's I joked about 'Mr. Roger's Neighborhood' being so bland and 'kidsy' and 'unhip.' Then years later when life became more complicated and I was battling my inner demons, I would watch him because he would always make me feel better about myself."

110   *"We made fun of him"*: Author interview with Sonia Manzano.

110   *"The puppet part"*: Author interview with Tom Whedon, 2010. Whedon passed away in 2016.

111   *"I certainly knew about and had watched Fred Rogers"*: Author interview with Joan Ganz Cooney.

111   *"Fred did something so spectacular"*: Author interview with Rita Moreno, 2019.

111   *"I was in the makeup room"*: Author interview with Bob McGrath.

112   *This Way to Sesame Street* is viewable on YouTube.

113   *"This finding has important implications"*: The ETS report was summarized and quoted from in Andrew H. Malcolm, "'Sesame Street' Rated Excellent," *New York Times*, November 5, 1970.

113   *"Besides the knowledge about letters and numbers"*: "If Kids Act Smarter, 'Sesame Street' May Be the Reason," *Nation's Schools*, March 1971.

CHAPTER TEN

116   *"disaster areas"*: Palmer as quoted in John Mathews, "Sesame Street a Hit but Doubts Remain," *The Washington Star*, January 12, 1970.

116   Memorandums concerning the itinerary and logistics of the 1970 *Sesame Street* cast tour may be found in Box 238 of the CTW Archives. The breakdown of the audiences' racial makeup is in an internal memo dated November 2, 1970, by CTW's Susan Greene entitled "Evaluation of Sesame Street Cast Tour by Steering Committee Chairmen."

116   *"When Big Bird came out"*: Author interview with Sandra Lindsey.

117   *"In Los Angeles, we had two or three thousand kids"*: Author interview with McGrath.

117   *"to further the meaning of black family life"*: *Southern Christian Leadership Conference Newsletter*, fall 1970.

117   The introduction of Reverend Jesse Jackson to CTW's Evelyn

Davis by Cecil Hollingsworth is explained in an internal CTW memo from Davis and Jay Levine entitled "Chicago Cast Tour Trip," December 14, 1970, Box 229, CTW Archives.

117 *"We were very anti-Nixon"*: Author interview with McGrath.

118 *"All the old ladies had been cooking for days"*: Author interview with Long.

120 *"changed, radicalized, by the objective of* Sesame Street*"*: Author interview with Beverley Stone.

120 *"Here's this Ivy League white boy"*: Author interview with Long.

121 *"There was no sense in which"*: Renata Adler, "Cookie, Oscar, Grover, Herry, Ernie, and Company," *The New Yorker.*

122 "Sesame Street *is changing its aim"*: This and the other letters of protest against Jackson's appearance on the program are from April and May 1972, Box 45, CTW Archives. The letters from parents protesting the appearance of Pete Seeger come from the same time span. More constructively, a nutrition-minded mother from Willowdale, Ontario, wrote to the Workshop on April 9, 1972, "I would like to see Cookie Monster changed to Apple Freak or Fruit Monster."

122 "Sesame Street *has enjoyed"*: Max Gunther, "What's Around the Corner for 'Sesame Street'?," *TV Guide*, July 10, 1971.

123 *"This administration is enthusiastically committed"*: Letter from Richard Nixon to Joan Ganz Cooney, January 28, 1970.

124 *"Suddenly, we had enemies"*: Cooney as quoted in Davis, 218.

124 The strange story of Cooney and Morrisett's *not* receiving the Presidential Prize for Innovation is described in detail in Deborah Shapley, "The Presidential Prize Caper," *Science*, March 8, 1974.

125 *"We would have accepted the prize"*: Author interview with Lloyd Morrisett.

125 *"It was heartbreaking to me"*: Author interview with Joan Ganz Cooney.

125 *"My father did not like Nixon at all"*: Author interview with Morrisett.

126 The story of how Cooney came to meet with Barry Goldwater about funding was relayed to me, in slightly differing forms, by Newton Minow, Morrisett, and Cooney herself. (It is also recounted in Davis.)

127 *"Barry was happy to see me"*: Author interview with Cooney.

CHAPTER ELEVEN

129 *"Why do you persist on picturing women"*: Letter from Sonja Sorkin to CTW, January 17, 1972. This and related letters from NOW's coordinated letter-writing campaign can be found in Box 45, CTW Archives.

130 Jane Bergman's article "Are Little Girls Being Harmed by 'Sesame Street'?" ran in the *New York Times* on January 2, 1972.

130 *"He felt that a woman's place"*: Author interview with Dolores Robinson, 2019.

132 *"While I certainly don't object to having our faults pointed out"*: Cooney's letter as quoted in Davis, 213–15. Davis himself sourced this letter from Lisa Grunwald's *Women's Letters: America from the Revolutionary War to the Present* (New York: Dial Press, 2005), 657.

132 A letter to Cooney from a woman in Orange, Connecticut, dated August 14, 1974 (CTW Archives, Box 45), alludes to an appearance by Jim Henson on *The Pat Collins Show* in which "he said that there were no qualified woman puppeteers." In his memoir, Stone makes a similar argument about the availability of female puppeteers in that era.

133 *"the woman's place is in the home"*: Letter to CTW's Bob Hatch from a Texas woman, January 10, 1975, Box 45, CTW Archives.

133 *"seems to be backing the new fad E.R.A."*: Letter to Hatch from a Missouri woman, March 3, 1975, Box 45, CTW Archives.

133 In 1977, CTW published a chart entitled "Curriculum Innovation" that showed, season by season for *Sesame Street*'s first eight seasons, which new goals were added each year—such as bilingual skills in Season Two.

133 *"the racist attitude"*: The circumstances of Cooney's meeting with the coalition of Hispanic leaders is recounted in Davis, 215–16.

134 *"That's a remarkable thing that Joan did"*: Author interview with Manzano.

136 *"At the time, the only parts that were available for young men"*: Author interview with Emilio Delgado, 2018.

137 *"The first year we did nothing"*: Stone's real-time outburst about CTW's shortcomings in terms of addressing Hispanic viewers, including his "Frito Bandito" allusion, comes from Herman W. Land, *The Children's Television Workshop: How and Why It Works.*

138 *"Things would come up like they wanted to have a character say"*: Author interview with Delgado.

139 *"We did not write a strong, delineated character for him"*: Stone, 150. Stone's remorse over Raul Julia's not getting a fair shake on *Sesame Street* never left him. "If I had to do it all over again," he wrote in the nineties, "I would certainly keep him on the show as long as he would stay. Raul would have found his character and *Sesame Street* would have been infinitely richer for his presence."

139 *"Except for Bob, who was always right on it"*: Author interview with Delgado.

CHAPTER TWELVE

141 *"Although Sesame Street's racial integration generally was commended"*: Lesser, 93–95.

142 *"some of the members of the commission were very much opposed"*: *New York Times*, May 3, 1970. The state of Mississippi announced its reversal of the ban on May 25 of that year.

142 *"too many black people"*: Internal CTW memo entitled "Information from the Coordinators Regarding *The Electric Company* as of Dec. 14, 1971," Box 219, CTW Archives.

142 *"Everybody is really making positive comments"*: Ibid.

142 Linda Francke's article, "The Games People Play on *Sesame Street*," appeared in *New York*, April 5, 1971.

143 *"Perhaps the most valuable, exciting use of the program"*: from CTW's promotional *Sesame Street* booklet that it published prior to the show's premiere, Henson Company Archives.

144 *"The intellectual achievement gap"*: Ibid.

144 *"any generally distributed social good"*: Author interview with Lloyd Morrisett, 2019.

145 *"Our judgment, however"*: Lesser, 95.

146 *"This aim to reach the disadvantaged child"*: "Kids Like It Short— And Kids Are Bosses," *Ebony*, January 1970.

147 *"I said, 'Jim, when I say'"*: Author interview with Loretta Long.

148 *"black revolutionary types"*: Author interview with Dolores Robinson.

151 *"I like the idea of black muppets"*: Memo from Jane O'Connor to Dave Connell, February 10, 1970, Box 36, CTW Archives. O'Connor's discomfort with Roosevelt Franklin is further explicated by Robert F. Morrow in his fine study *Sesame Street and the Reform of Children's Television* (Baltimore: Johns Hopkins University Press, 2006).

151 *"We ought to try this kind of thing in an experimental way"*: Memo from Joan Ganz Cooney to O'Connor, February 10, 1970, Box 36, CTW Archives.

151 *"Why insist on standard English"*: Robinson as quoted in Phylis Feinstein, *All About Sesame Street* (New York: Tower Publications, 1971), 49.

151 *"Somewhere around four or five"*: Ibid, 70.

152 The quotations and details of the debate about Roosevelt Franklin's merits and demerits among CTW's black employees come from the minutes of the October 6, 1970, training conference that the Workshop held for its utilization coordinators, Box 219, CTW Archives.

153 *"It was a sign of the times"*: Author interview with Robinson.

153 Cheryl Henson and Dolores Robinson both attested to the fact that Matt Robinson and Jerry Nelson were friends.

153 *"the Evelyn Davises, from the upper middle class"*: Cooney as quoted in Davis, 249.

154 *"Within the black community, we ask each other"*: Author interview with April Reign, 2019.

CHAPTER THIRTEEN

161 The formation and ascent of Action for Children's Television (ACT) is thoroughly chronicled by Robert F. Morrow in *Sesame Street and the Reform of Children's Television.*

162 *"I had been a reporter in England and France"*: Author interview with Evelyn Kaye (formerly Evelyn Sarson), 2019.

164 *"They were very clever at CBS"*: Ibid.

165 *"Our mandate was to somehow find a balance"*: Michael Eisner, with Tony Schwartz, *Work in Progress: Risking Failure, Surviving Success* (New York: Random House, 1998), 60–61.

165 *"brownie-points shows"*: "How Networks Are Upgrading Weekend Shows," *Broadcasting*, November 20, 1972.

165 *"appeasement gestures, and expensive ones at that"*: Ibid.

168 *"Its goals differ from* Sesame Street *and* The Electric Company*"*: Bill Cosby's doctoral dissertation, "An Integration of the Visual Media via *Fat Albert and the Cosby Kids* into the Elementary School Curriculum as a Teaching Aid and Vehicle to Achieve Increased Learning," (1976), is viewable in its entirety at Doctoral Dissertations 1896–February 2014, https://scholarworks.umass.edu/dissertations.

CHAPTER FOURTEEN

174 For details on Ira Nerken's campaign to engage advertising firms in the anti-war movement, I relied on Philip H. Dougherty, "Advertising: A Campaign to 'Unsell' the War," *New York Times*, June 8, 1971; Richard L. Gilbert, *I Was a Mad Man: A Madison Avenue*

Memoir (New York: Diversion Books, 2013); and Mitchell K. Hall, *Because of Their Faith: Calcav and Religious Opposition to the Vietnam War* (New York: Columbia University Press, 1990). Some of the "Unsell" TV spots are viewable on YouTube.

174   The "Mother Bombs" TV ad is viewable on the New-York Historical Society's website, at https://vietnamwar.nyhistory.org/videos/unsell-war-advertising-campaign-mother-bombs.

176   *"kind of a math junkie"*: Author interview with George Newall, 2016.

178   Newall, at the time of this book's publication, was the last surviving member of *Schoolhouse Rock!*'s founding team. Fortunately, I was able to hear his cofounders Bob Dorough and Radford Stone speak through the lively interviews conducted by the children's-book author Marc Tyler Nobleman, whose Noblemania.com is a mother lode of entertaining pop-culture sleuthing. Nobleman has tracked down not only multiple *Schoolhouse Rock!* alums for interviews but also various grown women who appeared, as girls or young women, in early MTV videos. Should you want to know whatever became of Bunty Bailey, the young woman who was pulled into Morten Harket's comic-book fever dream in A-ha's "Take On Me," Nobleman is your man.

180   The lyrics, backstories, and performance and writing credits of vintage-era *Schoolhouse Rock!* are collected by the series' two main creative cogs, Tom Yohe and George Newall, in *Schoolhouse Rock! The Official Guide* (New York: Hyperion, 1996).

183   *"It was something that we didn't have to do"*: Author interview with Newall.

CHAPTER FIFTEEN

187   *"aid broadcasters in being more responsive"*: The content of the FCC's Ascertainment Primer, as well as the story of ACT's influence on the FCC in the early 1970s, is detailed in "The Public Interest Standard in Television Broadcasting," *Current*, December 18, 1998.

189 *"so Paula would come to the theater with the baby on her back"*: Author interview with Carole Demas and Paula Janis, 2016. Demas and Janis continue to perform live as a duo and are thoroughgoing curators of their *Magic Garden* history.

193 Little footage survives of *Time for Joya* and its successor, *Joya's Fun School*, though Joya Sherrill's programs received a loving tribute on the TVparty! website, including audio of Duke Ellington's appearance, which may be found at http://www.tvparty .com/lostny2joya.html.

195 *"Of course, my mom being a good mom"*: Author interview with Doug Momary, 2019. Momary spoke to me at length about *New Zoo Revue*'s genesis and 196-episode run.

197 *"On commercial television, a lot of the Saturday-morning shows"*: Author interview with Stephen Jahn, 2019.

200 *"a lovely little show"*: Cooney's testimonial ran in ads taken out by WPIX in *Broadcasting* in 1972–73.

201 Morrisett's migration to the John and Mary R. Markle Foundation, and his mustering of the foundation's resources to support ACT, are covered in Lee D. Mitgang, *Big Bird and Beyond: The New Media and the Markle Foundation* (New York: Fordham University Press, 2000).

CHAPTER SIXTEEN

203 *"I remember saying, 'Oh my God'"*: Cooney, Television Academy Foundation. She tells this story nearly verbatim in Davis, 216.

204 *"the child in the lower half of the second grade"*: "A 'Right On!' for the Right to Read," *Children's Television Workshop Newsletter*, July 9, 1971, Box 2, CTW Archives.

204 *"some 20 million or 40% of elementary and secondary school students are reading cripples"*: Internal CTW memorandum, September 1971, Box 219, CTW Archives.

204 *"If you said it's beginning reading"*: Cooney, Television Academy Foundation.

205   Tom Whedon introduced me to the term "silhouette blending." He also explained how the CTW research department's findings on word placement were implemented on-screen.

207   *"Kids who are seven to ten aren't as containable"*: Author interview with Naomi Foner. Sam Gibbon also provided insight into *The Electric Company*'s development.

207   *"Paul had the idea of doing a show"*: Skip Hinnant as quoted in the DVD *The Electric Company's Greatest Hits and Bits*, Sesame Workshop, 2006.

208   *"A lot of it was simply a matter of"*: Author interview with Foner.

209   *"The interesting thing was that I talked to actor friends"*: Author interview with Rita Moreno.

209   *"Dave Connell was frantic"*: Author interview with Whedon.

211   *"I thought that was one of the great things"*: Author interview with Moreno.

212   Moreno related to me, with relish, the story of how she told Dave Connell that her *Carnal Knowledge* role involved a fellatio scene with Jack Nicholson.

212   *"But the black caucus said, 'You absolutely cannot'"*: Author interview with Whedon.

214   *"Our job was to get print on the screen in a lot of different ways"*: Connell as quoted in Martin Mayer, "*The Electric Company*: Easy Reader and a lot of other hip teachers," *New York Times*, January 28, 1973.

214   *"I looked at an early pilot of the show"*: Author interview with Whedon.

215   *"It was really a burlesque show"*: Author interview with Moreno.

216   *"I sat at my piano and I thought"*: Author interview with Gary William Friedman.

216   *"I found the show at times sort of tasteless"*: Cooney, Television Academy Foundation. She makes this observation nearly verbatim in Davis, 217.

217   *"one of the remarkable events in the history"*: Sid Marland as quoted in "Surveys Gauge In-School Audience," *Children's*

Television Workshop Newsletter, October 30, 1972, Box 2, CTW Archives.

217 *"Really bright three- and four- and five-year-olds"*: Boyd as quoted in *The Electric Company's Greatest Hits and Bits*.

218 *"But to her amazement and surprise and delight"*: Author interview with Moreno.

219 *"I've always felt that what we were doing"*: Ibid.

219 *"I saw myself as a political person"*: Author interview with Foner.

CHAPTER SEVENTEEN

222 *"It was just this incredible buzz"*: Author interview with Christopher Sarson, 2018.

222 WGBH is justifiably proud of its history and has a robust Web presence devoted to its past, which I relied on for background. Its historical and archival materials may be accessed at https://www.wgbh.org/foundation/history.

224 *"getting into their preteen ages"*: Author interview with Sarson. Sarson, who calls himself the "Zoom Papa," patiently explained the genesis of *Zoom* to me. Though he now lives primarily in New Zealand, he still flies to Boston semiregularly to reunite with the 1970s *Zoom* casts, many of whose members have remained in the area.

226 *"We're gonna zoom-a, zoom-a, zoom-a, zoom"*: Words by Newton Wayland. Copyright © 1974, Irving Music.

230 *"I called the hospital and, believe it or not, asked them to hold up the operation"*: Author interview with Sarson. This series of events was confirmed to me by the patient, Mike, who is now an artist and as an adult goes by his full name, Michael Dean. In an e-mail, Dean recalled that *Zoom* won an Emmy Award for the season he was on. "They sent me a nice note on *Zoom* letterhead saying that I deserved credit for a big part of that award," Dean wrote. "I also remember that after filming me back at home, the cameraman slipped me a *Playboy* magazine."

232   *"I don't know how WGBH found the school"*: Author interview with Bernadette Yao, 2019.

233   *"I was in a classroom with just twenty children"*: Author interview with Leon Mobley, 2019. Yao and Mobley are both now musicians: she composes music for meditation and yoga dance; he is a percussionist with Ben Harper & the Innocent Criminals.

CHAPTER EIGHTEEN

240   *"I was reading books to Dionne"*: Author interview with Marlo Thomas, 2010.

242   All of the Thomas quotations in this chapter come from my interview with her, but I am indebted to Lori Rotskoff and Laura L. Lovett's anthology *When We Were Free to Be: Looking Back at a Children's Classic and the Difference It Made* (Chapel Hill: University of North Carolina Press, 2012), which includes both written reminiscences from the project's creators and latter-day essays about the project's meaning, history, and impact.

242   *"She is very caught up with Women's Lib"*: Letter from Ursula Nordstrom to Mary Rodgers, March 22, 1972, as reprinted in Leonard S. Marcus, *Dear Genius: The Letters of Ursula Nordstrom.*

243   *"little girls' rooms that are so organdied, pink, and pippy-poo"*: Letty Cottin Pogrebin, "Down with Sexist Upbringing!," *Ms.* (then an insert in *New York* magazine), December 20, 1971.

244   *"I had not been paying attention"*: Author interview with Letty Cottin Pogrebin, 2019. I received further insight into Pogrebin's journey as a parent from her book *Growing Up Free: Raising Your Child in the 80s* (New York: McGraw-Hill, 1980) and by speaking with her daughters, Abigail and Robin, both of whom appeared in the 1974 *Free to Be . . . You and Me* television special on ABC.

245   *"This is a 8 year old girl speaking"*: Abigail Pogrebin, letter to General Mills, 1973, from Letty Cottin Pogrebin's collection. Young Abby's letter elicited a response from the company's manager of

consumer response, a woman, that was thorough if not particularly sympathetic:

> *Dear Abigail: Thank you for your recent letter concerning current Wheaties television commercials. In presenting the Wheaties story to the public we have endeavored to capitalize on the brand's long heritage as a male-oriented product. As you know, many products, such as Virginia Slims, Grape-Nuts, and Marlboro have spoken primarily to one sex. This is not done to the exclusion of the other gender. It merely speaks to those people that constitute the majority of the brand's consumers. This is true with Wheaties. For although many women do eat and enjoy the product, our research indicates that it is predominantly eaten by men. Our message for the product is that as a boy matures, his taste matures, and he is ready to eat an unsweetened, adult-tasting product. Wheaties is such a product. As we do studies concerning our advertising and promotion, we appreciate it when someone who feels strongly about a matter takes the time, as you have, to give us his or her comments.*

246 "*We examined gender stereotypes*": Carole Hart, "In the Beginning," in Rotskoff and Lovett, *When We Were Free to Be*, 36.

247 "*Civil rights, feminism, and other social justice movements*": Gloria Steinem, "Free to Be . . . a Child," in *When We Were Free to Be*, 67.

248 The composition of *Free to Be . . . You and Me*'s title song and the assembly of its soundtrack were described to me by Stephen Lawrence in an interview in 2019.

249 "*I stole those lines and never looked back*": Carol Hall, "Mommies and Daddies," in *When We Were Free to Be*, 55.

252 "*What would I want with a record produced by a bunch of dykes?*": Hart, "In the Beginning," *When We Were Free to Be*, 35.

252   *"blue eyes and curly eyelashes"*: Charlotte Zolotow and William Pène du Bois, *William's Doll* (New York: Harper & Row, 1972), 12.

252   *"a bit too earnest for our purposes"*: Hart, "In the Beginning," *When We Were Free to Be*, 36.

254   *"Not everybody wants to be a daddy"*: Author interview with Thomas.

256   *"It was as though the serious and provocative essays I had gathered"*: Francine Klagsbrun, "Beyond the Fun and Song," in *When We Were Free to Be*, 63.

258   *"I delivered it to the network"*: Author interview with Thomas.

259   *"not just a junior anthem"*: Letty Cottin Pogrebin, "A Thousand Fond Memories and a Few Regrets," in *When We Were Free to Be*, 44.

260   *"many children who did not own a copy"*: Lori Rotskoff, "Getting the Message: Audiences Respond to *Free to Be . . . You and Me*," in *When We Were Free to Be*, 127.

260   *"I would argue that back then"*: Author interview with Pogrebin.

261   *"To this day, I get mail"*: Author interview with Thomas.

261   *"I was singing 'It's Alright to Cry'"*: Author interview with Billy Eichner, 2015.

CHAPTER NINETEEN

263   The animated TV special *Really Rosie* originally aired on February 19, 1975, drawing upon material from Maurice Sendak's 1960 book *The Sign on Rosie's Door* and the three little books that comprised his 1962 masterwork, *The Nutshell Library*.

265   *"Now we can explain what happened to Grandma"*: Author interview with Loretta Long.

266   *"Product tie-ins, unfortunately"*: Author interview with Tom Whedon.

266   The saga of *Feelin' Good*, CTW's ill-fated health-education show for adults, is chronicled in queasy slow motion through various editions of the *Children's Television Workshop Newsletter* in 1974–75, Box 2, CTW Archives.

267 *"He led his readers to believe"*: article in *Children's Television Workshop Newsletter*, March 8, 1974, Box 2, CTW Archives.

268 *"a toaster with pictures"*: Mark S. Fowler as quoted in Milton Mueller, "Interview with Mark S. Fowler," *Reason*, November 1981.

268 *"To unregulate, and that's the difference"*: Ibid.

268 *"Broadcasters would often bury public-affairs and instructional programming"*: Ibid.

268 *"'the public interest'"*: Fowler as quoted in Peter J. Boyer, "Under Fowler, FCC Treated TV as Commerce," *New York Times*, January 19, 1987.

269 *"That was the death knell"*: Author interview with Carole Demas and Paula Janis.

269 *"Boys on active toys, girls on tea sets"*: Author interview with Letty Cottin Pogrebin.

270 James Dobson's *Dare to Discipline*, originally published in 1970, posited itself as a sort of antidote to the too-permissive philosophies of Benjamin Spock. Dobson believed that "minor pain" served a useful purpose in keeping children in line: "There is a muscle lying snugly against the base of the neck. Anatomy books list it as the trapezius muscle, and when firmly squeezed it sends little messengers to the brain saying, 'This hurts; avoid recurrence at all costs.'"

270 *"That was when we started to feel the pushback"*: Author interview with Pogrebin.

271 *"Houston will finish off the women's movement"*: Schlafly as quoted in Sean P. Cunningham, *Cowboy Conservatism: Texas and the Rise of the Modern Right* (Lexington: University Press of Kentucky, 2010), 189.

271 *"Increasing amounts of federal funds are no longer being directed"*: Morrisett as quoted in Lee D. Mitgang, *Big Bird and Beyond: The New Media and the Markle Foundation*.

271 *"I was in a rather despairing mood"*: Author interview with Morrisett, 2019.

273 *"I don't think the level was quite up"*: Author interview with Newall.

274   *"looking more like the South Street Seaport"*: Stone, 194.

274   *"wasn't as neurotic as Big Bird"*: Larry Rifkin as quoted in Pat Grandjean, "CPTV Celebrates 50 Years: Present at the Creation," *Connecticut Magazine*, April 1, 2013.

275   *"make the show more cutie-pie"*: Author interview with Sonia Manzano.

276   *"We've been able to keep the budget within the bounds we can finance"*: Author interview with Morrisett.

279   *"You stop to think about that"*: Author interview with Bob McGrath.

280   *"I was born to do this job"*: Author interview with Joan Ganz Cooney.

INDEX

Note: Page numbers in *italics* refer to illustrations.

ABOUT THE AUTHOR

David Kamp is an author, journalist, humorist, lyricist, and a charter member of the *Sesame Street*–viewing audience. His book *The United States of Arugula*, a chronicle of America's foodways, was a national bestseller, and his writing has appeared in *Vanity Fair*, *GQ*, and the *New York Times*. He began his career at *Spy*, the legendary satirical monthly. He lives with his family in New York City and rural Connecticut.